BowHunters' Digest

6TH EDITION

PATRICK MEITIN

Published by

Krause Publications a division of F+W Media, Inc.
700 East State Street • Iola, WI 54990-0001
715-445-2214 • 888-457-2873
www.krausebooks.com

To order books or other products call toll-free 1-800-258-0929
or visit us online at www.shopdeerhunting.com

Cover photography by Bill Kinney/windigoimages.com
and courtesy of Mathews Archery, Inc.

ISBN-13: 978-1-4402-4747-7
ISBN-10: 1-4402-4747-1

Designed by Dane Royer
Edited by Chris Berens

Printed in the United States of America

10 9 8 7 6 5 4 3 2 1

DEDICATION

As always, this one is for my wife, Gwyn, who means everything to me.

Photo Credit: Dustin Reid

TABLE OF CONTENTS

BOWTECH
BOSS
OCTANE

FOREWORD

I'VE HAD THE PLEASURE of knowing Patrick Meitin for more than 15 years. We met first at an archery trade show. I liked him instantly. Despite wearing a sport coat with leather elbow patches over a pressed dress shirt, it was plain to see that his environment was not among crowds or attending business meetings. His environment is the woods and wild places that most outdoorsmen dream of going to.

Patrick has hunted all over the world. He has harvested all types of animals in all types of weather and terrain. He enjoys the tough hunts, where comfort is a long ways from the small fire and tent he often calls home. He is addicted to the challenge of big-game hunting with a bow and arrow, and has bowhunted Alaska 18 times and been on nine African safaris with a bow. He has harvested animals with his bow from carp to bullfrogs, all the way up to African Cape buffalo.

I can speak of the frogs, as it was on a bullfrog hunt with our bows that I really got to know Patrick well. He had invited my family to go frog hunting with him in New Mexico, and to this day it still stands out as one of my family's favorite experiences together. Patrick was great with my kids and me as he showed us the finer points of frog hunting with a bow at night. What was great to see was how much fun Patrick had bowhunting bullfrogs, even though he has pursued some of the biggest game in the world.

Patrick is unique to the hunting industry, because although there are many people who write about the outdoors, archery and bowhunting, very few have his level of hands-on experience. When Patrick writes about archery, for example, he's not just regurgitating the words of others or basing his advice on research he has gleaned from the Internet. He is providing real information based on a lifetime of practical experience.

In truth, Patrick has exceeded one lifetime of experience and is working on two or three lifetimes of experiences, based on the amount of time he has invested pursuing his passion. Patrick's level of expertise covers a lot of arenas that all have to do with the outdoors. Besides being a very accomplished bowhunter, he also competes with both traditional equipment and compound bows, and has a multitude of wins under his belt while competing in 3-D tournaments.

He has worked retail, where he spent countless hours helping other bowhunters, as well as competitive shooters, set up and tune their archery equipment. He is a hugely prolific writer, selling more than 2,500 magazine articles, in addition to numerous columns and blogs that were all hunting or archery related. He was qualified to write these articles for a variety of reasons, including guiding hunters for 23 years, as well as having 37 years of bowhunting experience. He harvested his first deer with a bow in 1979 and has been hopelessly addicted ever since.

The advice and insight contained in this book is solid information that will make you a better shooter, competitor and bowhunter. I just hope that by reading it you become as passionate about the sport of archery as Patrick is.

– Fred Eichler, September 2016

Outfitter, Guide, Author, Photographer, Videographer and Host of "Traditional Harvests" DVD Series, "Easton Bowhunting TV" and "Predator Nation"

The late archery legend Jim Dougherty began his bowhunting addiction early at a young age, a passion that would endure a long lifetime.

CHAPTER 1

THE BOWHUNTING LIFE

EARLY IN LIFE ARCHERY AND BOWHUNTING became my way of viewing the world. It began with a Fred Bear Archery kit containing a cheap fiberglass recurve and wooden arrows, finger glove, small arm guard and paper FITA target with brightly colored score rings – something that represents archery to even those who've never touched a bow. I shot that little bow exhaustively, and with it hunted my first vacant-lot cottontails, for which the weakling bow was barely adequate. Shortly afterward I acquired a more powerful solid-fiberglass number, one made by Indian Archery and pulling 30 pounds. My take of bunnies improved dramatically, their skins stretched and salted for drying, becoming my first archery trophies. It wasn't long before I was pursuing larger jackrabbits (big game to a 12-year-old kid), and fashioning homemade bowfishing tackle to address invasive Asian carp in a nearby creek. I was bitten hard, my bowhunting dreams beginning to take on larger dimensions.

I went through an accelerated hunter's progression; killing my first mule deer buck with a rifle at age 10, my first rifle bull elk at 12, temporarily developing a fascination with muzzleloaders and everything mountain man during my teens. But deep down I always understood bowhunting represented my future as a hunter. I was lucky to live in a Western state where a youngster could pass a hunter's safety course, buy a license over the counter and bowhunt in early September, muzzleloader hunt in late September and, if things hadn't gone well, participate in the exciting, bustling, campfire-ring rifle camps of November.

I was also lucky to have passable mule deer hunting in the foothills close to my Roswell, N.M., home, peddling a bicycle 8 or 10 miles was the only

Archery and bowhunting are truly individual sports, but camaraderie is a big part of what makes the pastime so special.

price of admission. It was during those forays I did not have to depend on adults who organized, supplied and chauffeured those big November mountain forays. It was in this way I began bowhunting big game early in life, haunting a couple outlying ranches harboring scattered, stunted, desert mulies. With my cheap-but-trusty Shimbow 45-pound recurve and four-arrow, snap-on Kwickee Kwiver (which left broadheads dangerously exposed), I learned many harsh lessons while wandering lonely desert washes, stalking scarce bucks and putting an arrow through my first at age 14.

Since that time I've continued to bowhunt with simple longbows and recurves, but also increasingly modern compounds, first with fingers and no sights, eventually adopting the full catastrophe, including fiber-optic sights and peep, drop-away rest, carbon arrows, mechanical broadheads and laser rangefinder.

Thirty-seven years after that first small, velvet-antlered buck my bowhunting obsessions have taken me far from those Eastern New Mexico plains – from Alaskan barren ground caribou and Alaska-Yukon moose found on tundra wastes, to Cape buffalo and plains game animals in Southern Africa's veldts, and whitetails from harsh Old Mexico deserts to mossy Canadian boreal forests.

An early ambition of "Putting arrows through one of everything in North America" (before Chuck Adams copyrighted the Super Slam term) was slowly rendered into collecting 18 of North America's 29 species, and others – taking into account worthy game such as javelina and imported wild boars, for instance. But, my naïve dream hit a wall at the $10,000 mark for mandatory guided hunts and rich-man's game such as $25,000 sheep and $30,000 polar bears.

Still, my passions have remained undiminished. Nothing else beats archery and bowhunting as an outdoor sport. Here is a pastime that becomes a lifestyle, including long evenings on the lawn or back 40 honing shooting skills, fusing over equipment tuning and striving to break through current shooting plateaus, the entire year engrossed in planning and scheming for next year's big adventure, or simply ambushing that backyard whitetail, an entire language and assumptions shared with like-minded friends and acquaintances. The summer bowfishing outings and 3-D tournaments and scouting; winter

Some of the earliest stories and legends no doubt revolved around hunting tales, a tradition that remains strong with bowhunters today.

indoor leagues and annual equipment upgrades; the springs of wild turkey and black bears; falls filled with deer and elk that strain relationships and endanger gainful employment.

To label bowhunting a "sport," like golf or bowling, is to diminish its significance for so many. Bowhunting is not a sport in the traditional sense, because we compete with no one but ourselves (in a perfect world at least), while it is also true that with time it becomes as necessary for our mental health as nightly sleep.

While bowhunting allows the hunter to enjoy increased hunting opportunity with longer seasons translating into more days afield, the obvious advantages of often better seasons – access to September's bugling elk or November's rutting whitetails when gun hunters are excluded, for instance – for hard-core bowhunters this is only a fringe benefit fitting of the increased challenge that is bowhunting. For the real bowhunter longer seasons and increased opportunity simply offer more time to get away from it all, away from contrived living, the self-inflicted stress of the workplace and a modern existence, returning to our roots as a primitive being striving for mere survival. Of course, today the unfilled tag doesn't represent an empty stomach and potential starvation, but the inability to spend these quality hours in wild places does starve the heart and soul. A hard-core bowhunter deprived of time outdoors is a pitiful sight indeed, distracted, short tempered and irritable. It's the woods and deep absorption in this passion that makes a pleasant, patient person—though secretly the bowhunter's mind might very well be elsewhere; on a wind-swept oak ridge, alpine meadow or woodland hollow.

Bowhunting makes any person it touches a better human being, one deeply enmeshed with the natural world and better understanding our part in it, including, most importantly, making habitat better for the animals we so passionately pursue. We understand nothing comes without hard work, persistence, extreme patience and a smart application of slowly acquired knowledge and skills—the polar opposite of today's often narcissistic, instant-gratification crowd. So come along as we explore the finer points of this most awesome of pastimes, a "sport" which becomes a lifestyle, and a lifestyle that comes to shape the way we look at the world.

We bowhunt to get away from it all, but success is still sweet and a big part of what keeps us coming back for more.

Farmlands provide plentiful food that helps white-tailed bucks grow big and strong – like this Kansas buck taken by the author.

CHAPTER 2

WHITE-TAILED DEER & CLASSIC FARMLAND HUNTING

IT ISN'T DIFFICULT TO FATHOM why "Eastern whitetail," *Odocoileus virginianus*, are North America's—possibly the world's—most popular big-game animal. While they aren't the most majestic, nor do they wear the largest antlers, they are the most numerous, widespread and readily available of all of this continent's big-game species. From the alligator swamps of the Deep South to the snowy, mountainous regions of the Inland Northwest, from the birch big-woods of New England to the cactus and mesquite flats of West Texas, and from the Far North of Canada to Old Mexico, the whitetail thrives, providing challenge and subsistence for tens of millions of hunters.

Nothing seems to cultivate the kind of obsession that white-tailed deer do, whitetail fever sweeping the land border to border and coast to coast. As a Western bowhunter reared on elk, pronghorn and mule deer I bowhunted my first whitetails in Central Texas. While Texas has a reputation for producing *muy grande* bucks, Texas is also vast, meaning habitat varies widely and big bucks aren't found corner to corner. My whitetail initiation took place on Texas' Edward's Plateau, which is made largely of, shall we say, lackluster habitats afforded a destitute college student.

After college I discovered the secret to consistently killing big bucks: travel to only the very best habitats such as Illinois, Iowa, Kansas and Alberta, just to name some of the most obvious. Bowhunting destinations where genetics and habitat conditions are such that 2½-year-old bucks often make Pope & Young records. I quickly assembled an impressive collection of 140- to 160-inch whitetail bucks. I really couldn't understand what all the fuss was about.

Then my wife and I moved to northern Idaho, where we enjoy not only the usual Western suspects like elk, mule deer, Merriam's turkey, black bear and mountain lion, but abundant white-tailed deer. And I mean abundant, not scanty fringe herds like we had in eastern New Mexico, or the scattered deer of 1990s West Texas; where in the years since I graduated college whitetail populations have actually exploded and big bucks have become relatively common. My newfound immersion in solid whitetail habitat would completely change my perspective.

I might still travel to places like Iowa, Kansas and Alberta, but with each passing year I'm more inclined to stay home and pursue my generally smaller, certainly more challenging backyard whitetails. I've so much more invested in deer found close to home, the year-round scouting, the constant moni-

If you're looking for the biggest bucks in North America, the continent's rich farmlands will likely figure into your plans.

toring of trail cameras, so much so that I develop personal relationships with individual bucks, the intimate connection with the land, including my small part in its stewardship—planting and nurturing mast trees, creating watering sites and food plots on our own little piece of habitat. I have so much fun pursuing smaller, more elusive bucks in my big-woods habitats, I'm more than happy to stay home come November.

At long last I get it. Backyard whitetails are the bread and butter of North American bowhunting for all these reasons and more.

Hunting farmland whitetails is as classic as the sport itself; our productive farmlands help white-tailed deer thrive.

FARMLAND CLASSICS

When most hunters contemplate white-tailed deer they generally envision rich farmlands interspersed with patchwork woodlands and tangled riparian zones. This is no coincidence, as these habitat types create the whitetail ideal, generally painting a picture of the most consistently productive landscapes for trophy white-tailed bucks. In many cases, whitetails have thrived since the appearance of Europeans in North America, because of introduced agriculture alone. Thumb through the latest copy of Pope & Young's *Bowhunting Big-Game Records of North America* and states and provinces such as Illinois, Ohio, Wisconsin, Iowa, Kansas, Alberta, Saskatchewan, Kentucky, Missouri and Nebraska dominate the top listings. What do all of these places have in common? Top genetics—which are also found in places like South Texas, northeastern Washington and Maine, just without high-volume farming to boost population density—combined with abundant and high-energy alfalfa, soybeans, grain and especially corn, set beside ample woodlots, creek and river bottoms or vast CRP grasslands. This is a rich recipe for high numbers of behemoth bucks. Of course, quality wildlife management is also part of the equation and states like Minnesota, Indiana and Upstate New York often have the genetic potential and requisite agriculture, but intense gun-hunting pressure – often through the heart of the rut – spoils the stew.

Farmland habitats have traditionally provided the classic landowner-hunter dynamic, the private-land farmer happy to have a few deer removed from his land annually to protect crops, in exchange for the courtesy of a polite knock on his door and request for trespass permission, perhaps some summertime labor around the farm, a hunch of venison after harvest and a bottle of booze at Christmastime. This has been complicated in many areas, the high cost of trophy deer resulting in a proliferation of leases and outfitters, in other cases landowners leery of a litigious society and its hordes of blood-sucking lawyers. There are still places where knocking on doors, hat in hand, will get you into decent deer hunting, but it has become increasingly challenging. In general, you're more apt to find success in these endeavors by traveling farther from large population centers.

White-tailed deer live by their stomachs. Where there is food there are deer, and in farmlands food is abundant and deer numerous.

The tactics for pursuing farmland whitetails are as old as sporting periodicals themselves, the wary nature of human-savvy deer and noisy woodland settings making "stump sitting," or simply slumping against a tree bole and biding your time, standard operating procedure. The modern bowhunter has transformed this into climbing into the treestand or pop-up blind, literally raising above it all—most notably the whitetail's unsurpassed olfactory apparatus—or sealing scent inside a high-tech portable blind. Nearly all nimrods pursuing whitetails with bow—save the most traditionally driven—proceed in this manner today, so we all understand the drill. Success, as they say, comes through smaller details.

Bedding & Feeding Areas

A vast majority of whitetail hunting entails ambushing deer between where they retreat during midday, their bedding areas, and where they feed between dusk and dawn. Determining where these areas are located on the properties you hunt puts you well ahead of the game, providing known points at each end of a deer's daily travels to help you make educated guesses as to where to position yourself between these waypoints to create predictable encounters. We accomplish this by also understanding deer will generally travel between points A and B via the path of least resistance, which means not a beeline necessarily, but avoiding obvious barriers such as high, tight fences, steep or otherwise treacherous terrain, danger spots, even a newly plowed field that rain has transformed into a gooey, sticky mess.

In general, traveling deer prefer to remain under cover whenever possible, but will cut corners or take shortcuts when they don't feel overly exposed. For instance, a grassy or brushy ditch traversing an open field and connecting two woodlots often creates a deer highway. Shelterbelts and creek beds in relatively open farmland are generally well traveled. You'll commonly find deer trails paralleling agricultural fields just inside wooded cover, where deer can stage while awaiting nightfall or cruise while seeking other deer, funneling at points or corners as they hug cover while avoiding exposing themselves during daylight hours.

Micro topography also plays a big part in funneling farmland deer. Ridge points serve as "off-

Setting up a whitetail ambush near agricultural bounty is always a sound bowhunting approach and easy to do in farmlands.

ramps" into lower feeding areas, while a deep dip between a set of bedding headers and a corn field, for instance, are sure to see traffic, requiring deer to expend the least amount of effort possible while traveling between these points of interest.

Isolating Bedding Areas

Yet before any of this information does you any good it's important to first pinpoint specific bedding and feeding areas. In very general terms, bedding cover is thicker cover where deer can find shade from midday heat, perhaps even a breeze protecting their backside from undetected approach or detouring pesky insects during warmer seasons. It must also represent a secure place where deer are seldom, if ever, disturbed. I say generally, because depending on habitat, bedding areas can be wholly obvious, or quite obscure. At one extreme are Colorado's Eastern Plains and Kansas' "out there" western reaches, rich farmland where nearly any undisturbed patch of trees or brush is essentially guaranteed to act as a deer bedding area, though I've seen these open-country deer bed in a patch of weeds surrounded by open CRP grass and even along stubble rows of harvested grain crops. At the other extreme are places like my north Idaho back-

Feeding grounds are always one part of the Point-A to Point-B deer-hunting formula, and scouting should always revolve around food.

yard, or northern Wisconsin big woods or Kentucky oak-ridge country where bedding can take place nearly anywhere. During an exceptionally good acorn crop, feeding and bedding areas often lay side by side.

Scouting approaches are obviously contingent on the type of habitat you're addressing. In open country, or patchwork farmland, the most productive approach involves late-evening circuit driving. The idea is to use powerful optics to cover vast amounts of ground efficiently, parking on a rise to watch a creek bed with window-mounted spotting scope, climbing a grain silo or haystack to spy on distant fields, or hiking to a ridge crest to put quality binoculars to work. Note exactly when and where deer exit isolated cover, return several evenings in a row to see if this pattern persists, and you have a fairly solid stand game plan.

Thickly wooded or hilly habitats can prove much trickier. This kind of topography requires covering more ground afoot, visually earmarking obvious beds—matted swatches of grass, impressions in leaves, even pawed-out areas in rockier ground. The real problem with this approach is that rousting deer from their beds too often has the potential to alter their habits and cause them to choose another bedding site. This will send you back to square one, especially in hard-hunted areas where deer are spookier.

During hunting season I prefer scouting for bedding areas atop fresh snow, as it quiets progress and makes sign more conspicuous. Should I awake to a couple inches of fresh snow, I often skip a stand sit and dress light to cover ground. I start by walking the edges of likely feeding areas—farm fields, meadows, briar patches or orchards—looking for buck tracks (I've tracked big bucks directly from trail cameras after capturing nocturnal images) or concentrations of tracks indicating lots of does – which come in handy during rut hunts, and spoor them toward their beds. There are two basic approaches here; slipping along silently while carrying your bow and wearing snow camouflage, essentially hoping to slip into range of deer, or bumbling through country without stealth, giving deer plenty of advanced warning of your approach. The latter leaves bumped deer feeling more secure, believing they've picked a safe spot from which to detect danger easily. Slipping right on top of a deer before jumping him can make him feel the site is dangerous. If you should begin to encounter multiple beds during your wandering, it's normally best to quietly

The open nature of standard farmland country makes off-season scouting easier, so use quality optics to spy on deer from afar.

Climbing out of your stand after a fresh snowfall is a solid scouting tactic. snow will lay all bare and plainly reveal deer sign.

back out and minimize the disturbance.

A safer scouting approach is to wait until just after the season closes and canvassing your hunting area thoroughly. This presents many obvious advantages. By winter there may likely be snow cover, depending on your location, laying all sign bare, including bed impressions. Secondly, places where deer bed immediately following the season are places they obviously feel most secure—places they retreated to when the pressure was on, and where they survived the hunting season with hides intact. Finally, any disturbance created now won't hurt immediate hunting efforts, and deer will have plenty of time to forget the intrusion. No matter how arduous my hunting season has proven I always make time for thorough post-season scouting and taking notes toward next year's success.

Following Food

Scouting productive food sources can be simple or frustratingly difficult, again depending on the habitat type and topography. In productive farmland any appropriate foodstuff, generally harvested crops, will attract deer during evening hours. The question is what kind of deer are you looking for, just a deer, or a specific buck? Long-distance optical reconnaissance and leaning heavily on trail cameras (visited only during the warmest midday hours) are the only ways to know for sure.

Other habitats can prove more challenging. I've bowhunted Deep South whitetails where their entire world is made of potential food, from green briars, honeysuckle, acorns and persimmons to planted farms and food plots. In northern big woods or northwestern mountains vast clear-cuts or areas of scrubby willow and alder constitute grocery stores—which still doesn't necessarily exactly narrow things down to one single acre. In such extreme cases I've essentially given up trying to determine what deer are eating, concentrating instead on general topography to funnel deer from wider areas (see Big-Woods Whitetails later in Chapter 2). In the end, the more you invest in old-fashioned, eyes-on scouting, the more trail cameras you hang, the more you'll learn and the more effective your stand setups will become.

Hunting Edges & Corners

Hunters are naturally drawn to edges because we are visual creatures and want to see the world around us. But, there's a sound reason to hunt edges, as open areas typically represent the most reliable food sources, especially in farmland settings where crops like highly nutritious soybeans and corn are grown. Edges also funnel deer during rut periods, are places where deer can see each other readily, and bucks can keep track of does and competition. Scrapes and rubs regularly appear on field edges when hormones begin to flow.

The stand hung at the edge of the right agricultural field can prove to be bowhunting gold. This is often complicated by vast fields where deer come and go daily without discernible patterns. I encounter this often during early seasons – standing or recently harvested crops attract deer like ants to sugar – but leave hunters playing musical chairs while anticipating yesterday's pattern. Scouting and trail cameras may reveal a rough pattern, but on a micro level it remains a crapshoot in many cases. My general approach is to stick with the best intel available and gut it out in a single stand or blind, hoping lady luck will shine. Moving stands compulsively increases the risk of negatively altering deer movements.

In broken or hilly territory, or terrain well interspersed with creeks and draws, agricultural fields are often more irregular than the neat fields on

Farmland crops such as corn and alfalfa attract deer in droves, but don't discount natural provender like acorns.

flatter ground. These features include contours, rises and falls, and lobes of cultivated ground fitted around creek beds, headers, points and areas with poor drainage. These often create more inviting ground for feeding deer, providing security by minimizing exposure to human activities or including slightly better soil, moisture and forage that's more palatable.

These irregular edges also more reliably funnel deer past stands. A field contoured around a nasty thick or steep-walled header, for instance, might cause deer to swing around this point of brush or topography predictably. Ridge-point field "peninsulas" are some of my favorite stand sites, ridge points beyond cultivated ground offer gentler access into the field than ridge or bank edges, the compact crop lobe also offering security not found on open portions of large fields.

I always give field corners and field-lobe points extra scrutiny because these places naturally funnel deer movements, especially on fields edged by deep draws, ditches, creek beds or hillsides, or thick brush and timber deposited when the field was originally cleared. The natural inclination is for deer to follow edges while feeding, and especially while cruising during the rut. The corner or point serves as an intersection of opposing edges, mathematically doubling your chances of an up-close encounter.

Long-distance glassing during prime hours and trail-camera surveillance will help you discover concentrations of deer movement along field edges, but don't discount walking edges slowly during midday and noting beat-down trails entering fields, or concentrations of tracks on a particular patch of ground. During the days leading up to the rut keep your eyes peeled for scrapes and rubs indicating the presence of bucks.

Hunting corners is a sound ploy when pursuing white-tailed deer, since they serve as intersections from converging field edges.

Entrance & Exit Strategies

The biggest problem with field hunting is getting in and out of stands without clearing deer from the very field you hope to hunt. This is especially problematic during morning hunts, even more so during early seasons when deer adhere to strict early morning and late evening schedules due to daytime heat. Arriving well before daylight and taking the easy way to your stand by hiking across the open spaces will assure you've cleared that field of deer. Obviously a backdoor approach is in order.

To begin it is imperative to always heed wind direction, even if this requires a much earlier wakeup and a longer or more demanding hike into stands. If you walk upwind of deer—even under the cover of darkness, and even several hundred yards away—deer will clear out, leaving you guarding an empty field.

When possible, especially during early seasons, I generally avoid hunting open field edges in the morning, saving them for evening hunts when I can safely install myself on stand while deer are well removed. When no other options are available and morning hunts on field edges are neces-

Entrance and exit strategies are highly important to whitetail success, as spooking deer when coming and going turns good stands sour.

sary, I stick to stands with solid back door entrances that assure I spook fewer deer. Stands on field edges closely bordered by steep ditches or falling creek beds are one of my favorite setups. This allows sneaking up the bottom while wearing a red-lens LED headlamp, donning hip or chest waders when necessary (regular boots lashed to my daypack), remaining completely out of sight, scent and noise safely contained. I then climb out and straight into my stand. During evening hunts I reverse the procedure, slipping quietly out of my stand and into the creek bed to leave deer totally in the dark to my presence.

Sometimes approaching stands by way of the back door requires a bit more inventiveness, like using a steep ridge point, thick shelterbelt or irrigation dike and a low profile to disguise your approach. It doesn't matter if it's marginal, just as long as deer don't see, smell or hear you. In areas where they're abundant I've also issued turkey calls while entering evening stands, mostly while swinging through sensitive areas where deer are likely to be bedded within earshot, to cover any conspicuous movements through noisy cover or over blankets of dry leaves with nonthreatening calls that put deer at ease. If no other options are available, being dropped off by a friend or spouse via truck or ATV directly at your field-edge stand is often a viable option. In typical farmland settings deer are used to landowner traffic, often moving out of the way of a vehicle passing in the dark, quickly settling down and going back to business after the disturbance has passed.

Inside Cover

Another solution to addressing farm-country deer is to hunt inside cover hundreds of yards to maybe a half-mile from proven food sources to catch deer returning to or departing from bedding areas. This presents a couple real advantages. It allows you to sneak to stands while being assured deer are somewhere else, to minimize the chances of alerting them – be that farm fields during morning approaches or in beds when you return in the early afternoon. It also gives you a jump on vampirish bucks inclined to leave fields well before shooting light to beat the daylight, or those that wait until full nightfall to enter open areas. In other words, removing yourself from the immediate feeding area can mean deer move by your stand later in the morning or earlier in evening when getting a shot off during legal shooting hours is more likely.

During the rut, setting stands deeper into thick cover is a smart move to catch bucks scent-checking for does on adjacent fields.

Inside cover is also useful for ambushing bucks well away from open fields when they're not on specific bed to feed patterns. During the rut, for instance, finding trails well inside edge cover and downwind of open feeding areas is a sure bet for intercepting rutting bucks cruising for estrous does — the bucks remaining safe in disguising cover while scent checking the upwind field for potential mates.

I also like stands situated well inside thick cover, but otherwise sitting between two patches of obvious food sources. Let's say you have a corn field coming to a corner on a bend of a major drainage or woodlot, and another field, holding standing soybeans, is on the east side of that drainage or woodlot and terminating above a point. It's safe to assume deer regularly travel between these two obvious feeding areas. Somewhere between these points, let's say at a creek crossing or deep trail cutting a steep draw bank, is a pinch point where sitting a downwind stand is sure to result in deer sightings. There is a stand that is easy to get into without being seen, heard or smelled, and also a place where deer might feel secure moving at nearly any hour of the day. Such stands can prove priceless with reliable winds, producing year after year. Online aerial photographs are often invaluable for locating such sites, providing a bird's-eye perspective difficult to garner on foot.

Hunting inside cover in my area means short-stopping deer headed out of higher elevation big-woods sanctuaries and into outlaying areas (in our case, lower ground where recreational feeding by rural residents and the elevation limit of area agriculture—winter wheat, oats and peas—concentrates does and increased breeding opportunity). Our neighborhood is zoned in 40-, 80- and 120-acre parcels, many of them occupied by full-time, weekend and summertime residents and avid deer hunters that have turned area bucks largely nocturnal. While deer move freely nearly all day long at higher elevations, down in the farmlands it's rare to see a mature buck inside legal shooting hours. To hunt these bucks you must back well into wild woods for daytime encounters.

I've developed an approach for addressing such

Deer hunters gravitate to open fields because they can see long distances, but sometimes getting into the thick of things offers more encounters.

bucks, a time-consuming ploy requiring some amount of tracking savvy and persistence. This involves starting at a known point with trail cameras (multiple cameras shortens the process) and a buck making regular nighttime appearances. Feeding deer to create this starting point, where legal (for instance, feeding deer is legal in Idaho, though hunting over feed is not), is not out of the question. The idea is to then push cameras back from that starting point, using multiple cameras to cover multiple entrance points, attempting to capture a buck farther and farther from that starting point. My record with this approach, I believe, is about 2 miles from my starting point. I would like to say I tagged that buck—a beautiful 145-inch 4x4—but he was shot by a neighbor before I received an opportunity.

Inside Staging Areas

Some of the most useful pieces of inside cover are staging areas. These are usually a small opening, glade or patch of cover where bucks pause while awaiting the cover of darkness, and they create the ideal evening ambush site. I first detected this phenomenon while conducting back-track trail-camera scouting as described above. I would find that a particular buck showed up at a particular site, say a fruit tree, agricultural field, food plot, pond, fence corner or feed pile well after dark, something to the tune of 9 or 10 p.m. But after pushing trail cameras back only 300 or 400 yards I would discover a small meadow or glade where that buck hung out well before sundown, sometimes an hour, pausing to nibble and loiter before moving on. I had even captured images of such bucks bedded in these spots immediately prior to dark.

This is exciting stuff. Better yet, I soon discovered that I could improve this situation to my own needs by creating intimate "shot-plots" in natural openings by raking out debris, roughing up the soil and broadcasting fertilizer and "throw-and-grow" food plot seed. These weren't full-blown food plots, just a small patch of ground, say 10 to 20 yards across, where I offered a little snack while bucks cooled their heels awaiting the safety of darkness. These are also great spots to construct a mock scrape (see Understanding Rubs & Scrapes Section). I recently took an 8½-year-old warrior over such a setup.

Creeks & Ditches

It's rare farmland that isn't diced by an array of creeks or ditches. For the farmland bowhunter these often subtle topographical features figure significantly into bowhunting ambush, as not only do they dictate the layout of farm fields and roadways, but how deer are able to move about a given piece of property. Gentle swales with sloping banks often hold cover deer crave, but don't offer the aggressive funneling features of narrow creeks and draws with steep or vertical banks that prevent crossing without great effort. These steep-walled creeks and draws should be studied carefully, as they often dictate deer movements with precision.

One spot I've bowhunted in Kansas offers the perfect illustration. A brushy, 500-yard stretch of

Using trail cameras to locate staging areas—places deer pause before entering open fields at dark—helps pinpoint prime stand sites.

windbreak running between a rocky ridge and a sizable river separates two farm fields, one of irrigated corn, the other food-plot clover. The windbreak represents nothing more than a fence line and two-rut road segregating individual fields. But as you follow the windbreak downhill and toward the river, within 200 yards you'll discover a sudden erosion cut filled with rock and rusted appliances to help check further erosion. The cut starts with a sudden 3-foot drop and quickly turns into a major diversion 20 feet deep and walled like a house hallway, its impassible bottom a tangle of exposed roots and accumulated debris. Not incidentally, the very head of that abrupt draw includes a wide, beat-down trail, multiple trails fanning out to each side and showing that every deer paralleling that river bottom must detour up to the draw head to proceed up or downstream or while traveling between those fields.

At another site on that same Kansas farm, as another example, you'll find a wide, shallow shoal on that sizable river, the only viable crossing for miles in each direction. At that place are several deep trails cutting the steep, crumbly bank, offering passage across that major barrier and offering another obvious stand site. These crossing cuts are often more common in cattle country, but deer happily use them to ford major water barriers. In other cases farmers have employed heavy machinery to create access roads across creeks or small rivers which deer certainly aren't averse to employing.

Rest assured, unpressured deer will not risk injury or exert themselves unnecessarily to cross a steep-walled creek or draw in a treacherous or demanding spot. They would rather walk 200 yards out of their way than scramble across challenging obstacles. Walk out any steep-walled creek, ditch or sustained erosion cut traversing farm country and you'll invariably discover a place where walls slope more gently, a bank has been cut by wildlife or farm equipment, or erosion has been checked or naturally stalled. At that point you'll also find a narrow convergence of widely spoking trails where many white-tailed deer have passed. You have just discovered a prime stand site to intercept deer traveling between bedding and feeding areas, adjacent feeding areas, or just cruising during the frenzied days of the whitetail rut.

Funneling creek crossings are always good for ambushing a trophy buck, especially when these barriers include steep walls.

Big woods can spell big bucks, both in antler and body size. The author took this 250-pound trophy buck in Idaho mountain habitat.

CHAPTER 3

BIG-WOODS WHITETAILS

YOU'LL FIND CLASSIC BIG-WOODS habitats in many far-north states like the border regions of Maine, Michigan, Wisconsin and Minnesota, and especially Canada. Big woods might also constitute wilderness like New York's 6-million-acre Adirondacks Park and Minnesota/Manitoba/Ontario's 70-square-mile Lake of the Woods and its 14,552 islands. In my portion of whitetaildom, the Inland Northwest of eastern Washington, northern Idaho and western Montana, big-woods also means major mountain ranges and bowhunting whitetails alongside Rocky Mountain elk. Perhaps the biggest challenge with big-woods or wilderness hunting is the obvious intimidation factor brought on by an overwhelming expanse of country. To top it off terrain is often foreboding, vegetation impenetrable and deer densities inherently low. This isn't farmland habitat where food is super abundant and bedding areas, travel ways and food concentrations are easily identifiable. This is habitat where every square acre constitutes bedding possibilities, the sky is the limit regarding movement patterns, food is highly scattered, normally nonspecific or even sparse.

On the positive side, most big-woods habitat is made of wide-open public lands, human hunting pressure often low to nonexistent (though wolves and mountain lions keep deer on their toes in many regions), especially if you're willing to travel off the beaten path. A good percentage of big-woods bucks mature and die of old age without encountering hunters. This produces a healthy percentage of 4- to 6-year-old bucks growing the largest antlers. And while most big-woods deer can't access the fat-producing crops that corn-fed Midwestern bruisers are privy to, Bergmann's Rule says the farther north and colder the geographic range, the larger the animals' body sizes. Hence, it's not uncommon to tag big-woods bucks weighing 225 to 250 pounds or more; a trophy in itself.

Although big-woods population densities never match even marginal farmland settings, the upside includes a more defined rut sparked by healthier herd dynamics – a higher percentage of mature bucks seeking a balanced ratio of receptive does and the natural competition that results. This, combined with relatively low hunting pressure, results in abundant daytime movement and success while hunting directly over scrapes and along rub lines. This success can also include building mock scrapes (see Understanding Rubs and Scrapes chapter) and bringing bucks beneath stands with aggressive calling ploys such as rattling and grunting (see Calling

Big-woods habitats give deer room to grow old. Even in an area with intense rifle hunting pressure the author tagged this 8½-year-old buck.

All Deer chapter). Big-woods deer truly encourage all-day vigils, as you simply never know when they will appear.

Make no mistake, big-woods deer hunting is extremely demanding. Lower deer densities mean fewer opportunities, longer sits between sightings and more demanding scouting. Deer prove highly scattered when given unlimited room to roam, though during the rut big-woods deer tend to cluster in specific patches of habitat, leaving lots of empty space between honey holes. One bright spot is that deer normally return to these chosen honey-holes annually, save a major alteration to habitat like extensive logging activity. Finally, big-woods weather can prove brutally nasty, including mixed rain and snow—or just lots of snow—killing temperatures and wind. While extreme weather typically encourages deer movement in these habitats, surviving all-day sits in those conditions can prove demanding. This can also make getting around interesting, especially when your best stand requires a 20-minute ATV ride and 30-minute hike to access.

Big patches of woods can prove intimidating. Narrow down hunting prospects by carefully studying maps for potential hotspots.

Overcoming Big-Woods Intimidation

The sometimes rugged and always enormous scope of big-woods whitetail habitat can prove daunting, the prospect of plucking a trophy buck from seemingly endless landscape appearing as hopeless as locating the proverbial needle in a haystack. This isn't Iowa or Illinois—where guarding obvious agricultural crops or isolated, acorn-bearing oak groves virtually guarantees sightings. The big-woods and mountain whitetail's supermarket is typically less defined and often spread thinly. Highly physical, ground-gobbling scouting is the name of the game.

Early season scouting requires a sharp eye since subtle tracks and droppings are not as obvious as the rubs and scrapes appearing by late October. Watering sites, normally secreted springs or seeps, can prove productive during early seasons in drier Western habitats, as well as north-slope benches where daytime temperatures are cooler. Trail cameras are indispensable in this vast habitat.

Big-woods whitetail hunting really heats up with the approach of the rut. Low population densities mean bucks travel more widely, and more importantly, scrapes and rubs become pivotal to herd communication. Scrapes are visited more regularly in the search for highly scattered does, and freshened more frequently due to generally wetter fall weather patterns. I regularly sacrifice stand time during the rut for intense in-season scouting to seek the latest intelligence. I travel light, toting a recurve holding a mini quiver and arrows in case I encounter a volunteer, and a daypack containing water, topographical-map-equipped GPS for marking hotspots, folding saw and two dozen screw-in steps to ready discovered stand sites, mock-scrape makings, plus several compact trail cameras to set as sign dictates.

I might traverse 50 miles of logging roads by ATV and hike another five to eight in a day, sometimes accomplishing nothing more than eliminating dead ground. Should I discover copious sign, a rub line or especially a major scrape, I conduct some quick trimming, install screw-in steps and deploy a camera. It's not uncommon for me to have 25 or 30 trees prepped for quick stand deployment, many of which are never used but stand ready nonetheless. This makes it easier to toss up a stand as needed, namely after returning to find intriguing images on a trail camera. In the heat of the rut I normally check cameras with a lightweight, aluminum-frame stand strapped on my back (or at least on the ATV), allowing me to set up and hunt within the hour should the need arise.

Trail cameras are important to any whitetail hunting, but in the big woods you're literally hunting blind without them. It's difficult enough to sit three of four days without a deer sighting, but having proof a big buck is frequenting an area allows you to confidently gut it out. In these cold, harsh conditions I demand three things of a trail camera: It must be affordable – $150 to $200, any priced lower are frequently troublesome; it must be dependable; and it must be AA-battery powered. I often have 20 to 25 units scattered across 150 square miles of mountain habitat and don't have time for failures. The rut offers only fleeting opportunity. Losing an entire week of intel due to a malfunctioning camera is infuriating. I choose only AA-powered units because lithium batteries (offered only in AA) last eight times longer than alkaline and are unaffected by extreme cold. Alkaline batteries freeze when temperatures hit single digits, rendering cameras inoperable.

I pair every unit with two 8 GB SD cards, coded with indelible ink to avoid cross-use in other units, especially those of another brand. This allows me to walk in, power the unit off, swap cards, switch it back on and be on my way, reviewing cards on a more detailed home computer at my leisure. But, scouting cameras with viewing screens or a handheld card reader prove useful when hunting on the fly. It's not uncommon during the rut for a cold stand to turn suddenly hot when a single doe comes into estrous.

On-the-ground scouting—and a little help from strategically placed trail cameras—is vital to finding big-woods whitetail success.

When habitats are seemingly endless, trail cameras become that much more important for scoping out many potential sites.

Topography & Natural Barriers

Obviously, funneling influences differ widely based on the kind of big-woods settings under discussion. Relatively flat and swampy northern boreal forests, for instance, share little resemblance to Appalachian or Rocky Mountain terrain, or smaller ranges like the Northeast's Adirondacks and Catskills, Green and White mountains or Arkansas' Ozark plateau. Each requires a unique approach according to prevailing habitat types.

Mountain Bucks

When seeking mountain bucks I concentrate efforts on three basic terrain features: benches, ridgelines and especially saddles. Benches can mean wide, flat spots formed on ridge points, or long shelves running along canyon walls. In timber country defunct logging skids and grown-over landings also serve as benches, offering easier travel through thronged second growth or steep terrain. Ridgelines are often used by deer to traverse terrain with less effort, ridge crests serving as virtual deer highways in jumbled or steep terrain and effectively concentrating deer movement. This is usually evidenced by well-worn trails. Saddles offer the path of least resistance between adjacent bowls, hillsides or valleys. As an added bonus, all of these terrain features also happen to be places where scent is most easily managed. Scouting is accomplished on foot, putting in miles tracing out sinuous ridges, exploring remote benches and investigating saddles for converging trails, fresh sign, and especially major sign-board scrapes during the rut—not smaller frustration-displacement scrapes that are seldom visited again (see Understanding Rubs and Scrapes chapter).

In new territory I normally spend hours poring over topographical maps, earmarking interesting terrain features and access roads, ATV trails or abandoned logging skids that can get me near these features with minimal effort. This saves time and makes scouting trips more productive. Developing an eye for a topographical map's system of contour lines used to show elevation changes eventually allows you a virtual bird's-eye view of real estate, which helps to pare down vast country into manageable pieces. Each contour line represents a particular elevation snaking around ridge points, saddles, mountains and hillsides. They can be continuous or closed, a hill peak, for instance, indicated

Natural funnels such as saddles and points are easy to find on detailed topographical maps, but you must still inspect each on foot.

It's physically impossible to cover every acre of mountain habitat. Start by carefully studying maps to better grasp the lay of the land.

by a series of small circles resembling a bull's-eye. The closer together the contours, the steeper the terrain; the more widely spaced, the more gentle that piece of ground is. Popular 1:25,000 scale topos, for instance, include contour lines showing 40-foot spaces in elevation and offer enough detail to read terrain fairly precisely.

So a ridge point, for instance, might appear as a series of open arrowheads, all pointing downhill, closed contours representing small peaks or rises on that ridge. On each flank will run long, generally parallel contours showing hillsides to each slope of the ridge crest, broken occasionally by arrow points or jogs indicating small canyon heads flowing off that ridge. A flat-topped ridge with steep sides may reveal a welcoming travel-way, while a gentler ridge point would prove more inviting while accessing lower ground than one falling vertically. Benches show where contours are more widely spaced but surrounded by more constricted contours of the steeper terrain above and below the flat shelf. Saddles appear as hourglasses, opposing points with a gap between. A wide bowl, showing horseshoe contours that are moderately spaced would make a more inviting bedding area than a straight contoured hillside with closely-spaced contour lines indicating steep terrain.

Often, if I stare at topo maps long enough, I begin to see how I might traverse a piece of landscape; walking through a saddle, side-hilling to reach a slightly lower bench, hitting a pinch point at the bench's end, side-hilling to reach a ridge point and descending into a meadow below. Then when tracing these routes afoot it's amazing how often the route I've conceived on paper also contains beat-down game trails and concentrations of sign on the ground. Deer are lazy by nature, or maybe it's more fair to say their survival depends on conserving energy whenever possible. Deer will not work for or give up elevation when unnecessary, nor will they fight tangled brush or blowdowns when an uncluttered route is offered.

Mountain terrain generally makes scent management easier on stand, if you just avoid obvious traps. These traps include confined bottoms, bowls or headers where breezes eddy and swirl. Prevailing winds aside, mountain air can generally be counted on to flow downhill when it's cool—early mornings and late evenings during early seasons—and uphill when warming during midday. Typically the safest approach is to hang stands on points or ridges situated 90 degrees to prevailing winds, or downhill but slightly higher than benches and ridges where deer are traveling. Saddles are trickier since their corners own the potential for producing back-curling eddies. The safest bet is to hang stands on the downwind gap or in the high point of the saddle where funneling breezes shoot straight through and into treetops where terrain falls away beyond. The idea for hanging any mountain stand is to climb high enough to allow human scent to ride breezes into open space well above a deer's head, while situated just above the line of sight of passing deer. In many cases, this involves climbing 35 to 45 feet off the ground to address deer only 18 or 20 yards away and slightly below your position, due to terrain climbing away quickly from the stand-tree base.

Only very rarely, under very specific circumstances, have I found pop-up blinds useful in mountain terrain. The problem is normally one of falling terrain, as often thronged vegetation provides very limited visibility to the point that deer must be standing on a very specific patch of ground to offer a viable shot. Treestand elevation simply opens up more shooting options.

North-Woods Bucks

In lower elevation Northern habitats broken terrain features may factor in to some degree, but normally on more of a micro level than the bigger ranges already discussed. From my experience the Far North's abundant waterways and swamps do more to influence deer movement than geological formations. I could also say the same of Deep South settings, where woods may not be as expansive when translated into square miles, but habitat is just as nasty and challenging. Creek and river crossings are always worth investigating in these circumstances, as while deer are certainly strong swimmers – I've seen white-tailed deer swimming far from shore on the mighty Mississippi River, for instance – given a choice they would much rather traipse across water barriers without getting their bellies wet. Find a shallow shoal on an otherwise deep or swift river or creek and you'll likely discover deep-cut trails revealing evidence of frequent crossings.

To this affect beaver dams often create welcome crossing spots. I recall a small, likely unnamed creek in New York's Adirondacks, deep in the wilderness and accessed only after a full day of paddling and several arduous portages. The late-September foray was largely a fishing expedition, with bows and arrows tossed in as an afterthought because the season opener coincided with our plans. The area wasn't exactly filthy with deer, but wading up a tannin-stained creek one afternoon tossing streamers on a

In northern whitetail habitats water barriers often become more reliable funneling aspects than saddles or ridges.

light fly rod, stringing up a few rock bass for dinner, I encountered a small beaver dam stretched across the creek. I couldn't help but notice the trails at each end, carved deep into the steep, mossy banks. Now this wasn't much of a creek, sluggish water I could easily wade across nearly anywhere, but here was this beaver dam and those conspicuous trails. To make a long story mercifully short, I invested just a single evening there and tagged a small-antlered but heavy wilderness buck, my hunting partner collecting a black bear there a couple days later. In all of that trackless wilderness of low-density game we managed to fill two tags in a week on a single seemingly insignificant beaver dam. Imagine the possibilities on a larger beaver dam bridging a more significant waterway.

Beaver ponds and waterways are also the deflection barriers that topography is in mountain areas. Even on skinny water an ambitious beaver dam can create a sizeable pond with deep upper channels that work to funnel deer from a wider area and through a narrower corridor. Chain lakes and ponds or intermittent beaver ponds are also attractive, acting as watery saddles for deer passing from one side of a valley to the other.

River and creek bends are always reliable deer funnels, as they push deer around these points on the path of least resistance.

On large far-northern Idaho lakes I always take the time to explore the head of lakes fed by major rivers, especially the long finger ridges of mature trees often jutting out into open water. Deer frequent these snaking points because they are seldom disturbed (it requires some effort, and a shallow-draft boat, to reach them) and feed is abundant. These fingers are narrow enough that a bowhunter with a compound bow need only to locate a gap in the trees to cover the strip of land bank to bank, though blow-downs and swampy spots generally encourage distinct trails that are easily guarded.

Contour maps also come into play in seemingly topographically featureless Northern whitetail country. These maps can prove especially useful in swamp country and reveal high hummocks of dry ground, or slight ridges traversing wetter surroundings. These are features that could prove difficult to simply stumble upon while hiking. More pointedly, who makes a point of wading through nasty swamps on the off chance of stumbling across such places? Maps establish a destination and real motivation to don waders and slog in for a closer look. Again, whitetails don't mind getting their feet wet – in fact when heavily pressured they often take to nasty wetlands like African sitatunga, a water-loving antelope – but when undisturbed they certainly prefer to tread solid ground instead of mucking through deep mud. "Bridges" or "ridges" of higher ground traversing wetlands, or an "island" hummock of hardwoods, can prove to be a deadly stand spot in swampy big-woods settings.

I've also killed a good number of bucks in places as varied as northern Idaho, southern Georgia and Saskatchewan by setting up over river, swamp and beaver-pond edge transition zones that naturally funnel traveling deer.

No matter the scenario, careful attention to wind direction is, as usual, imperative. This is complicated by the fact that so many Far North and Deep South habitats involve bottoms where wind eddies and swirls are possible. The best possible use of bottoms is finding a situation where breezes flow harmlessly over open water where deer obviously won't walk. I've also found situations where climbing high enough gets you above the heavy coolness

Far North deer habitats often include low-lying, swampy terrain with few sizable trees. Pop-up blinds are an obvious answer.

of ground-hugging dampness, which allows scent to tower away on rising thermals. While scouting, the liberal use of wind-detecting powder often reveals these wind-friendly spots.

Pop-up blinds can also prove quite useful in these situations, granted visibility is sufficient. The safest bet in low-lying areas is to dig a foot-deep or deeper pit to match your blind's footprint, then set the erected blind inside this excavation and backfill to seal its skirting. The blind is then backed with nasty brush to assure deer don't travel downwind and only windows facing probable shooting lanes are opened. This approach effectively seals scent into the blind (some models actually include scent-control technology) and allows setting up in places with swirling winds or swampy settings where an appropriate stand tree is absent.

Paddle Bucks

I can't think of Far North, big-woods whitetails without also envisioning canoes or kayaks, campfires and fishing poles—likely a result of my adventurous New York Adirondack experiences. I can also recall many Deep South locations where a canoe or kayak would have come in handy for bowhunting white-tailed deer—*Deliverance* style, but without the dueling banjos and psychotic hillbillies. Canoes, and more recently kayaks, offer an obvious mode of transportation along remote big-woods waters for obvious reasons, but also because they require no boat ramps or gentle banks to launch, and also prove more versatile on shallow waters. These small watercraft are plenty stealthy, allowing you to silently access riparian habitats commando style and catch deer completely off guard.

Most often I break this style of hunting into day trips or full-scale expeditions.

Be it a quick crossing to access little-hunted ground beyond a deep or swift river, slipping into that secreted swamp hummock while remaining dry, or a sneaky backdoor approach along a large pond or lake, a compact and maneuverable kayak and climbing stand are ideal for day-trip sits.

Larger lakes and rivers invite more extensive exploration, paddling into remote areas and camping to provide quick access to untouched whitetail ground. In general, canoes are best here, and allow packing more gear like stands, bowhunting duds and archery gear, though larger, sit-inside kayaks can be used with prudent packing. Whether traveling by canoe or kayak, packing for prolonged adventures requires careful planning. Think in terms of backpacking, as while you can carry a bit more gear and luxuries in canoes and kayaks than on your back, you obviously don't have the unlimited space afforded by a truck or SUV base camp. The issue isn't so much weight as space, especially when hunting gear is added to necessary camping gear and food. Backpacking stoves and tents, nesting cook kits, mini lanterns, water filtration system and your lightest, most compact sleeping gear are best. Dehydrated food is also a real space saver. Remember, too, to place all gear—especially clothing and sleeping bags—into rubberized dry bags, or at least plastic lawn bags, to protect them from paddle drip and spray.

No matter the trip, short or long, don't leave home without a life vest – an absolute necessity during cold fall seasons and on any flowing water.

Paddling into remote deer country is a classic mode of operation in northern whitetail woods – kayaks and canoes are your vehicles.

Big-Woods Attractions

Whitetails are always hungry and food is always the main attraction. In big-woods settings whitetail food isn't as cut and dried (no pun intended) as farmland fields of corn, soybeans, alfalfa and such. Whitetail far from croplands must scrounge for subsistence, often living the "twig-burning" existence of the mountain mule deer. I have experienced worthwhile success on big-woods deer by creating simple throw-and-grow food plots with hand tools and no-till seed where legal. This includes a tremendous amount of work, despite the "no-sweat" sales pitches offered by plot-seed companies. It starts by locating a small opening in the forest, or opening up a thin spot, where wind is also beneficial to bowhunting. This normally includes an ax and handsaw, though schlepping a small chainsaw into a remote spot isn't out of the question where it's legal. Definitely check into the laws and regulations regarding this practice on public land before proceeding.

There are then two basic approaches: apply herbicide to eliminate competition, lime to neutralize almost certain soil acidity, and after waiting the appointed amount of time for herbicide to dissipate, rake, hoe and sow no-till seed or hardy clover purchased from a local farm-supply outlet. Or, you simply rake to loosen soil, seed and rake again to maximize seed-to-soil contact, hoping for the best.

Natural food plots, of sorts, are found in big-woods settings via beaver dams and clear-cuts. Beaver-pond edges, especially those that have been breached to leave a drained patch of rich earth, normally harbor lush forbs that deer relish. While new clear-cuts are ugly to behold, removing old-growth or mature-succession timber and burning slash piles creates instant new growth like broad-leaf forbs, tender grasses and second-growth shrubs deer enjoy—mature trees mostly good only for bedding cover, winter shelter and spotted owls. In North Idaho I scout clear-cut edges as carefully as I do Midwest farm fields, looking for concentrations of sign and vectoring trails.

How About Those Apples?

One of my favorite big-woods whitetail draws are feral apple or pear trees, or ancient homestead orchards gone to seed. Deer have a universal sweet tooth, and sweet fall apples and pears will not go unnoticed by deer in any habitat—even the Midwest land of milk and honey. It is simply amazing the places I run across wild fruit trees, and when I do, I don't care if I'm three steps behind a bu-

Food is everything when pursuing white-tailed deer. Small "shot plots" are one place to find scattered deer; feral fruit trees another.

gling Idaho elk or have a New York spring gobbler coming in hot and heavy, I'm going to stop, dig out my GPS posthaste, mark that tree and label it with exclamation marks. A feral apple or pear tree that has volunteered near some unnamed spring or miraculously survived to maturity along a lonely ridge, a hardscrabble farm marked only by a crumbling chimney and a few hoary heirloom apple trees, translates into a big-woods whitetail bonanza. While those trees may not produce fruit every year due to vagaries of frosts, heavy winds and moisture, when they do you can rest assured you'll put an arrow through a buck feeding beneath its branches.

When I discover one of these lost jewels I treat it like a newborn, nurturing it, feeding it, helping it remain healthy. Pruning is a good start, but always proceed with caution on antique trees, as you can send them into shock with too much cutting all at once. Simply eliminate obvious water shoots on lower branches and the trunk, any branches that abrade one another and all dead wood. Sprinkle tree-specific fertilizer beneath its branches or drive fertilizer stakes around its drip line according to directions. Pack in bails of old hay or bags of grass clippings and spread them at its base for mulch during dry years. Take care of that tree and it will yield much big-woods venison.

In other big-woods settings, from the Allegheny Mountains of Pennsylvania to the Ozark Plateau of Arkansas, acorns and persimmons prove the huge natural draw. This is ridge-line hunting for the most part, creating perfect settings for concentrated deer and automatic scent management. You'll normally find that deer prefer one acorn species over another, white oaks typically number one, with species like bitter red oak acorns consumed only after white oak nuts are exhausted. There is also the business of one tree proving regularly more appealing than others around it. It might be a matter of superior soil chemistry or moisture intake, but the nuts on that oak are simply sweeter and attract more attention from deer. I've conducted experiments by fertilizing specific trees with some success, the added nutrients making acorns from that tree more desirable. No matter, in big-woods settings you'll normally be required to figure this stuff out through old-fashioned scouting, first determining what the desired acorn species is in your neck of the woods, and then scouting out trees garnering the most attention in the form of fresh tracks and especially droppings – which are much easier to age accurately than tracks.

Knowing what deer in your area prefer to eat is highly important. Consulting with an area game biologist can be very helpful in this respect.

The secret is out: North America's open spaces, once neglected, produce some of the highest-scoring white-tailed bucks around.

CHAPTER 4

PLAINS & PRAIRIE WHITETAILS

I NOW RECALL MY FIRST time bowhunting Colorado's Eastern Plains whitetails with amusement. The night before we'd motored east out of Denver, pushing farther from the Rocky Mountains with each minute and driving across some of the most desolate and forsaken countryside I'd ever witnessed. Even pronghorn hunts enjoyed in New Mexico, Wyoming and Montana included more topography than I witnessed on that ride. Leaving the motel in the dark morning we sped east toward Kansas, negotiating a labyrinth of square-cornered county roads following random section lines, dipping only occasionally to cross shallow draws. I rode in silence, confident a great river or major canyon lay out there somewhere in my future.

When my friend parked at daylight and began to assemble gear I wondered if an elaborate joke was afoot, waiting for him to say something to the effect of, "Just joking! But you should have seen the look on your face!"

To the south lay a seamless plowed field, rolling away to the horizon in dizzying monotony. To the north, the direction my friend indicated we'd be hiking, was an ocean of CRP grass nodding gently to a sharp-edged November breeze, interrupted by only the occasional weedy swale or tight barbed-wire fence stretching to obscurity over a distant skyline.

Pronghorn? Definitely! Mule deer? Maybe... But whitetails?

I knew whitetail habitat, and this wasn't it. Where were the woodlots, the riparian corridors, or at least some scattered patches of thorny scrub that might serve as daytime bedding cover? Even if we did see a white-tailed deer—which I seriously doubted—how was I supposed to get within range?

I won't cliff hang you here. It took only an hour in that drab landscape to see the light, finding a pretty 140-ish 4x4 shadowing a small knot of does, dodging and crawling until he was 40 yards away and mine for the taking. But I passed – my curiosity was peaked and I wanted to see more. By lunchtime I'd been within bow range of three different bucks wearing antlers large enough to pass P&Y minimums. I stalked another gorgeous 4x5 scoring around 145 inches, but was just never able to close the deal. By that evening I'd passed another 140-inch 4x4 bedded in an open field of harvested milo, thin stubble strips and rattling wind covering our approach to 45 yards before I passed. Then that evening I had another near miss with the 145-inch 4x5 we'd stalked that morning.

I fell into contented slumber, knees sore and raw, palms filled with sand-spur spines, and visions of big-antlered whitetail bucks dancing in my head.

Before noon the following day I'd put an arrow through that wide 4x5 with a very long shot, as

The author tagged this bruiser buck on the desolate, wide-open plains of eastern Colorado, though he observed much larger bucks.

whitetail shots go, collecting one of the prettiest whitetails I'd tagged to that date and forever changing my perceptions of what constitutes trophy whitetail grounds. Since that day I've taken open-country whitetails in places such as western Kansas, Nebraska's northern Sandhill country and the pan-flat shadows of South Dakota's Black Hills. Today, to my mind, prairie habitat equals behemoth white-tailed bucks.

Spot & Stalk Primer

What comes as the biggest shock during any plains-whitetail initiation—after the initial shock of the landscape itself—is the standard mode of operation. We have been brainwashed to believe whitetails are unapproachable afoot through decades of stationary pursuit, so it is somewhat worrisome to arrive on foreign ground to discover you'll be required to slip into bow range using nothing but your wits and the scanty cover provided. You glance around at all that wide-open space and are not inspired, your confidence draining away like an emptying bathtub.

But you must shake away the doubt, gird your determination and jump in with both feet. It also helps if someone has reminded you to pack knee pads and leather gloves. Rancho Safari offers quiet fleece-covered knee pads made for bowhunting that work quite well, instead of hard-shelled numbers meant for home flooring projects. One of those stretch-fit arm guards pulled over each elbow never hurts either. This isn't going to be pretty, but the most undignified and painful snake-belly crawls eventually result in the biggest rewards.

It's a funny thing about prairie habitat, only when you get down on hands and knees do you notice the subtleties, what constitutes disguising cover and begins to make what appears impossible completely feasible. Let's put it this way, go barreling across an average piece of prairie ground in your pickup at 50 mph and you're gonna break something vital beneath its undercarriage. There is a vast array of small erosion cuts, shallow gullies, dips and humps and clusters of yucca cactus, broomgrass or snakeweed, tumbleweeds and swales of knee-deep CRP grasses. I've used irrigation-pump heads, sorghum round bales, rusted farm implements and a single hoary cottonwood bole as cover during prairie stalks, keeping that seemingly insignificant object between me and a buck's eyes while scrambling closer. Of course sometimes you have to wait deer out, allowing them to vacate impossible terrain like grazed-down pasture, 2-inch-tall winter wheat—and wander into ground more beneficial to your cause.

Deer are at several disadvantages in such settings. Most importantly, they can't conceive of anything stalking them in that wide-open terrain, convinced their sharp eyesight and noses will warn them of approaching danger. Second, it's a rare prairie set-

It's easy to dismiss wide-open prairies and plains habitats, but some of the nation's biggest bucks are found in such places.

ting that doesn't include daily wind, or at least a stiff breeze. This helps cover the occasional crunch of dried grass, gravel or the clatter of archery equipment scooted ahead while crawling, most especially while approaching from the necessary downwind angle, which pushes sound away from them more thoroughly. Finally, believe it or not, it's infinitely easier to stalk deer that are readily observed than their woodland counterparts, timing moves when a deer's eyesight is obscured, attention focused elsewhere, holding stock still should they glance your way or stand to stretch.

The Spot In Stalk

To begin you must obviously find a target of interest. While I normally abhor road hunting, it is actually most productive in many open prairie habitats. Deer will often tolerate a parked truck in plain sight when they wouldn't tolerate a skylined human at the same distance, especially in busy ranch or farm country. This also allows you to cover more ground efficiently, driving ranch and farm roads, section lines, even county roads, stopping on slight rises and putting quality optics to work. Also, don't hesitate to make use of man-made structures like windmills, grain silos, haystacks and even oil-field pumps and storage tanks to gain elevation for more productive glassing in flat terrain.

The prairie hunter needs top-quality binoculars, 10x42mm binoculars are my standard workhorse, plus a decent variable-power spotting scope in something like a 15-45x60 configuration with a window mount for road hunting and tripod for foot hunts. It's normally easy enough to spot deer in open country at reasonable ranges, but you soon learn to seek them at distances measured in miles instead of hundreds of yards. This is where the spotting scope comes in, sizing up not only antlers, but planning sensible plans of attack according to terrain and wind direction while still at a safe distance.

Once a desirable buck is spotted you have a decision to make: start a stalk immediately, or wait for that deer to bed. That decision really depends on the time of day, weather conditions and forecast, and especially terrain. There might also be other considerations such as property boundaries; where you're allowed to hunt versus where a buck travels during daily patterns. For example, I once pursued a monster buck in Eastern Colorado, a true Booner, that fed each night on an open winter wheat field, passing over a patch of ground we had permission to hunt, but retreating to a strictly off-limits national park each morning to bed. The challenge was to catch him on 500 yards of wide-open grass separating the two properties, a mission I obviously failed despite five days of concerted effort.

Traveling deer—more common during the rut

In the right prairie habitats the bowhunter shouldn't dismiss spot-and-stalk tactics, as they can prove highly productive.

Open prairie habitat makes scouting more productive when using optics to cover vast amounts of land more quickly.

when the weather is cooler—offer the option of circling to arrive in front of them, granted the wind direction is useful, and waiting motionless for an approach. Should a deer cross a coulee or patch of sandhills, as examples, the stalking hunter is given the chance to approach quickly, sometimes literally running to close the gap before dropping to crawl to the coulee lip or sandhill corner for the shot. Bedded deer are sometimes easier, allowing you to take your time, crawling ahead slowly, catching your breath between pushes. This might also allow a friend to sit well back and hand signal adjustments to your trajectory so you never have to expose yourself, instead just rolling over and glassing back for instructions instead of peeking out of cover to relocate your bedded buck.

Open country also welcomes the use of calls and decoys, especially useful when you have run out of cover or become pinned down by too many does surrounding a rutting buck. When all other options are exhausted, offering a quick rattling sequence, grunt or tipping a challenging buck decoy into view can turn things around in a hurry. Getting a clean shot on a curious or charging white-tailed buck—now that's a different matter altogether, but calling is exactly how I killed one of my best prairie bucks to date.

Skimpy Cover Concealment

Though the situation is often complicated by a lack of trees, or more commonly a lack of trees in exactly the right place, stationary hunting can be quite deadly when bowhunting prairie bucks. Even the most barren portions of the Great Plains harbor spotty trees of some sort, many of them introduced by man—windbreaks, "timber claims" or abandoned homesteads—others occurring naturally along low-lying areas, seasonal creeks or rivers. Some of these strings or patches of trees don't amount to much, but typically prove productive for bowhunters, especially from late October through November when love is in the air.

Having hunted Great Plains whitetails on many occasions, a region that has resulted in two of my all-time best white-tailed bucks from country most serious whitetail hunters would label worthless and blast right past, I've learned even the skimpiest trees

Most modern bowhunters are programmed to hunt from stands or blinds, but open areas welcome stalking.

are like a "Field of Dreams" for prairie whitetails. When the rut arrives, if there are trees, bucks will come, as even prairie whitetails must rub and scrape as part of their mating rituals.

Windbreaks & Crooked Trees

I recall an abandoned and rerouted county road dead-ending at a scrawny strip of exactly eight Dutch elm trees jutting into wide-open CRP field. It was a place I nearly dismissed out of hand, uglier than homemade soap but for the profusion of scrapes and rubs. I killed one of my all-time best bucks on that unattractive tree line.

I also remember a 10-acre West Texas pasture I was allowed to hunt for free – nearly unheard of in the Lone Star State – because it was so unremarkable. Marking the back property boundary was a 200-yard shelter belt, a line of cottonwoods marking one edge, a neat row of Russian olives set a few yards inside those, the windbreak connecting a vast CRP field and sandy, shin-oak pasture. That shelter belt always held scrapes and rubs, though the biggest bucks seemed to appear only after darkness – and this was before trail cameras, so I never did know what might live there. I never killed a book buck there but did tag two eating-fat bucks during those lean college years when fresh meat was a godsend.

I also recall arriving on Colorado's Eastern Plains one November to unseasonably hot and dry conditions, deer movement minimized by the heat and stalking complicated by crunchy ground. In desperation, I hung a stand in a lonely windmill occupying a cattle-trampled flat. The last evening of my hunt I arrowed a 150-inch 5x5 buck that sprouted from open ground as if by alchemy to drink from

Limited trees can force stand hunters to get creative by hunting from pop-up blinds, windmills or inherently unsafe cottonwoods with strap-on steps.

Portable ground blinds are a plains staple. The author has found that setting them conspicuously is often better then camouflaging them.

an overflow puddle 40 yards away.

The problem with wind-tortured prairie trees is they seldom offer ideal stand platforms. Common shelter belt Osage orange and elms are either crooked or scrawny or both, while mature cottonwoods can prove outright dangerous with bark too thick to allow safe use of screw-in steps, branches often brittle and unreliable. This can demand creativity in regards to crooked or slender trees, though a couple manufacturers like Twisted Timber and Swivel Seat offer stands designed specifically to address such situations. Regarding cottonwoods, I'll only use strap-on steps and only attach stands to healthy trees and on the main trunk below any forks.

Making Use of Ground Blinds

I once believed pop-up blinds came into existence strictly to serve open-country bowhunters. That isn't completely true, of course, but nowhere is a portable ground blind more at home than on the open plains. Those twisted or too-skinny trees that make hanging a conventional stand so challenging create excellent background clutter for disguising pop-up blinds, helping them melt into landscape and pass scrutiny from wary whitetails. How you deploy pop-ups really depends on whether you live near your prairie hunting ground or are traveling there with limited time. No matter what your approach is, I always prefer to stab pop-ups into a shrubby line of vegetation or tall grass along a brushy draw, field edge, shelter belt or CRP field, surgically trimming out an exact footprint and replacing the void with the camouflaged blind. A liberal application of grass, brush and branches then helps the blind blend right in, making it ready for immediate use. Blinds with sewn-on material loops are especially helpful when light material like grass and weeds must be used to disguise a blind.

When handy access allows you to set up blinds well ahead of the season, say two weeks minimum – the longer the better – placing a blind dead in the open where camouflaging material simply doesn't exist isn't out of the question. This is especially true where farming activity is common, since deer are accustomed to machinery and hay bales here today, gone tomorrow. In fact, newer bale blinds are often just the ticket in prairie country, especially where round hay bales are common. I've actually discovered that when hunting wide-open places—say near a cattle-trampled watering site or on a harvested field—deer are often more comfortable with the glaring appearance of a blind than slip-shod attempts to brush blinds over in the same settings. Deer don't even seem to trust pop-ups with ragged, 3-D camouflage edges in these situations. It's as if making the blind obvious makes it less threatening in their minds.

There was a pop-up blind I occupied in South Dakota recently that was erected and occupied in the same hour, but set amongst a jumble of defunct farm machinery, car parts and assorted junk without any brush cover. A good number of deer passed within easy range on their way to alfalfa fields without giving me a second glance.

Just another day of whitetail hunting on the wide-open plains.

When bowhunting whitetails from pop-up blinds, it's normally best to place them out weeks ahead of the season so that deer will become accustomed to them.

Unlike most North American big game, whitetails thrive close to man. This has made suburban whitetail hunting more common. *(Photo credit Thomas Kirkland)*

CHAPTER 5

SUBURBAN WHITETAIL

THE WIDESPREAD DISTRIBUTION OF white-tailed deer is a testament to their extreme adaptability, being able to thrive in Southern swamps, Northern woodlands, Midwest farmlands, Great Plains prairies and Texas deserts. Add to this list of disparate habitats America's growing suburban sprawl. Around large and small towns across the nation surprisingly productive whitetail hunting is found at the edges of populated metropolitan areas where the sounds of traffic, barking dogs and neighborhood pick-up games often supplant chirping birds and hammering woodpeckers. Hunting pressure varies from nearly zero—due to a non-hunting public or difficulty obtaining hunting access—to intense in areas where residents demand culling to minimize vehicle collisions, exposure to Lyme's Disease or garden destruction.

While it can prove difficult to establish a foothold on many suburban properties, those in the loop actually kill some of this country's most impressive bucks each year. Living in the neighborhood or knowing the right person is wonderful, but sometimes it's simply a matter of actively soliciting trespass permission, knocking on doors or perusing county tax records to discover who owns vacant woodlots, locating contact information and giving the landowner a jingle. Many suburban woodlots are owned by land developers that really don't care what you do on that property, as they see only an eventual future of cleared land and pay dirt. You may be surprised to find no one has gone to the trouble of running these landowners down and actually asking to hunt. It's no mistake the best suburban hunting sites are often found on the ritzy side of town with larger land parcels, sometimes even sprawling, or adjacent undeveloped lands overlooking real estate too rough to build on, periodically flooding or large in-holdings set aside as wildlife preserves or state parks and acting as sanctuaries for large numbers of deer. These deer venture into outlying suburban areas daily to forage. In some areas residents grow weary of deer reaping havoc on expensive landscaping, making trespass permission fairly easy to secure.

I recall, for instance, an area on the outskirts of Omaha I once bowhunted quite frequently. Town abutted wooded bluffs overlooking the sprawling Missouri River. A railroad bed passed between the bluffs and the river, creating a long strip of cover connecting corn fields to a large preserve where hunting was not permitted. We had permission to hunt that half-mile-long but narrow strip of land, and with two friends along, spreading out became necessary. I couldn't help but note a large patch of woods above the tracks and bordering the preserve, a literal mansion occupying the head of the wooded hollow. I asked our local host about this

The author took this handsome white-tailed buck close to civilization, in a woodlot only a couple acres in size.

Keeping scent under control in suburbia is even more important, as blowing your cover can leave you with nowhere to hunt.

property and was informed the owner was a rich banker and it was doubtful he would grant hunting permission, though he admitted no one had ever inquired. With nothing to lose I drove to the house and knocked on the door.

The owner answered the door in a bathrobe with a phone pressed to his ear, looking a bit irritated. He held his hand over the receiver while I quickly blurted out I was from out of town and would like to set up a treestand on his property to bowhunt deer—emphasizing I would be using only bows and arrows. He gave me a curt "Go ahead," the dismissed me with flicking fingers and closed the door in my face. I tagged my first Nebraska buck on that 10-acre parcel.

One close friend in Upstate New York, only an hour outside New York City, said it was once impossible to obtain hunting permission to bowhunt in his Westchester County neighborhood. But since the arrival of Lyme's Disease landowners are practically begging people to hunt. Some of the state's biggest bucks also happen to come from this bowhunting-only area.

Big Things From Small Places

A common theme with nearly any suburban bowhunting situation is postage-stamp parcels of property. While large whitetail ground might be measured in tens, hundreds or thousands of aces, a productive suburban woodlot might be measured in square yards. This doesn't leave a lot of room for error. Spook a buck only once and that spot is instantly burned out, the buck will choose an alternative route and avoid your little patch of ground for the remainder of the season. This can leave you without a place to hunt.

With this in mind, bowhunting suburban whitetails requires an extremely conservative approach, as unlike other whitetail habitats where you often have the option of hunting many stand sites, suburban hunting often means you're by necessity occupying the same stand site many days in a row, or for an entire season. To succeed in such a setting you must proceed with extreme scent control, first by assuring you aren't inadvertently depositing alerting scent while entering and exiting stands. This also means you should never hunt a stand unless the wind is absolutely ideal for the site. Remember, you aren't just trying to avoid spooking a particular buck, but the many does that will keep that buck around during the rut. There are those who would argue suburban deer are used to encountering human scent, and this is certainly true. So while tedious scent management might not be 100 percent necessary for young bucks and does, rest assured the mature bucks that any bowhunter wants the most haven't survived beyond their fourth year in such habitats without well-whetted survival skills, in-

Giving deer a reason to pass your stand instead of an adjoining property can increase your odds of success in suburban settings.

cluding a neurotic approach to human scent.

In this regard, climbing stands are a boon for suburbia bowhunters and allow you to shift stand positions according to changing wind directions. They also make the best choice in areas frequented by civilians, as you take them with you when finished hunting so they are less likely to be stolen, sabotaged or to attract attention from curious youngsters who could then hurt themselves monkeying into your stand.

It's also vitally important to avoid bumping deer while coming and going. This can be complicated by suburban whitetails' highly nocturnal inclinations, which can demand installing yourself on stand well before legal shooting light, sitting in the dark a full hour if necessary, and leaving stands well after dark when deer are assured to have passed. Many times I've been stranded in suburban stands, enduring teeth-chattering cold, waiting for deer to clear out before climbing down. It's a major inconvenience, but necessary to keep stands fresh.

Of course, one of the biggest dilemmas on small suburban properties is public disturbances like kids playing on weekends or people walking dogs. I once actually had a pimple-faced teenage couple arrive beneath my stand, carrying a sleeping bag, anticipating a covert tryst. When clothing began to be shed I felt inclined to inform them of their logistical error, sending them scrambling in embarrassment. There is no way to foresee such intrusions, but they somehow seem to affect deer movement less negatively than being discovered perched in a tree, which savvy suburban deer seem to understand poses a real threat to life and limb in areas where they have been shot at before.

In fact, while bowhunting those Omaha suburbs years ago I discovered an alarming number of mature deer walked around with their necks craned skyward. I really began to wonder if ground blinds held the answer, though never tested the theory. No matter, leaving a pop-up in place long enough to be accepted as a natural part of the scenery wouldn't have proven feasible since that would invite theft or nonhunting vandalism. I've often wondered if an old-fashioned pit blind covered with natural vegetation might hold some merit.

It's also necessary at times to make a site more attractive by offering mineral, feed or even water held in a small trough—where absolutely legal of course—as suburbanites regularly engage in backyard recreational feeding, creating competition for deer traffic. You might also think in terms of a small throw-and-go food plot, with landowner permission obviously, to funnel daily deer movement. No matter how you approach a suburban site, first assure there are no city or county ordinances restricting

Mineral licks and baiting are great ways to get bucks to stop by suburban stands—of course, only when and where legal.

weapons use in relation to residential areas, as it's just not worth getting into hot water with authorities.

Micro Sanctuaries

The key to regular suburban success really hinges on discovering places, however small, where public traffic is minimized or nonexistent, and where deer feel secure moving during legal shooting hours. The most common scenario I've already touched on, involving actual preserves or parks where hunting is not permitted. These are normally places deer feel completely secure and where they retreat to during the light of day or when the pressure is on. Yet, too many deer using too small a patch of ground for sanctuary can cause over-browsing and a scarcity of food, which will coax them out of these safe havens and into surrounding suburbia in search of food. Hunting the very edges of such places is always an obvious starting point whenever possible.

Other de facto sanctuaries are created by swatches of ground the average person just won't go to the effort to access, like swampy areas that require donning waders and slogging a few hundred yards, places requiring scooting across a small piece of water via kayak, nasty thick areas most see as too much effort to traverse—or ground simply too ugly to garner attention. Of the latter, I remember a weed-choked lot behind a utility company power transfer station. You had to wade across a shallow, mucky ditch, duck through a gap in a chain-link fence and walk around the half-acre humming, razor-wired facility to access a 1-acre patch of nothing more than brush and pigweed. There was not a single tree in the area, so hunting there meant sitting on the ground in a natural blind carved from a patch of weeds. The interior of that nasty patch of brush and weeds proved a reliable bedding area and a great morning spot.

Patches of ground adjacent to busy highways can also present habitat too ugly to attract attention. One friend of mine in the Minneapolis-St. Paul area tells me of bowhunting, successfully, in long-abandoned and overgrown sand and gravel yard behind a major grocery store. It doesn't have to be pretty – it just needs to harbor deer. An amazing number of bucks grow to old age on such properties simply for lack of hunting pressure.

Nocturnal Tendencies

One aspect most indicative of those days I spent pursuing Omaha's suburban whitetails was their tendency to skirt the very edges of legal shooting hours. This was before fiber-optic sight pins, so our outfits normally held primitive, sometimes blinding sight lights, helping us discern solid pins in the gloom of deep woods or under a heavily overcast sky just after sunset. Today, of course, that is no longer an issue since the best fiber-optic sights (generally the more fiber backing each pin, represented

Working around human traffic is normally your biggest hurdle when bowhunting suburban habitats—weekdays are usually best.

by extended, aperture-wrapped or spooled fibers, the brighter they are) allowing distinct pin resolution during any legal shooting hour. Also, in states where they are legal, encapsulated sight lights that eliminate blinding bleed-over, or tritium-backed pins, offer a solution for those with failing eyesight or during the most challenging days when heavy overcast skies or fog blocks daylight.

Still, white-tailed deer are adept at molding their schedule around human activities. In general, fewer people will be out hiking or kids out roaming during early morning hours. During early seasons when days are longer, evening intrusions are more likely, although as days shorten and temperatures dip most people are indoors well before nightfall. This makes weekends your only real problem, as this is also when disturbances are most likely to occur—bad news for weekend warriors. This makes the early morning vigil most productive, though I've also experienced good luck on Sunday evenings.

There are other solutions as well. The most productive approach is to hunt only weekdays when the masses are toiling for wages or incarcerated inside school buildings. It's always interesting to see how deer immediately adjust to work schedules and move more freely Tuesday through Thursday than the remainder of the week. Midday hunts are often productive during midweek days as well; deer simply adjust to those periods when woodlots are invariably empty and neighborhood vehicle traffic thins. Brutal weather also opens doors for suburban success, even on weekends. When temperatures plummet, wind roars and snow flies deer must move and eat to stay warm, and they also know through experience that the nastier the weather the fewer humans they'll normally encounter. This can require some serious and expensive cold-weather gear, but it is a sound investment toward suburban success.

The Suburban Contract

Bowhunting in settled suburban areas comes with greater responsibilities. No hunter wants to wound any deer, to cause one second more suffering than necessary, and especially to lose an animal

Finding a place to hunt can be the biggest challenge of suburban hunting—depending on how residents feel about their deer.

due to a bad shot. Yet in populated areas there is more weight on your shoulders with each shot, as a marginally hit animal that travels far enough to die on a homeowner's lawn quite visibly can cause bad feelings, even if that person isn't necessarily opposed to hunting. Some residents could care less, of course, but others do, and tipping a nonhunter off the wrong side of the fence is something best avoided. Worst yet, is a wounded deer running around a neighborhood with an arrow hanging out of its side, with a liberal local newspaper printing pictures posed as news but meant to do nothing more than sway public opinion against hunting. This is how petition drives to end local hunting get started. For this reason alone an extra measure of caution is necessary any time you draw on suburban deer, waiting the perfect angle, and even passing shots on deer that appear wound up and likely to jump the string.

Remember, while many residents don't oppose hunting—even if they would never kill an animal themselves—they really don't want the death of a "cute" wild animal rubbed in their faces. It's important to be discreet in suburban settings and wait until after sunset to remove deer from the field, or cover them with a tarp during daylight hours. Keeping dead deer under wraps during transport, while stopping for fuel or while enjoying lunch at the local café is just good common sense. I know the pride a bowhunter feels after tagging an impressive buck, but lashing that buck, bloody and tongue lolling out, to the hood of the family sedan won't win us any converts. When operating under the scrutiny of the masses, it really is best to keep deer covered, which also equals cleaner meat in the end.

Suburban bowhunting certainly requires an initiation period, especially for those used to pursuing deer in more idyllic habitats. The wrack and sputum of daily human activity can convince you no deer in its right mind would frequent such a spot, but the evidence says otherwise; intrepid bowhunters each year collect some of the nation's largest-antlered whitetails right in the middle of civilization. White-tailed deer are adaptable that way. Success depends on your own adaptability.

All-day sits can prove the trick while bowhunting suburban deer, since deer quickly learn to live around human work schedules.

The white-tailed deer lives by its nose—whether to find food, breeding or avoiding danger. Successful deer hunting is all about scent. (Photo credit Thomas Kirkland)

CHAPTER 6

MAKING SENSE OF SCENTS

IT'S NO SECRET THAT WHITE-TAILED deer live and die by their remarkable noses. In everything from finding daily sustenance to breeding and avoiding danger, a whitetail's nose factors in heavily. Of all the big-game animals bowhunters passionately pursue perhaps only the wild hog and black bear hold superior olfactory gear, but even that is debatable. Nor does it really matter… The fact remains that whitetails are this continent's most popular big-game animal, putting us more regularly at the mercy of what a deer does or doesn't smell. There is also the detail that while bowhunting many big-game animals, such as elk or mule deer, we are on the ground actively scurrying to remain on the right side of the wind while closing the gap. But, while stranded on stand or inside a blind, wind direction and schemes to assure deer do not intercept our foul human odor become our primary concern, and instruments for success.

We can easily fool a deer's eyesight by wearing camouflage clothing and holding still, and their ears by wearing soft clothing that doesn't rustle or whoosh while drawing our bows, and holding still. But you'll only rarely fool a deer's nose. Give deer a whiff of human odor, even from distances measured in hundreds of yards, and they'll invariably react by removing themselves from the situation hurriedly.

The elongated snout of the average white-tailed deer holds millions more olfactory receptors than humans, added to a Jacobson's organ in the roof of the mouth that also helps them sort out various aromas. Also, while the human brain is plainly much larger than that of the white-tailed deer, a much smaller portion of our brain cells are dedicated to detecting and deciphering aromas. So though deer have smaller brains, a decidedly larger portion is used directly in analyzing aromas. This also makes deer much better at differentiating between minute olfactory stimuli. One study showed that deer could easily sort through six mixed scents simultaneously. In other words, a white-tailed buck likely doesn't simply smell the overall perfume of that magic buck lure you've dribbled near your stand, but individual ingredients contained within that bottle.

Biological testing has also shown that under ideal conditions bucks can smell doe sexual pheromones from up to a mile away, meaning his powerful sense of smell can also work in positive ways to aid the bowhunter. In the whitetail game it's vitally important to heed scent and how it can work for or against you. For the sake of clarification let's call positive aromas scents, and negative aromas odors.

Attraction Scents

For bowhunters, proactive uses of scents are generally employed with the straightforward hope of luring deer, especially mature bucks, near our stands. This is certainly possible, especially during rut dates, but I've found scents most useful for steering deer into wind-friendly areas or open shooting lanes for cleaner shots, coaxing traveling deer to pause for standing shots, and as a prolonged program to urge deer to revisit a particular site. Scents can be broken into three basic categories: food, curiosity and sexual. Each has its place and time and can expand the deer hunter's bag of tricks and help tag more deer.

Food & Curiosity Scents

It could be argued that food scents and baiting are one in the same, but there is a distinct difference, namely in the fact that many states that institute strict penalties for hunting near bait like shelled corn, for instance—are A-okay with the use of scents. In other words, scents are 100 percent legal almost everywhere. Check regulations carefully, though, just in case. The one true distinction is that bait can be consumed in some way by deer, including licking residues, while scents feed only the nostrils.

Curiosity scents are much the same, formulated with exotic extracts and oils that somehow perk the interests of passing deer, much the same as if you were to detect an alluring perfume in a crowded room and wonder where it came from. It doesn't bring to mind food or sex, it's just something that makes you say "Huh, that smells good, I wonder what it is?" Though the new trend here are products claiming to include ingredients proving either addictive or calming to deer, or both, so deer actually seek them out and invest in repeat visits. I've used such products in front of trail cameras, and while deer are certainly captured pausing to thoroughly inspect these alluring scents—beneficial in of and of itself—I haven't observed specific bucks returning repeatedly for a needed fix.

From this standpoint, food and curiosity scents are generally most useful on a one-time, sit-to-sit basis. This isn't a bad thing. If you can get a deer to pause, or just stick around a moment longer, the more opportunities you receive for a standing broadside shot.

There is an exception to this rule. One manufacturer of a food and curiosity spray scent tells me he has experienced exceptional success baiting during the off-season in a state where feeding is legal but hunting directly over bait isn't, applying his product each time. A couple weeks before the season opener he eliminates the bait but continues spraying down the site with his sweet-smelling food and curiosity scent. By then deer have been habituated to associate his spray scent with food so they continue to investigate each time new scent is applied. Now, understand that individual states may have very specific rules about how much time must pass before a baited site can be legally occupied. They may even state that if bait has been deposited at any time in the past the site may not be hunted. There is a fine line between laws not clearly defined and a game warden's interpretation.

In general, food and curiosity scents work best during early seasons, becoming an either-sex proposition.

Some scents are meant to perk curiosity or play on the constant search for food. Such scents work well for early seasons.

Gland & Urine Scents

Scents become another matter altogether when rut dates arrive. Food scents without tangible reward are one thing, but when a buck has sex on the brain all bets are off, especially in areas where buck-to-doe ratios are closer to even and more competition for does exists. This is especially true in areas, like my northern Idaho backyard, where vast mountain habitats result in highly scattered deer, decent herd dynamics and highly defined ruts that cause bucks to travel widely while aggressively seeking does. One quick note: due to concerns about Chronic Wasting Disease (CWD) many states now disallow scents containing natural urine or glandular components, though synthetic scents are allowed. Check regulations in your state to assure you don't innocently break the law.

One of the most useful ploys for use of sex scents is to help create better quality bow shots. For instance, a scent wick hung in the middle of a wide shooting lane can cause bucks to pause in the open, where you won't have to shoot around branches or take the gamble of a moving shot. I also create short drag lines spoking out from a point where the scented drag is placed behind a large tree bole or stump. This not only coaxes a buck to pause for a standing shot, but places his head behind an object that blocks his vision and makes drawing a bow undetected much easier. I've also experienced positive results from such setups while using reusable containers, or simply unscrewing the cap on a clean bottle of buck lure and setting it where I want deer to pause. This allows me to replace the caps after each hunt so a bottle of lure lasts longer than spilling it on the ground or dipping wicks or branches into the bottle that quickly dissipate or wash away with the next rain.

Proactively, drag lines are a time-honored method for bringing randy bucks beneath stands. Again, the level of competition for area does dictates how well this ploy plays out. Bucks in habitats where they're significantly outnumbered by does have no need to chase down every hot doe trail they encounter, while in areas where does are more scarce every lead must be followed if a buck wishes to effectively spread his seed. The standard procedure was once boot pads soaked in scent, but I contend this poses too much potential for spreading or introducing unwanted scent that can alert savvy bucks to the ruse.

There are many ways to distribute whitetail scents for bowhunting purposes, including (from top to bottom) scent drippers, scent pads to create a scent trail into your stand, and scent drags to create a scent trail to direct deer movements.

A much safer approach is to attach your clean, scent-soaked wick or rag to a long length of clean cord attached to a 5- to 6-foot branch collected on site. This branch, with its trailing scent, is held at arm's length while trekking toward your stand, or dragged along field edges, trails and other paths while effectively separating potential human scent from the lure trail. Furthermore, while setting down this scent trail I walk downwind of the paths, making sure that scent is deposited on actual trails. This can make for more tedious walking, but further isolates potential human scent from the lure you hope will bring bucks dogging near to your stand. Now, many will advise replenishing the scent as you progress, the idea being this produces a fresher trail as it progresses. But common sense tells us a hot doe, after urinating (the spot where scent is dribbled onto your wick or rag, or splashes onto a real doe's legs and hooves) will walk away from the site, scent diminishing with each step. So adding fresh scent as you proceed might actually confuse a buck and cause him to trail backwards and away from your stand.

Another obvious proactive scent tactic is the use of mock scrapes, a subject I'll address in great detail in the Understanding Rubs & Scrapes chapter. For the time being let's just say the effectiveness of mock scrapes, in habitats containing healthy buck-to-doe ratios and age structure, is very real and potentially deadly effective.

The Odor Wars— Minimizing Repelling Odors

Game animals think you stink. This is well-known bowhunting lore no matter the quarry. So while it's true preventive measures taken to assure your human odors don't reach the noses of big-game animals is highly important—and some small-game and predators—it is also true that scent management becomes more emphatic while bowhunting white-tailed deer. I'm often amused by testimonials claiming a "deer walked dead downwind without smelling me." Wind and how scent is carried on it is a fickle thing. You might be sitting in a stand with the wind blowing on the back of your neck as a pair of unsuspecting does pass downwind, without suspecting that updrafts have carried your scent safely over their heads, just as an easy example.

Ultimately, the most reliable approach to keeping your scent out of a deer's nose is by keeping deer upwind of your position.

There are countless variations. So such statements are always suspect in my mind.

We work diligently to minimize scent, but if you take a moment to give the matter critical thought it's easy to see 100 percent elimination would require a scent-free bubble from which it would be impossible to shoot a bow. Breathing produces odor. The smallest patch of exposed skin off-gasses CO_2-borne odors. Anything you touch with bare hands carries human odors. Playing the wind is still the most important aspect of all successful bowhunting.

Is odor management then unimportant? Absolutely not! We do the best we can because bowhunting is about playing the odds. It just might make us appear farther away than we really are and quell immediate alarm, and while depositing fewer odors less time will be required for them to dissipate – in regards to odors left behind while entering or exiting stands.

Bathing and Laundering Away Odors

Don't be alarmed, but your skin, every square inch of your epidermal covering, is one vast bacteria factory. It is these bacteria that are largely responsible for producing human odors as they consume dead skin cells and die, in addition to natural and food-borne secretions (hormonal and residues caused by, say, eating garlic or onions) and respired carbon dioxide. These bacteria especially thrive in moist areas, like armpits and the crotch area. This is why we bathe regularly as civilized beings who must often work in close proximity to one another. But when bathing in preparation for bowhunting, that perfumed Lifebuoy, Irish Spring or Zest that smells so nice to us proves alarming to white-tailed deer. It screams human and danger. Nowadays the hunting industry is bursting at the seams with scent-free antimicrobial soaps and shampoos that all claim to be the best, some include silver, others active enzymes. Don't anguish over such decisions, just pick one and keep it handy during hunting season. There are now even scent-free products designed to cleanse bad breath, including gum and toothpaste, as a good deal of human odor is produced by our hot breath.

Now that our bodies are as scent free as possible (though far from 100 percent, which is impossible), give your hunting duds the same treatment. The same perfumes that make most hand and body soaps and shampoos "stinky" to deer apply to laundry detergents as well. Also, nearly all commercial laundry detergents include UV brighteners, ingredients that make colors pop and whites appear whiter. In bowhunting you obviously don't want clothes to pop, and more importantly, the UV residues left behind are highly visible to a deer's sight. Deer eyesight operates more efficiently in dim to dark light because of a higher incidence of cones, while in contrast human eyes contain more rods,

Savvy bowhunters work to keep gear as scent free as possible. Scent-free laundry detergents are a big part of this.

thus more color fidelity. Plus, whitetails' eyes do not include the UV filter the human eye naturally processes. In short, hues on the UV end of the color spectrum are completely visible to deer and not humans. If your clothing contains UV brighteners, your clothing essentially glows to a deer's eye, especially in dim light during prime shooting hours. The company Atsko provides kits to eliminate UV glow, then you can wash them in UV-free, scent-free detergents thereafter to keep camouflage togs hunt ready.

Neutralizing Scent & The Cover-Up Myth

In a world where advertisers make hyperbolic claims in the interests of separating cash from wallets it's easy to grow skeptical of any claims made by manufactures regarding scent-killer sprays. I was understandably skeptical in the beginning, but science has proven them legitimate. Scent-elimination products operate on one of four principles: absorption, neutralization, oxidation or antimicrobial qualities. Absorption products contain elements that are microscopically highly porous. Basic baking soda is

Storing hunting duds in scent-barrier containers and donning them only when ready to hunt is normally the best approach.

You just can't cover one scent with another, as deer simply smell both. The only way to eliminate a scent is to destroy it.

an example, odor control people have been using it for ages. More sophisticated Abscent crystals, as an example, include more pores to lock up additional scent and are less affected by moisture. The downside is that these odor traps, while useful, are generally short lived and the pores quickly fill and absorption is diminished. They're effective in sprays if reapplied frequently, and especially powders sprinkled into boots when shaken out and replaced regularly.

Neutralization formulas contain agents that chemically attack odor-causing particles and alter them to create neutral compounds. Such formulas can be especially effective on nonorganic compounds such as gasoline or diesel fuel, food odors, and tobacco and campfire smoke. Oxidizers work much the same, but instead of chemically altering an organic or inorganic compound, they accelerate the rate of oxidation (the same as decomposition or rusting) to turn odor molecules into inert elements. Antimicrobial products do nothing more than kill odor-causing bacteria on contact, but don't touch organic or man-made odors already in place. Today the best scent-elimination products remain in clothing long after they are dispensed, neutralizing new odors as they appear, and employ more than one of these technologies to offer a multipronged approach to fighting odors.

Which brings us to cover scents… Recall that earlier we discussed how test deer were able to easily separate six mixed scents. This should serve as a warning that cover scents just don't work. You can cover yourself in all the pleasant pine or vile skunk cover scents you want, but a downwind deer will smell that scent, and just as easily, your human odor. The human nose has so little capacity for scent interpretation it is easily overwhelmed. This just isn't true of animals with superior noses. Ever watched dogs stick their noses in a pile of overpowering poop and sniff away, wandering how they could stand it? Cover scents should never be used as a substitute for a careful scent-free regimen. Although lately a couple cover-scent products have appeared claiming to essentially short circuit a deer's olfactory senses, so-called nose-jamming products. The verdict is still out on this approach, but many bowhunters swear by it, so they might hold some merit.

Clothing & Footwear Systems

The newest space-age bowhunting weapons are odor-elimination, or perhaps more accurately, odor-filtering outfits. This started with scientifically designed activated carbon, or charcoal, embedded in camouflage attire, a material universally known for aggressively attracting and absorbing scent. A controversy followed, challenging the notion that these outfits could be "recharged" by subjecting them to the heat of a home clothes drier for half an hour, essentially flushing out the carbon pores and making them available again for odor absorption.

A class-action lawsuit ensued, and the manufacturer's claims were eventually validated. The science has been settled to my satisfaction. Will such a suit eliminate 100 percent of your human odor? Certainly not, but it will certainly put a dent in it, and as I've hinted this can be just enough to create the illusion of a safe space between you and a deer, giving

Avoid depositing scent while coming and going from stands. Spray boots and pants cuffs with scent-killer spray.

you a few extra seconds to get off a clean shot. This original activated carbon technology has evolved, as all things do, now also containing antimicrobial agents to kill odor-causing bacteria on contact. In my opinion these products are most useful when worn directly against the skin and less so in outer garments, unless you are sweating profusely enough to soak them through. Now many use zeolite compounds (think in terms of microscopic "lava") that attract and absorb odors on spectrums activated carbon and original charcoal cannot. Newer, synthetic "filtering" technology has followed.

The problem with scent-elimination clothing is that it's only as effective as the coverage provided. Wearing only a jacket and pants, for instance, leaves scent pouring from the head, hands and mouth. Scent-filtering clothing is an entire system, including hats, face masks, gloves, and sealed openings – including cuffs and neck opening. Due to this, it never hurts to douse scent-escape routes thoroughly with scent-killer sprays.

The author believes in an entire scent-control regimen consisting of bathing and spraying down with scent-killer products, and wearing scent-containment clothing. It's an approach that has helped him tag plenty of big bucks.

One garment that many hunters forget is footwear. They wear their boots while fueling their truck, introducing leaked motor oil and fuel, and they drive to their hunting area while wearing them, also introducing food and pet odors at the minimum. That's why it's important to keep a single set of boots set aside—or more, dependant on weather conditions—used strictly for bowhunting. I store my hunting boots in a baking-soda-scrubbed, air-tight plastic tub with my other hunting clothing, suiting up only after leaving my truck or ATV in preparation for hiking into my stand or blind. Knee-high rubber boots seem easiest to keep scent free, as rubber doesn't soak up odors as readily, but I also regularly hunt in insulated neoprene-topped or leather boots that are thoroughly doused with scent-killing sprays. In fact, no matter what my footwear design, I always spray down boots—including soles—and pant cuffs before entering any stand or trail-camera site to assure I leave as little human odor behind as possible.

If you want to kill big bucks, or keep limited stands fresh when occupied day after day, keeping deer in the dark requires leaving no scent behind. Any deer that knows he is being hunted becomes that much more difficult to kill, and deer survive mostly by trusting their noses. So while it is obvious that removing 100 percent of human scent is statistically impossible, you can increase your odds of success by keeping human odors to a minimum.

Bowhunters accept calling as part of elk and turkey hunting, but often fail to understand how white-tailed deer can also be called into range.

CHAPTER 7

CALLING ALL DEER

WHITE-TAILED DEER AREN'T AS OPENLY garrulous as more vocally conspicuous species such as spring's gobbling turkeys or fall's bugling elk, yet many hunters fail to understand just how vocal white-tailed deer actually are and how this can translate into successful bowhunting. By this I'm thinking beyond the obvious rattling or even grunt tubes, which have their place, certainly, but are only part of the overall picture. Subtle as they are, the soft bleats of young fawns, social grunts of the doe or pecking-order sparring of bucks can also help bring more deer near your stands.

There is something truly enthralling about calling game into range of your bow, that element of communicating with another species that both fascinates and, as often, leads to desperate measures. I include the latter only because it seems many whitetail hunters habitually apply the wrong calling techniques even when they have little to show for their efforts, doing little more than setting deer on edge. Better understanding helps us avoid these pitfalls.

The problem with calling to whitetails is readily available information, be it magazine articles or call manufacturer's videos, most normally originates from a singular perspective – namely the Midwest, though a few Texans and Canadians are allowed to weigh in. This is understandable; we are a results-oriented society and whitetail "experts" are made by virtue of living in the best whitetail habitats available and killing bigger bucks than the average guy. I offer this not in the way of sour grapes, but to illustrate that whitetail hunting differs greatly from region to region. The one-size-fits-all mentality of the Midwest whitetail "expert" just might not fit the area you hunt, and this is especially true of aggressive ploys such as loud calling and decoying. To better understand how whitetail calling can work for you, no matter where you hunt, we must first understand what deer are saying, and why.

A variety of vocalizations bring white-tailed deer into range, including doe bleats, buck grunts, snort-wheezes and rattling.

Whitetail Vocalizations 101

Whitetails are relatively simple creatures. Their entire existence is one of basic survival; eating, avoiding danger and procreation. They're also fairly social, regularly operating within tight-knit groups like the doe-fawn unit, loosely assembled does with a matriarch leader and early season buck bachelor groups. There is also the rut when deer mingle to breed, which is another matter altogether. So the vocal range of white-tailed deer is relatively limited, including combinations of basic bleats, grunts, snorts and bawls, each delivered with various degrees of intensity.

The tending bleat or grunt is a short, single-toned call all deer use to maintain contact with one another. Fawns hear this call from the day of birth from mothers issuing contact bleats, and well into maturity while identifying approaching deer or maintaining contact within a group with soft grunts. Translated into simple human terms these single-tone calls mean "Here I am." For example, a fawn wanders too far and mama bleats, "I'm here, where are you?" The fawn answers, "Here I am."

The two-toned "Come here" grunt is a tad more assertive. Its utility ranges from maintaining herd cohesion to demanding something of another deer, again depending on inflection. A fawn strays too far from its mother and she issues a sharp "Come here" like a mother reminding her child to stick close in a crowded shopping mall. When bucks grunt at does during the rut they are essentially saying "Come here!"

Be it a simple contact bleat or tending grunt, real meaning is imparted through inflection, duration or volume. So while a soft bleat might say "Where are you?" when junior wanders slightly, a louder, more frantic "Where are you!?" might follow as a fawn's anxiety increases after becoming separated from its mother. By the same token, a soft grunt issued by a calm doe says to her fawn, "Come here," while a loud, aggressive grunt says the same with an exclamation point—something that might follow after a doe spots a coyote nearby.

Anthropomorphizing again, picture yourself in a tavern and facing two polar opposite scenarios: Someone across the room says, "Hey buddy, come over here, how have you been?" That's a nonaggressive grunt. Or, you walk into a tavern and someone sees you and shouts, "Hey you! Come over here! Where's that money you owe me?" That's an aggressive grunt.

The snort generally carries negative connotations. The snort, as any deer hunter knows, is the universal signal for danger. But it can also denote a frustrated or "mad" buck warning another buck to back off, especially when a hot doe is involved, which can also denote possible danger if you are a physically weaker buck. It can also represent a direct challenge.

The bawl is normally produced by deer under duress, such as when being attacked by predators, for instance, or when an estrous doe is desperate to be bred. It actually holds some usefulness for hunt-

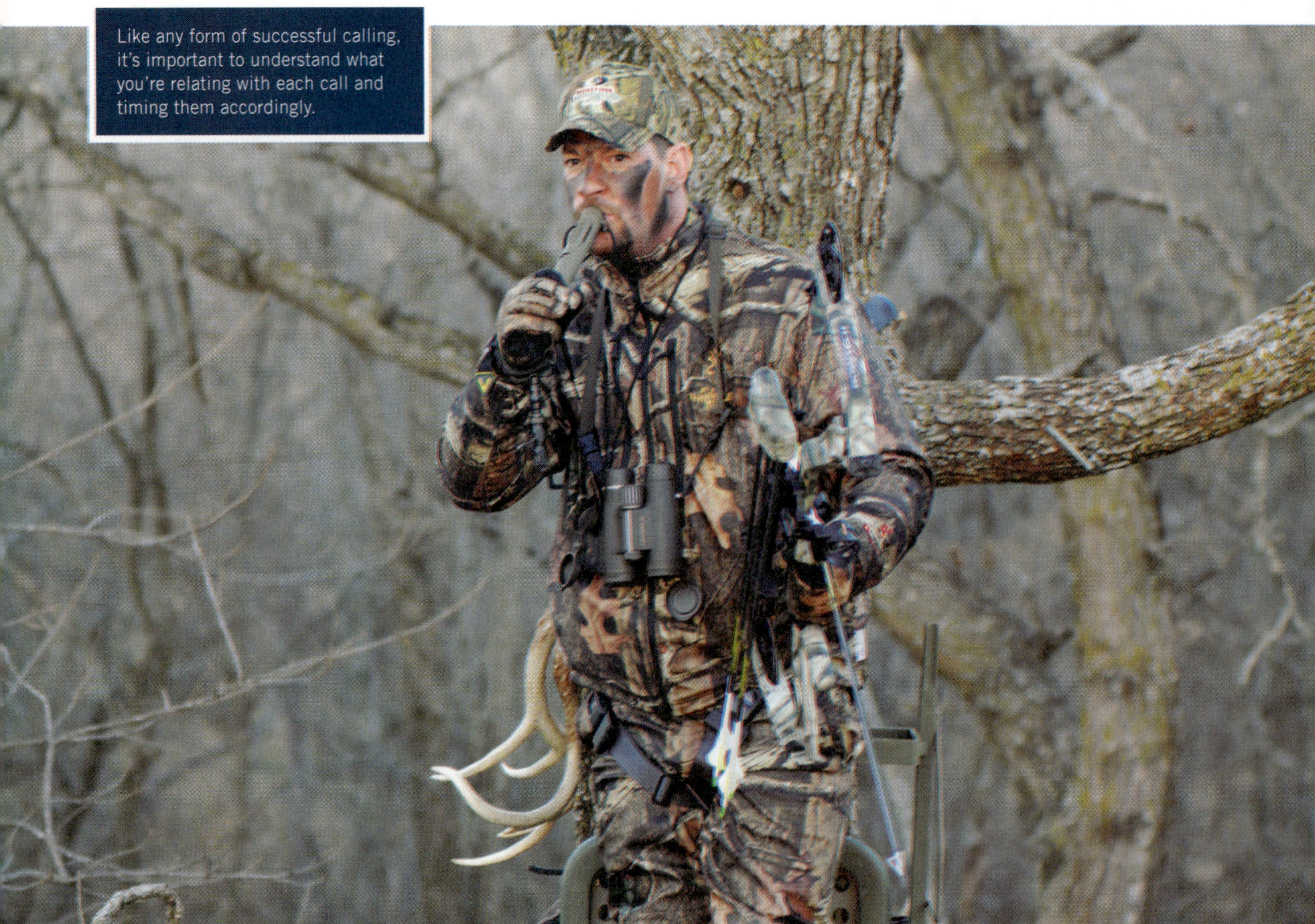

Like any form of successful calling, it's important to understand what you're relating with each call and timing them accordingly.

ers, a fawn bawl often bringing protective does on the run, a breeding-bawl useful in habitats where competition for does is intense.

Knowing how to proceed really depends on understanding the differences in habitats and how they dictate calling approaches.

Calling Biology

It's critical to understand that for aggressive whitetail calling to prove regularly effective certain biological criteria must reign. Most importantly is a healthy ratio of bucks to does. Opinions vary, anything from 1:2 to 1:5 ratios have been offered, but in basic terms ideal calling situations are created during the rut when there is intense competition for limited does. Deer herds including healthy age-class structure are also important. Aggressive calls generally attract fewer immature bucks because they lack confidence in their physical stature and will not risk physical confrontation. It also helps when bucks aren't subjected to intense rifle-hunting pressure through the heart of the rut to turn them understandably wary and nocturnal. This, not incidentally, also correlates directly to healthy age-class structure, as rifle hunting during the rut allows fewer bucks to survive into their third or fourth year.

Skewed buck-to-doe ratios simply make aggressive calling less productive. This is generally regional, although exceptions exist where properties are large enough and quality deer management pursued passionately. Ideals are found on lightly hunted properties in well-known trophy states, or regions big and wild enough to absorb rifle-hunting pressure without negatively affecting breeding activities. Then there is the rest of whitetaildom, which we will address a bit later on.

Aggressive Ploys

Rattling to white-tailed bucks in better habitats is one of hunting's biggest thrills. I cherish the memory of a pre-rut, do-it-yourself bowhunt on a sprawling West Texas ranch that for all practical purposes hadn't been hunted for decades. We approached these deer in a straightforward manner,

Aggressive grunting and rattling works best in areas or regions where buck-to-doe ratios are high and mature bucks are common.

setting up in likely looking areas and calling from the ground. We rattled in 18 mature bucks in three days, a friend and I both putting arrows through old warriors showing significant tooth wear. It was one of the most exciting weeks of whitetail hunting I've experienced anywhere.

My first Pope & Young quality white-tailed buck—after years of frustrating bowhunting in lesser habitats—came through rattling. In fact, that 127-inch Illinois buck was called back three times before he finally presented a clean shot. So, obviously, I endorse rattling wholeheartedly – in the right time and place.

Experience has shown that the right time for productive rattling to be during the pre-rut, when mature bucks' hormones are just beginning to flow, does are fickle and pecking orders are being assertively established.

I prefer rattling from the ground whenever possible. This allows mobility, the opportunity to explore and more importantly, avoiding burning out prime stand sites – though there are exceptions to this reasoning. Playing the wind is the most difficult portion of this run-and-gun game. In West Texas it was easy enough to find places backed by falling topography where downwind ground was unavailable to responding bucks. In Midwest habitats I seek spots backed by water, swamp or tangled brush that discourages bucks from swinging downwind to discover my scent.

Aggressive rattling to mature, lightly hunted bucks is just that—aggressive. The object is to imitate all-out battles. This is partly why I prefer calling from the ground. In addition to clashing antlers violently, I pound the ground like hooves grappling for better purchase and smash any brush within easy reach. I usually add loud grunts to the mix. The illusion you're striving for is two bucks trying to kill each other. Bucks respond to see a fight, like kids ringing school-yard fisticuffs, or to pinch disputed does while the brawlers are preoccupied. Most bucks respond with hackles on end and nostrils flaring. But, just as many bucks will slip in quietly, so remain alert for this contingency.

The exception to this approach occurs while occupying stands, especially after observing a cruising buck passing out of range. Even so, I normally try a grunt call first. Yet, when bucks are too far away or wind obscures their hearing, a bit more volume is needed. If I receive no response after grunting, I create a quick series of antler cracks before setting the horns aside. You always risk being spotted when rattling from trees since deer are amazingly adept at pinpointing sources of noise. Any time a

Rattling works best where competition for does is intense and battles for dominance are common. The author and his friend Steven Tisdale rattled in this buck in Texas.

buck looks your way, freeze, then set the horns aside when given the opportunity, continuing only with grunt tube.

Grunt-tube success hinges on a buck believing either an estrous doe is available for the taking or another buck is taunting him. The responding buck must then be confident enough in his physical abilities to face a fight. This is why I generally prefer to have a visual on a buck, so his body language is easily observed. The first grunt or series of grunts is offered to grab a buck's attention, then increasing in volume until he acknowledges your call(s). A couple more grunts should do the trick. If he doesn't come, I'll switch tactics and offer a snort-wheeze or rattling sequence. Of course some deer just won't commit. In these cases there's just no use pushing the issue and educating him for another day when he might prove more receptive to your calls. Grunt calls seem to produce the best in one of three situations: any buck anxiously seeking the first estrous doe of the season, bucks that have just lost their doe and are frantic to re-establish contact, or bucks that are obviously worked up and rubbing trees or pawing scrapes.

When faced with a buck that is just out of bow range, allow him to distance himself slightly before calling, as a buck that's too close can easily be spooked by a sudden grunt, as if you walked into a room, pre-occupied, and someone yelled "Boo!" The ideal engagement distance seems to be about 80 to 100 yards.

The snort-wheeze is a relatively new development to whitetail calling. It's basically a belligerent challenge, akin to calling a barroom bully something unpleasant to illicit a response. I consider it a last resort with lone, passing bucks showing no interest in either grunts or rattling. It's especially effective when combined with a buck decoy.

In the realm of doe calls, the so-called "estrous bawl" is another aggressive call effective in areas where competition for does is fierce. This is an inhale-exhale call producing a short doe grunt,

Most bucks are called in by offering grunts in ideal habitats, or a doe bleat in average settings.

Bucks rattle antlers while sparring to establish pecking orders, or engage in all-out fights during arguments over the possession of hot does. (Photo credit Thomas Kirkland)

followed by a more prolonged, tapering bawl. It's the vocalization produced by a doe desperate to be bred. In habitats where buck-to-doe ratios are closer to even it produces predictable results. One of my prettiest bucks—a solid 150-inch Kansas bruiser with a clean 4x4 frame—was diverted from a distant, determined trajectory and past my stand with a breeding bellow. He turned on a dime and came on a string, leaving me scrambling to prepare for the shot.

For the hunter with a pocket full of doe tags, nothing works better, or speaks more aggressively, than fawn-distress bawls. Think in terms of predator calling and you get an accurate picture. These are raucous, ear-splitting calls imitating a fawn being attacked by coyotes or wild dogs. Does with strong maternal instincts come to the rescue all hackles and pinned ears. The occasional buck has been known to investigate, but this remains a doe-tagging ploy most of all.

Subtle Social Calls

In most portions of the whitetail's range, where buck-to-doe ratios are closer to 1:50 than 1:5, where few bucks survive beyond their third year, where rifle hunts interrupt ruts, the aggressive stuff is a sure bet to literally blow your chances of success. Yet calling still remains a viable success strategy. This requires subtler social calls that deer hear regularly; nonthreatening calls they've heard since birth. Social calls, especially during the rut, can bring bucks and does near your stands largely out of curiosity, but also through social tendencies. Better yet, if a buck chooses not to respond and refuses to deviate from his course, no harm is done. Deer will accept it as part of the natural landscape and go about their business.

Perhaps surprisingly, rattling still fits into this program, though "antler tickling" may be a more apt label. Better yet, antler-tickling works as well during early seasons when bucks are just out of velvet, as it does during rut dates. I use the rattling analogy of Midwest bucks living in the 1800s Wild West, harder-hunted bucks more reminiscent of an average high school setting. In the Wild West "Might makes right." In high school boys typically establish pecking orders through shoving matches and posturing. Bucks living in a world of low buck-to-doe ratios have no real motivation to risk injury by fighting. There are plenty of does to go around, but bucks still need to determine pecking orders. This results in frequent shoving matches and posturing, but rarely all-out battles.

I've watched this innocent sparring on many occasions while sitting early season stands, bachelor groups of younger age-class bucks and occasionally mature bucks pushing, shoving, rattling antlers, but without real malice. Any dominant buck within earshot, curious to see who is in his immediate area, perhaps welcoming company, is inclined to mosey over and investigate.

Sparring sessions are easily mimicked with standard rattling bags. By simply rearranging interior

Whitetail does are generally more vocal than bucks, so doe vocalizations can also be used to bring bucks into range.

parts and rolling the bag between your hands periodically, you produce the effect of two bucks shoving each other around to see who is the toughest. I've called in many bucks using this approach—including a couple Midwest behemoths. In lesser habitats where younger bucks are typically the prize, this is your avenue for rattling success.

Grunts are also part of social calling, but to a lesser degree. Bachelor groups grunt at each other frequently, keeping tabs on one another while traveling. By degrees I'm talking volume and duration. A simple buck contact grunt is quiet and short. An aggressive grunt is loud and longer in duration. The subtle grunt, offered periodically, can coax a nearby buck or occasional doe to swing by to see what's up. Or they will ignore you, and no harm is done.

How often to offer social calls while on stand is a common question – and a good one. Think of this in human terms: you hear someone say "Hi there" and find it comforting. Yet, you hear someone repeating that "Hi there" over and over again and you begin to believe he's strange and best avoided. Deer are no different. I'd consider social calls offered at 15- to 20-minute intervals a maximum.

When producing social-based vocalizations, calls producing quieter doe grunts and bleats are also preferred. Anyone who has spent a good deal of time on stand where does and fawns are numerous understands just how vocal whitetails can be. Does issue frequent tending grunts to keep fawns from wandering, fawns send short bleats to remain in contact with mom. These are calls even the biggest bucks have heard since birth. I really believe there's an instinctual residue buried deep in every buck's subconscious, his mama's come-here call remembered well into maturity. Doe calls, therefore, can cause a buck to investigate out of purest instinct or simple curiosity.

During early seasons, the same curiosity factor remains. Nearby deer hear a subtle tending grunt or come-here bleat and swing by to investigate, or they go about their day, and your stand remains fresh. But during the rut, even in lesser whitetail habitats, a come-here call carries the potential for love. Even when does are quite plentiful and competition nearly nonexistent there's really little effort involved in swinging 100 yards out of their way to pay the perceived doe a visit. Keeping calls subtle means these bucks will likely slip in quietly, but also without anxiety, so they aren't keyed up and on edge.

Another recent development is a subtler brand of lost fawn calls. These are subtle calls producing fawn vocalizations saying basically, "I'm lost. Where are you?" This isn't the obnoxious distress bawls discussed earlier, but quiet, nonaggressive calls that deer are used to hearing regularly. Nearby does respond out of maternal instinct or social curiosity, so they arrive calmly and with defenses down. If you have some doe tags to fill – this is your answer.

Calling whitetails is exciting stuff and should be part of every deer hunter's bag of tricks. This applies no matter what kind of whitetail habitat you ply. The trick is choosing the right calling approach for the right time and place, perhaps a mix of both if you operate in habitat not exactly ideal, but not exactly lacking. Save the aggressive stuff for the best whitetail grounds, erring on the side of caution where deer are hunted harder and keep in mind that subtle, nonthreatening calls are also right at home in the very best habitats.

Decoying Whitetail Success

We're all likely familiar with the concept of decoying waterfowl, if not on a firsthand basis, then at least in practice. Well, decoying white-tailed deer is nothing like that. Decoying wildfowl is a matter of setting up where birds already want to be, tossing out decoys of the prevailing species to encourage them to land or pass closely in front of your blind. In other words, even without decoys and calling you'd likely still get some shooting. Waterfowl are also inherently gregarious and prefer to travel, feed and raft in large flocks. Finally, the basic precepts of decoying waterfowl in conjunction with calling are fairly universal; the same approach that nets positive results in northern Saskatchewan can be just as effective when plied on New Mexico's Rio Grande.

Conversely, while decoying whitetails you're most often coaxing them off of an established trajectory and pulling them from 100 yards away or more to near your stand with the promise of sex or a fight. White-tailed deer, especially mature bucks during season dates when decoying is most effective, are largely loners, not exactly looking for company for company's sake. In fact they're most often inclined to ward other bucks from their turf and are interested only in estrous does, taken one at a

In areas with healthy herd dynamics, a buck decoy tending a doe decoy can bring the best results from mature, confident bucks.

time. Perhaps most importantly – your approach to decoying whitetails hinges largely on habitat dynamics, where you hunt and the amount of hunting pressure bucks in your area endure.

This in no way should be construed as discouragement against decoying deer, but it is important to understand that like calling, there are big differences in approaches when faced with the ideal habitats already discussed in conjunction with calling, and lesser areas. You can't just stake out a deer decoy and expect every buck that spies it to come running in to investigate. How you proceed—the direct approach or deflection schemes—depends largely on the very facets dictating how whitetailed deer react to calling.

Straight-On Decoy Ploys

In the very best habitats decoys make a great addition to aggressive calling ploys. A buck hears a call, reacts to it and is rewarded by a visual target. When used in conjunction with stand hunting and tolling passing bucks it is first important to place your scent-free decoy where cruising bucks can actually see it from afar. The edges of agricultural fields are the most common arrangements, though don't dismiss a wind-swept oak ridge, clear-cut, natural meadow or swamp rise. Before it is set the decoy should have been cleansed of all foreign odors, handled only with scent-free gloves and sprayed down with scent killer spray again once it's staked out. A dash of commercial tarsal-gland scent or dominant buck urine is a nice touch, as bucks are apt to swing downwind of the deke before moving in and it adds a little more realism to the ploy – keep this all in mind while setting the decoy in relation to stands and blinds.

Deer decoys are normally unisex, plug-in antlers removed to create a doe, plugged in to represent a buck. Generally, in ideal habitats the best results are elicited by decoys wearing small- to average-size antlers, sparking conflict and encouraging fights. This may seem counterintuitive in direct relationship to rut dates and bucks who are actively seeking does, but this is something other decoying deer

Keep deer decoys free of human odors, and add a touch of deer sex lure to make them more appealing to a scent-checking buck.

hunters relate as well.

Another proven approach is to use a small buck decoy hovering over a doe fake. Position it to appear ready to mount her or standing over the bedded decoy as if tending her. This sparks heated jealousy and direct competition for a perceived doe.

Encouraging direct approaches from mature, aggressive bucks is typically aided by including calling in the mix. A common theme is to spy a buck cruising out of range and sending him a series of aggressive grunts, increasing frequency and volume until you grab his attention. If he should ignore you or somehow fails to hear these calls—say on a windy day when sound carries poorly—a short burst of rattling can sometimes be used to grab his attention. A loud and challenging snort-wheeze should be used only as a last resort—and understand that less aggressive bucks may shy away from this most belligerent of whitetail calls. But, it can enrage a confident buck and get him to take the bait.

Try to set up a buck decoy upwind and about 25 to 35 yards from your stand or blind and quartering toward your position. In this way any confident buck arriving on the scene will instinctively swing around in an attempt to look his opponent in the eye (turkey hunters should remember this ploy as well). This means the approaching buck is more apt to present a broadside or quartering-away shot, also making it easier to get your bow drawn undetected while his attention is riveted on the decoy.

It is also possible in better habitats where aggressive bucks are more common to go on the prod and in search of rutting bucks to cajole with calls and a decoy. Put in basic terms, the hunter glasses up a buck and moves closer or still-hunts thick cover setting up and calling randomly. In either case the decoy – lightweight, two-dimensional fold-up models work well for this – is used both for attraction and concealment, and turned on its stake as the angle of approach changes, your bow drawn behind the deke and peeking over its top to shoot. The trick is to choose setups that make it difficult for bucks to swing downwind and discover your scent. A combination of calling, decoying and bow-

In areas where competition for does is intense, buck decoys works best. In other areas a doe decoy aids in deflection schemes.

hunting on the ground when bucks are in the right frame of mind can prove one of the sport's most exciting tactics.

Deflecting Maneuvers

In less-than-ideal habitats decoying must be a bit more devious, as fewer mature, confident bucks exist to make a direct approach as likely. In such cases deer decoys normally play a larger role in deflection schemes. Since fewer older-class bucks survive in such habitats and a fighting-mad buck is less likely, antlers are normally removed from decoys to imitate does. One thing is certain while dealing with less confident or outright wary deer – if they react to your decoy at all it will be to swing well downwind and scent-check the fake. Also, expect many does to outright blow at your decoy and eventually vacate the area. Does are often a bane while decoy hunting. Young bucks seem to remain the most curious, the reckless teens of their species.

The general approach often requires some adjustment to local conditions. In a nutshell, the decoy is installed 100 to 300 yards upwind of your position—this distance will largely be dictated by vegetation density and terrain. The exact range will be adjusted through several hunts until you get a better feel for the general disposition of deer in your region and how they react to decoys. Just as importantly, since all deer will swing downwind of your faux deer, is to spray your decoy with doe urine after making it scent free, of course, to make the decoy smell legitimate, possibly even getting a responding buck to hang around longer. Otherwise the same conditions apply, including setting the decoy where it can be easily seen, and using calls to grab the attention of bucks passing out of range and unaware of the decoy's presence.

The plan is that a buck passing out of range spots the decoy and becomes curious or even suspicious. That buck, if it doesn't spook outright, will cautiously circle downwind to investigate further. The trickiest part of this program is to position yourself at just the right distance that when that buck swings downwind he appears within bow range of your stand—but not so far downwind that he also smells you—and you receive a clean shot at an unsuspecting deer whose attention is focused hundreds of yards upwind. Admittedly, this approach isn't foolproof, but it can work to guide deer away from wider areas to near your stands on properties where bucks are otherwise unlikely to approach your decoy directly.

As you can see it isn't necessary to sit in your stand silently and wait for something to happen. Calling and decoying allows you to bring the whitetail action to you. But this requires a careful reading of the conditions at hand and adjusting your tactics accordingly. No matter where you hunt, calling and decoying not only prove productive – but highly exciting.

Successfully calling whitetails requires special stipulations, but when it happens there's nothing more exciting.

Some rubs are nothing more than frustration displacement, though signpost rubs are important to whitetail communication. *(Photo credit Thomas Kirkland)*

CHAPTER 8

UNDERSTANDING RUBS & SCRAPES

AN ARRAY OF CLOVEN TRACKS reveals the presence of deer, but tells us very little about their sex, age or trophy quality. Droppings reveal with greater accuracy when deer passed, but again leave a lot of unanswered questions. Conversely, rubs show deer hunters that without a doubt a buck is in the area and may also reveal clues to his size. Scrapes signal the beginning of the rut, show a buck or bucks are in the area, and also leave a solid lead as to where he might appear again. Scrapes and rubs are also the most conspicuous of deer sign, an important factor when scouting large parcels of ground. Scrapes and rubs allow hunters to gain quick insight into deer density and movement patterns.

The utility of rubs and scrapes to deer hunters is multifaceted, from signaling rut activities to come and revealing what phase the rut has entered, to gaining better insight into general buck patterns. They can also provide productive stand sites in habitats where deer are more thinly distributed or competition for does more intense. Much misinformation and outright old wives' tales surround rubs and scrapes; i.e. rubs represent nothing more than damage done while "scratching the itch" of velvet shedding, or these sites serving as the strict territorial markers of individual bucks. While rubs and scrapes do serve as territorial markers to an extent, there's much more involved – including important roles in the white-tailed deer's breeding ritual.

The Rub

Rubs, in their simplest capacity, represent aggressive displacement behavior prior to the rut, reflecting the tremendous rush of testosterone triggered by decreased photo periods. This begins as buck bachelor groups disperse and begin to establish pecking orders. However, they soon discover the gals aren't especially amorous and, in fact, want nothing to do with them. To vent their frustration these bucks abuse defenseless saplings and tree branches. This aggression intensifies as the rut progresses, when rubs appear almost randomly.

Many hunters mistakenly believe that rubs are created during velvet shedding due to itching antlers. This just isn't so, as velvet and antlers beneath, are dead when shedding begins. The entire velvet-shedding process and antler polishing normally take place within just hours or days. So velvet shedding produces only a fraction of the vegetation damage caused by frustration displacement or signpost rubbing.

Communication rubs, generally labeled as signposts, bring whitetail forehead glands into play. This gland produces a pheromone, a communicative scent unique to a particular animal that acts to establish a buck's presence. Whitetail researchers have several theories regarding the purpose of the forehead gland, but the most popular is this scent actually primes does for the rut and suppresses tes-

Major rubs not only reveal a buck is around, but major rubs – especially rub lines – are often revisited by other deer.

tosterone production in lesser bucks. Part of this theory is based on the observable fact that ruts string out longer where fewer dominant bucks are available; so without the forehead scent of dominant bucks, does fail to produce estrogen. It has also been shown that dominant buck urine also affects doe reproductive cycles.

Signposts are typically created by dominant bucks in places where other deer are apt to encounter them, such as near available water, ridge-point trails, fence corners, breaks in rock walls or any other topographical funnels. The observant deer hunter will often notice a specific tree species is preferred, sometimes something odoriferous or aromatic, cedar or sumac for instance, but more often a hardwood, especially in forests dominated by pine or fir. The rub serves mainly to register a buck's status and condition, among other information. Larger bucks normally rub larger trees, 6 inches or larger; younger bucks trees about 2 inches in diameter. A fence post planted at a strategic location will often serve as a signpost for area deer.

Unlike frustration-displacement rubs, signposts are revisited, but not necessarily on set schedules. A buck might simply become fond of a particular tree, or more strategically, the tree might offer geographical advantages. A hunter wishing to use this rub as a focal point can only hope that visits become regular, though it's more common for a buck to simply swing by when in the area and he finds time. Regular visitors are just as apt to appear during nighttime as legal shooting hours. Does and lesser bucks often share a dominant buck's signpost. Save unusual circumstances, I typically find an overall rub line—a connect-the-dots pattern of major rubs—more useful than concentrating on individual rubs, though there are exceptions to every rule, because some bucks simply become awful fond of a particular rub and return frequently.

The Scrape

It was once believed scraping was a rut behavior that began only after bucks became concerned with breeding. Strictly speaking this is accurate, though I've observed bucks and does scraping well ahead of the rut, once watching a young buck start scraping only days out of velvet. There is much about whitetails we don't completely understand and this is one of those instances, though it certainly has to do with communication.

Most deer hunters are familiar with the generalities of the scrape, but confusion arrives with specifics. In general, scrapes are pawed-out patches of ground almost invariably beneath an overhead or licking branch that appears chewed or rubbed. When it comes to specifics, much more is involved. The area below the tree must be open to allow construction of the pawed-out area. The scrape site

The diameter of the rubbed tree can reveal buck size; generally the larger the tree the larger his antlers.

must also include a low-hanging branch to provide a licking branch. Due to a buck's finicky nature in choosing scrape sites, the same spot may be utilized from one year to the next. The licking branch's worn appearance is caused by bucks gumming and rubbing antlers on that branch. Gumming deposits saliva to help better hold scent from the lachrymal gland, while sensors inside the deer's mouth allow him to read scent left by other animals.

Bucks begin the scrape sequence by chewing the overhead branch gently. He then rubs scent from the lachrymal gland—also called the pre-orbital gland—located at each tear duct. The lachrymal gland deposits scent unique to the animal making the scrape. The buck also paws out an area beneath the licking branch. This pawing provides visual sign for deer upwind and unable to smell the scrape and as a medium to better hold scent. The buck then urinates down his tarsal glands, located on the inside of each rear hock.

Dominant bucks return at least once and sometimes twice a day and go through a full scrape sequence using the overhead branch and pawing. Smaller bucks visiting another buck's scrape will normally employ the licking branch but skip pawing and urinating. Dominant bucks are also sure to return after a fresh rain or snow to put the scrape back in order. Dominant bucks sometimes guard their scrapes, warding off other bucks from the area. The scrape, in all, is a complex signpost where bucks trade information, and is also used to attract estrous does.

As does come into estrous they stop by scrapes to leave their calling card scent by urinating into their interdigital glands located between the front hoof cloves. This mark tells bucks they are ready to breed. The buck, while making his rounds, then discovers the doe's scent and trails her in hopes of breeding. In many areas the scrape isn't an essential part of the breeding cycle. Deer density around most of the nation ensures a buck will be on hand should any doe slip into estrous. Scrapes are most important to breeding—and bowhunters—anywhere there is competition for limited does or in big-woods settings where deer are highly scattered. In my northern Idaho backyard, for instance, scrapes are highly important to my annual success. In places I've hunted in central Texas, the Deep South or Northeast suburbia, not so much.

Many hunters consider scrapes pure territorial markers, but as you can see this isn't necessarily the case. Generally, territorial markers are respected by animals within the same species. Deer are more gregarious and scrapes more often used by multiple bucks and does. Any number of bucks from a given area might make use of a single major scrape. Another common stumbling block is that scrapes, like rubs, don't all hold the same importance. Just like rubs, some scrapes often appear randomly due to displaced frustrations or a younger buck's wishful thinking. These lesser scrapes are seldom visited again. They're useful as sign alone, but not as focal points to base stand locations around.

Scrapes can appear as early as September, but are used during the rut as communication centers for all deer.

Scrape Timing

A buck will visit his scrapes once or twice every 24 hours, but these visits are just as likely to occur at midnight, especially in areas where hunting pressure is intense. Whitetails don't have schedules to keep like we do—unless this includes keeping hours to avoid humans. Daytime visits are obviously what we hope for. Trail cameras are a boon to discover any

A scrape's pawed-out area is most easily observed, but the licking/overhead branch is likely the most important to deer communication. *(Photo credit Thomas Kirkland)*

scrape patterns, revealing schedules and exposing daytime visits.

But, another problem with scrapes arises. Just because an area harbors a trophy buck doesn't mean you'll be able to ambush him on a signpost, rub line or scrape. Some bucks make rubs and scrapes, some do not. I recall one of my Range & Wildlife professors at Texas Tech University, Dr. Steven Damarais (now with Mississippi State University), relating experiences with two penned research bucks, both of equal age and trophy quality. One buck was quite placid. He loved being scratched behind the ears and patted. Another buck in another pen was full of vinegar, constantly tussling and wanting to fight. When the rut arrived, the placid buck's pen rarely held a rub or scrape. The aggressive buck rubbed and scraped his pen from one end to the other. This shows that just because the buck you're after wears massive antlers doesn't mean he can be counted on to appear at rub lines or scrapes.

The bowhunter who pays close attention to scrapes also receives insight into what phase of the rut deer are in and how to hunt them.

I also use scrapes to gauge what phase the rut has entered—which also tells me how to approach ploys such as calling, decoying and even where I set stands – over food before the rut and funnels during. The sudden appearance and aggressive maintenance of scrapes signals that bucks are growing anxious and putting out feelers. This is the so-called pre-rut or seeking phase. This signals the ideal time to apply aggressive rattling or grunt calls in ideal habitats, or offer more frequent does bleats and grunts in lesser habitat. At some point during the rut you might notice scrapes have gone cold. It's easy to assume the rut has come to a screeching halt, but more likely you're witnessing its peak. During the peak bucks are more likely to camp out on hot does, which translates into diminished traffic. Be patient and keep an eye on those scrapes. A week or so later you'll notice that action at scrapes resumes after the majority of does are bred and bucks become desperate to mop up any stragglers. This also means the party is winding down.

The waning days of the rut can actually present one of the best times to ambush a buck at a scrape. The rut has run its course and bucks understand the end is near. Ready does are more difficult to locate, but bucks' reproductive drive is peaked by prior action. Bucks remain hopeful, some even desperate, searching for that last elusive doe that wasn't covered during her first cycle and will come into estrous again. The scrape becomes more important to unbred does as well, biology driving them to reproduce and pushing them to leave more frequent calling cards. Bucks continue to make regular visits to scrapes well after the rut has ended hoping against hope for such a scenario. It is also at this time the woods normally begin to quiet down as hunters fill tags or throw in the towel.

Hunting Rubs & Scrapes

How you approach rubs and scrapes really depends on the kind of habitat you're dealt. While in the thronged big woods of my Idaho backyard I tend to hunt directly over scrapes, while in hard-hunted areas this can be a mistake. Vegetation here is so thick, travel patterns so random; I really have little other choice. Also, being a bowhunting stand hunter in a gun-happy land does have advantages—scrape sites receive zero hunting pressure. Of course extra care is necessary when hunting such sites, since getting busted just once will likely burn the spot for the duration of the season and at the very least turn that buck nocturnal. Just as importantly, since I've got all of the elbow room imaginable, killing a buck off a single scrape leaves me with plenty of other options if I blow the spot out permanently. On smaller properties, this is best avoided.

On smaller ground I tend to leave plenty of room between rubs or scrapes and stands, just to assure my presence isn't correlated to those sites. The basic approach in those situations is to position yourself between two points of interests—sign post or rub line, scrape or cluster of scrapes—and find trails or topography linking the two. Remember, during the heat of the rut many bucks won't visit scrapes directly, instead swinging downwind to scent-check the site from a distance. Situating stands well downwind takes advantage of this common trait. This requires a bit more thought and scouting effort, but playing it safe pays big when forced to hunt the same places repeatedly. Good places to wait for rub- or scrape-patronizing bucks include ridge points, deep saddles, sags or open gates in tight wire fences, creek-bottom crossings, shelterbelts and obvious trails between two sites or field edges. Let trail cameras show you the way.

Mock & Seeded Scrapes

Another problem with scrapes is that they aren't always positioned to the hunter's best advantage, sometimes situated in spots with wind issues or where a suitable stand tree is unavailable. When a natural scrape isn't situated ideally – the next best thing is to build your own. Mock scrapes can really tip the odds in your favor in the right habitats and

In hard-hunted areas bucks might visit scrapes only at night, but deer will visit scrapes any time they're in the area.

sites. The right habitats are those where competition for limited does makes scrapes more crucial to breeding, and where dominant bucks are more common. The right sites are those where it's easy to remain on the right side of the wind while guarding it from a stand or blind, and in a place where many deer, including your targeted buck, travel naturally.

I once strived to find places where the right combination of natural licking branch and clear ground beneath it invited a convincing scrape, but lately have taken a more aggressive approach by constructing scrapes exactly where I need them. I find a place along a natural path, funnel or feeding area overlooked by a perfect stand tree. I've developed a good feel for what area bucks prefer after observing countless natural scrapes in my hunting areas—always a good point of reference to assure you get it right, including ground type, licking-branch height and scrape positioning.

Wearing scent-free gloves (surgical gloves are best) and boots, I trim an appropriate branch from a tree species that the local deer prefer. I wouldn't be averse to cutting an existing licking branch from a distant scrape that is of no use to me. I also cut a second branch of about the same length. At the scrape site I use clean cord, wood screws and screw gun or even nails to secure the generic branch at the extent of my reach, then the designated licking branch about chest to head height. The higher

Mock scrapes can prove highly productive, and Wildlife Research's Magnum Scent Dripper an easy way to maintain such sites.

If you look closely, you can see a scent dripper hanging above this mock scrape—the reason for this buck's regular visit.

branch serves only as a scent-dripper hanger, the lower as the actual licking branch. I fill the scent dripper with a "scrape-mate" type product to start, transitioning to estrous doe urine when the rut heats up, and attach the dripper to the upper branch so it must drip through the lower licking branch. After determining where dripped scent falls I use a stout branch collected on site to dig out an exaggerated and highly visible bare spot beneath the licking branch. Then I dump a bag of Code Blue's Grave Digger into the scrape (sterilized soil containing time-release scent capsules releasing scent each time they get wet or are pawed) and finish by dribbling "dominant buck" scent on the licking branch. I often experience overnight results at better sites, though I have seen mock scrapes sit for a week or more before being investigated.

The advantages of Wildlife Research Center's Magnum Scent Dripper is scent is continually dispensed while you work or hunt in other areas, and the special design dribbles scent only after a quick increase in ambient temperature, meaning it will dispense only during daylight hours. This helps to encourage daytime visits. Mock scrapes serve two purposes: duping a dominant buck into believing another mature buck has moved into his territory, causing him to remain more vigilant, or believing a hot doe is present—or both. Both of these factors will coax an aggressive buck to visit the scrape more frequently.

Increased vigilance can also be encouraged by seeding existing scrapes. I often seed scrapes when simply curious to see what type of buck is tending it, then deploying a trail camera to determine if additional effort is warranted. In these cases I normally carry a bottle of buck lure and another of doe-in-heat urine to produce a double whammy of territorial tendencies and lust.

This mock scrape was created by wiring a licking branch into place and adding some scent. The buck appeared within 24 hours.

Wildlife Research's Magnum Scent Dripper encourages daytime visits by dispensing scent only after ambient temperatures rise.

Seeding existing scrapes can elicit more frequent visits by making bucks believe another buck is horning in or an estrous doe has left her calling card.

To really turn up the volume, add a mock scrape beside or very close to an existing cluster of scrapes or major sign-board scrape. In so doing you'll make the dominant buck who built them believe he is being moved in on, often sparking competitive over-marking and more frequent visits. When a super-aggressive buck is involved it can really turn the tables in your favor.

In my own Idaho backyard, where habitat is vast and deer density relatively low, scrapes have become my go-to ploy for regularly putting tags on mature bucks, including a couple oldsters whose tooth wear revealed they were 6½-plus and 8½-plus years old. On Kansas' trophy grounds guarding a pickup-hood-size scrape resulted in one of my all-time best bucks and my first clean 5x5. In West Texas, many moons ago, sitting a windbreak scrape line resulted in my first DIY whitetail buck. While scrapes don't attract consistent attention in every part of the whitetails' range, and though they are far from a bowhunting cure-all, they offer yet another part of the puzzle to make you a more well-rounded whitetail hunter.

The author tagged this ancient buck from a mock scrape, a technique he has perfected in his challenging big-woods haunts.

As whitetails become a more valuable, more hunting property is tied up. Luckily we live in a country with abundant public lands.

CHAPTER 9

THE PUBLIC-LAND CHALLENGE

THE MOST IMPORTANT INGREDIENT to any productive whitetail hunt is access to a quality piece of ground. But in the times we live in reality means that not all of us have a private hunting spot to call our own. Knocking on doors for trespass permission isn't as lucrative as it once was; landowners understandably wary of strangers in an age of less basic respect and a public with a decidedly litigious bent. More pointedly, today it's just as likely any prime piece of whitetail property is already spoken for. For many deer hunters public lands are the only viable option if we wish to hunt at all. Hand in hand, there are also properties that are private in name, but the landowner so contemptuous of depredation inflicted by area deer the farmer's land becomes open to literally anyone who wishes to hunt there. The problem then becomes that many others are in the same boat as you are and you'll surely be sharing these properties with others—sometimes plenty of others.

Now, I'm not complaining. Thank God we live in a great country where, unlike Europe, we have properties open to all for egalitarian hunting opportunity. Gazing on the current scene it is sometimes easy to imagine we're headed down a European path, with hunting reserved only for the rich and well connected, but the reality is that we're far from that actuality in this country—even if the cost of hunting does increase annually. The United States, with a very few exceptions like Texas and maybe Delaware, is well interspersed with public lands; national forests, Bureau of Land Management, state-administered lands, Bureau of Reclamation and Corps of Engineers properties, state and national wildlife refuges, "Walk-In/Access Yes!-type sportsman's easements, corporate timberland or mining reclamation made available to the public', and sometimes even military posts. The deer hunter with a little ingenuity and willingness to do plenty of desktop research and in-field snooping will find there are plenty of public lands offered to hunters—even in private-land dominated Texas.

Of course, not all public properties are created equal. In north Idaho, on the seam between vast private farmlands and public mountains stretching into Montana, though I have access to at least one productive private farm I typically experience my best hunting on public timberland and national forest. But this is the Wild West, where public lands are measured in hundreds of thousands of acres and the largest cities are smaller than an average burg in the burgeoning Northeast.

Any bowhunter with the knowledge and gumption could've tagged this buck, as it came from Idaho public land open to all.

"No Trespassing" signs are more commonplace today, leaving more deer hunters with few options but public lands.

Public-land hunting can certainly prove productive. Quality white-tailed bucks are taken on public ground across the country every season. But public-land hunting also comes with inherent challenges, namely, the public. Only those hunters willing to work harder and smarter will find regular success.

Hunting as Competition

Plying public lands means you're no longer "competing" with only deer (for lack of a better word, as hunting as competition has always bothered me greatly). Not only will you be competing with other deer hunters, but sometimes upland, waterfowl and small-game hunters, plus trappers, bird watchers and joggers, and maybe even ATV, mountain bike or horseback riders and firewood cutters. All such activities can potentially alter or wholly shape deer movement patterns. Some of these activities are relatively predictable and easy to work around. Others are wildly unpredictable and impossible to anticipate.

Lets return to my Omaha suburban hunts as a good example. While the property we hunted was technically private, the adjacent nature preserve, complete with public hiking trails, scenic overlooks, interpretive centers and restrooms, provided regular spillover. On weekends in particular you could pretty much count on some adventurer wandering off the preserve and beneath your treestand, usually accompanied by an unleashed dog lifting his leg on everything in sight. Then there was the morning I was presented with an attractive redhead swathed in puffy down, expensive German binoculars swinging on her delicate neck, high stepping with the look of someone on urgent business. Not until she paused, produced a wad of tissues and exposed her superlative rear end did I understand what was happening. Luckily I was on hand to prevent that foul odor from being deposited near my best whitetail stand. True story.

Such realities also require deer hunters to take precautions against treestand theft by unscrupulous "hunters" or sabotage by misguided antihunters believing their actions will directly save poor Bambi. Chaining or cabling and padlocking stands to trees has become standard public-lands operating procedure, though I prefer to employ quick-deploying, strap-on ladder sections that are taken

Succeeding on today's public lands requires that you work harder and smarter than your "competition" – sometimes both.

out of the woods between hunts to make stands essentially inaccessible. Public lands also welcome climbing stands, taken with you after each hunt and providing increased adaptability in changing conditions. The only drawback with climbers is that they require a straight and limb-free tree—which might not be available in your hunting area. I've never seen such trees on the Kansas public walk-in areas I've bowhunted in the past, for instance. Though, I've left many stands and pop-ups in Kansas coverts for days on end, unlocked and unattended, without losing one. Of course this says as much about the general moral character of Heartland residents as the lack of traffic on those public-access lands.

No matter the property under discussion or number of hunters an area hosts, bowhunting public lands—or private lands wide open to all takers—must usually be approached a little differently, first anticipating how your competition will attack the area and influence deer movement, and on highly popular ground working around the schedules and movements of others. Of course, some public hunting areas are larger than others, some painfully small, others close to major cities and receiving more traffic than those situated in the hinterlands where before-work and after-school hunts are impossible. Some public lands allow public camping, others require a motel room. In other words, no two public-land areas are alike. But one thing is certain: the public always poses the potential for wreaking havoc on hunting plans, meaning bowhunters must generally work harder and smarter to find success.

Hunting Harder

There are some general rules to live by while bowhunting public lands. As a serious bowhunter you already have an advantage, as many public areas that are hammered during general firearms sea-

If you're to outmaneuver public-land hunters you must walk farther, or find more creative ways to access land that others do not.

sons see little traffic during early archery seasons. Still others are bowhunting only, even during later rut dates. Despite these realities, when bowhunting public or heavily hunted private lands I avoid weekends like the plague, for obvious reasons. The only time I break that rule is during exceptionally brutal weather. When the snow flies, temperatures dip into the teens and wind rocks your stand tree most modern bowhunters are inclined to remain inside watching football. When weather turns nasty, even on a long-awaited weekend, you can count on seeing fewer hunters in the woods, and increased daytime deer movement.

Find me a regularly successful public-lands bowhunter and I'd bet my best bow that person works harder than the average guy. This can translate into more thorough scouting than the average hunter is willing to invest, spending the time and effort required to canvas every square inch of a public hunting area during the off-season to find those especially appealing spots and instilling confidence that the grass isn't greener somewhere else, which eventually makes it easier to buckle down and put in that all-important time on stand.

On the best public lands—which are also generally the biggest parcels and sometimes the most rugged—the obvious way ambitious hunters beat their competition is by simply outdistancing them. For instance, near home many of my best mountain stands require a cold, muddy 20- to 30-minute ATV ride before initiating a mile uphill slog to reach the stand itself. This indicates rising earlier to reach stands before legal hunting hours. In other areas, simply traversing a patch of rugged, swampy or difficult ground that the masses are unwilling to tackle can get you into little-touched ground and better hunting. In north Idaho, again as an example, I find regular success by crawling into the nastiest, thickest patches of cover possible and locating a small opening to hang a stand over. Darn few hunters, especially rifle hunters with their long-range weapons, are willing to fight into such places.

This is where careful map research pays huge dividends, providing a bird's-eye view of likely access points, surrounding terrain and insight into how deer hunters will begin each day. It also provides better clues as to how deer might react to daily pressure. You can then pore over terrain details and make educated guesses as to where deer might retreat to avoid this hunting pressure. When dealing

Water access is one creative way to get into little-hunted public lands. Paddling across water barriers can do the trick.

with finite areas—unlike essentially infinite Inland Northwest or Far North big woods—it is sometimes relatively simple to decode potential escape patterns with a fair degree of accuracy.

Hunting Smarter

It is often said that young hunters get the job done through pure brawn, while the older hunter learns to find success with less effort by hunting smarter. On hard-hunted public lands I say you must have both, but smart will normally trump determination any given week. Brains come into play after physically determining where on a public hunting area deer are most apt to retreat to, then how you intend to get into that area with minimal effort without being detected. Let's look at a couple scenarios as food for thought.

In the first situation, while studying a map of a Bureau of Reclamation property open to whitetail hunting on a bowhunting-only basis, you discover a large oxbow created by a sluggish but deep river unequivocally preventing chest-wader crossings. This lobe of land comprises perhaps 2 acres of prime bedding cover with a bottleneck opening that can be covered with a single treestand. This public hunting area provides only two access points: a designated parking area and footbridge two miles south and downstream, another public parking area only a half-mile from that oxbow, but across the river. Viewed in a straightforward manner, you're looking at a two-mile bushwhack to reach that oxbow opening, while also potentially spooking deer on the way in. But the smart hunter sees this same situation, acquires an inexpensive skiff or lightweight kayak, drags it the half mile, paddles across the river in five minutes and situates himself in that pinch point well before daylight, and deer are none the wiser.

In the next scenario you're dealing with three sections of land set end to end and encompassing a stretch of a small, brushy, widely wandering creek. This Kansas Department of Wildlife & Parks Public Wildlife Area has but a single access point, a county road spur dead-ending at a locked gate at the very corner of the upstream section. You must walk from there—three miles if you wish to reach the far end of the hunt area; and you'd better pack waders if you wish to wade across that muddy, steep-walled creek. On the opposite boundary of this long stretch of property and the shallow creek it encompasses is a major highway, four lanes with very little shoulder and signage every 300 yards warning that parking is not permitted. But those signs don't say a thing about having a hunting partner, family member or spouse drop you off quickly, summoned again with cell phone when you're ready to climb out of your stand. Problem solved, other than the issue of recruiting an early morning chauffeur…

These are actual scenarios that I've faced in the field, the first in Nebraska (where a friend eventually arrowed his first whitetail), the second a place where I missed a gorgeous 5x5 buck with my recurve. The point is to study each situation with an open mind and a willingness to get creative.

Another aspect of hunting smarter involves setting up where others will not simply because the spot is too ugly or so wholly obvious it just never occurs to anyone to hunt there. This really demands keeping an open mind and actually reminds me a lot of suburban hunting in many respects. Given a large piece of real estate the average hunter is going to automatically dive into its heart, or engage in what I call end-of-the-road syndrome, at least in areas where roads are even available. Follow a public road to its very end during any general deer season and you'll invariably find a parked vehicle. What about all of that country you passed on the way in? Show me a patch of public ground sitting behind a wildlife refuge administration building, adjacent to a public parking area or behind the county trash dump and odds are good very few deer hunters have hung a stand there. Setting a stand beside a busy highway? Heresay! Which is exactly why it just might work...

Allowing Crowds To Work For You

If you can't beat them, join them. When hunting crowded public areas, especially when work regulates you to weekends only, sometimes you're better off playing the hand you're dealt and letting the crowds work to your advantage. This is the ultimate game of hunting smarter because it requires reading the country precisely and accurately predicting how

Carefully studying maps can reveal overlooked areas, or how to allow the public to work for you by pushing deer past your stands.

the masses will move into or through it, and setting up an ambush to take advantage of the resulting movement. This also means slipping into your treestand well before legal shooting light to assure you're properly positioned for the public drive to come, or using clever backdoor entrances to reach stands well ahead of driven deer without becoming part of the general mayhem. This may sound like a big order, but with a thorough understanding of the landscape – gained through diligent boots-on-the-ground scouting and poring over detailed topographical maps – and a touch of putting yourself inside a deer's head, it can work remarkably well.

While the early morning rush is an obvious highlight (many hunters don't head into their stands until they can see without a light), don't forget the late-morning exodus around 10 to 11 a.m. in most woods when most hunters are cold, bored, hungry or in need of a restroom. Midday hours can also be productive, since hunters begin hiking around seeking a better stand site or scouting in general. Then while you're at it, you might as well stay put for the evening arrival rush around 3 p.m., and the last hour of light when bored hunters who haven't seen anything begin to climb down from stands to assure they reach their vehicles before dark. Maybe it would just be easier to say that during the weekend bustle, deer might arrive beneath your stand at any hour of the day.

Ambush sites in these situations are 100 percent topographical or barrier oriented. We have visited this concept in great detail in earlier sections, so this should now come as second nature. In the most basic terms, locate stands in places where terrain, obstacles or natural barriers act to deflect deer through a predictable point. While hunting the so-called October lull, when bucks are just out of velvet and movement slows to a crawl, I actually welcome a bit of activity to stir things up and get deer moving. On public lands this can act in the same manner on nocturnally inclined bucks during any season date.

The author tagged this buck by being dropped off on a highway and slipping in the back door of an open state wildlife area.

Hunting far from home can include "roughing it," another allure of road-trip hunting—getting outside your comfort zone.

CHAPTER 10

DO-IT-YOURSELF ROAD-TRIPPING WHITETAIL

BACKYARD WHITETAILS ARE A HUNTING mainstay because the average deer hunter relegated to average habitat fully understands trophy quality is relative, and furthermore, making the best of what home has to offer includes its own intrinsic appeal. Still, while living outside classic habitat I spent two decades traveling eastward to find my whitetail fix, visiting only the best places promising the biggest antlers. I mean, really, why endure TSA manhandling or 18-plus hours behind the wheel for average hunting?

This is largely why whitetail hunters travel; looking for better hunting, bigger antlers, though there's also a definite sense of wanderlust for many. There's a seemingly endless world of whitetail possibilities awaiting the intrepid hunter, the next state over presenting the opportunity for an additional tag, or a cross-country trip providing grand adventure. While guided hunts remain out of reach for the majority of us, do-it-yourself forays can be funded cheaply and executed relatively easily. Seeking new horizons means continually encountering fresh perspectives, experiences making you a more versatile whitetail hunter. The rooted "whitetail expert" dogmatically lays down the rules, but what does he really know? He's hunted only a single place. Road tripping serves as a continuation of that backyard spirit, with basic ingredients including a license/tag, a place to hunt, travel funds, time away from work and an open mind.

The possibilities are inexhaustible whether you're seeking an on-the-fly opportunity or more involved preparations, but I offer these options to spark the imagination and set you on the path to

Bowhunting whitetails on limited time far from home requires you to hit the ground running, which means lots of research up front.

Oklahoma has become one of the author's favorite out-of-state whitetail destinations – giving up two bucks on two hunts.

enjoyable out-of-state hunts. All offer good trophy potential, as there's really no reason to leave home if the grass isn't greener, right?

Easy Access Do-It-Yourself Destinations

Oklahoma Sooner-Than-Later Bucks

With affordable over-the-counter (OTC) deer tags, generous bag limits and a long October through January 15 archery season, Oklahoma is one of my favorite whitetail destinations. This might also have something to do with tagging two gorgeous bucks in as many hunts there, but all of the ingredients are present. Oklahoma offers pure DIYers 1.6 million acres of wildlife management areas alone, in addition to scattered national forests and grasslands, and at least one coveted military reservation hunt. Oklahoma ranks number 17 overall in Pope & Young entries, with 51 percent of harvested bucks 3½-plus years old.

I especially enjoy hunting the western portion of the state, which is dry habitat reminding me of the West Texas country I started bowhunting whitetails in many moons ago. Baiting is legal in Oklahoma and especially productive during the dry early seasons.

Delve into specifics by visiting www.wildlifedepartment.com.

Washington Big-Woods Busters

Northeastern Washington is one of the greatest sleepers in whitetail hunting, a place where hunters quietly tag monster whitetails with little fanfare. These are big-woods bucks with big-antler genetics and Hercules body mass hunted on vast tracts of public national forests. Challenges come through the mountainous western landscape, but placing bait and or minerals (both legal) helps to concentrate deer from larger areas. License fees are on par with most western states, which means relatively pricey, though tags are available over the counter.

Hotspots include the Okanogan National Forest north of the Colville Indian Reservation, and Colville and Kaniksu National Forests north of Spokane. For those who find baiting repellent or don't have the time, the 40,000-acre Little Pend Oreille

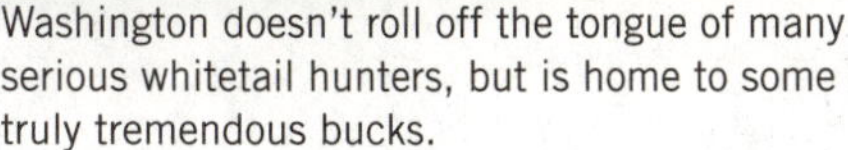

Washington doesn't roll off the tongue of many serious whitetail hunters, but is home to some truly tremendous bucks.

Whitetail fanatic Daniel Hawthorne took this awesome whitetail in northwestern Washington during a late bow season.

National Wildlife Refuge north of Spokane offers excellent bowhunting-only opportunities where baiting isn't allowed. Archery hunts span most of September, mid-November and mid-December.

Find out more by visiting wdfw.wa.gov.

Nebraska Prairie Prowlers

Nebraska is another one of my favorite whitetail destinations because I've done well there, but also because the Cornhusker State has a lot to offer, including one of the lowest hunter densities in the entire country, midpriced OTC licenses/tags and generous seasons. Nebraska ranks number 15 overall in Pope & Young buck production. I've bowhunted whitetails from the populated suburbs of Omaha in the east, to the corn-field countryside along the Republican River in the south, to the forsaken Sandhill country between the Niobrara and North Loop rivers up north. Each relinquishes its own charms—eastern hardwoods, Midwest farmland, traditional buffalo plains. I've taken respectable bucks from all of these places.

Nebraska also offers a cornucopia of public lands—state and national wildlife refuges, national forests and grasslands, state recreation areas and Nebraska Game & Parks Commission wildlife management areas. But it's also true that Nebraska landowners aren't as guarded as residents of other prime whitetail habitats. Even amongst the crowded Omaha outskirts I was able to knock on doors and gain permission to respectable properties.

Learn more by visiting outdoornebraska.ne.gov.

Kentucky Oak Ridge Boys

A recent report by the Quality Deer Management Association charted the incidence of Boone & Crockett bucks per square mile of habitat. To my surprise the top spot was not Iowa or Kansas or Illinois, but Kentucky. And why not? Kentucky has made a conscience effort to improve trophy quality through aggressive game management, and the home to bluegrass music, thoroughbreds and world-class bourbon also harbors some of the best whitetail habitat around. My single visit to the Bluegrass State includes memories of a juxtaposition of Midwest-like woodlands and Southern hospitality and cooking.

There is also plenty of room for DIY adventures,

Nebraska has always been good to the author, recently relinquishing two beautiful whitetails in areas open to all.

Kentucky has emerged as one of the best trophy whitetail states in the Union in recent years, and also includes abundant public ground.

This handsome buck is just a sampling of what the Dakotas have to offer, this one coming from South Dakota.

as affordable licenses can be purchased on arrival and early September seasons make Kentucky a velvet-antler hotspot, plus seasons proceed through the end of the year. Crossbows are welcomed during specified dates. National forests abound east and south; all under the romantic moniker Daniel Boone National Forest. Kentucky also features a wide variety of state recreation areas, Bureau of Reclamation lands and private logging and mining lands open to public hunting—though knocking on doors in less populated regions can still prove profitable.

Find out more by visiting fw.ky.gov.

Dakota Knock-Knock Bucks

The fly-over states of North and South Dakota remain a place where polite knocks on farmhouse doors still net great hunting. Maybe it's the weather that keeps the irritating masses away. Last time I was in North Dakota thermometers stuck at 10 below zero the entire first week of November and 5-foot-deep snowdrifts prevented access to our best stands. My latest South Dakota foray included nonstop 50 mph winds. But I kept meeting ranchers who beckoned me to barns to inspect lines of 150-inch-plus whitetail antlers nailed to rafters. I'd ask if I might hunt their land, you know, like you'd jokingly ask a rich friend if you might take his Ferrari for a spin. Except these ranchers always shrugged and said, "Sure."

North Dakota has some quirky rules, like all season openers commence at noon, and you must buy not only a $250 bow license, but any number of nickel-dime permits according to weapons choice and hunt dates. South Dakota is less complicated and more affordable. Archery seasons are generous here, generally August through early January.

To learn more see gfp.nd.gov (North Dakota) and gfp.sd.gov (South Dakota).

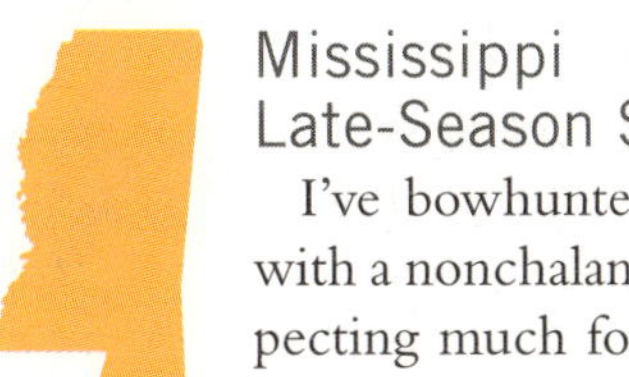

Mississippi Late-Season Swampers

I've bowhunted much of the South with a nonchalant approach, seldom expecting much for trophies, but participating so I can enjoy the total Southern experience. The Deep South provides its heralded Southern Hospitality, of course, complete with fine Southern Cooking. There's also the important facet of Deep South opportunities peaking well after the Midwest closes shop.

The one exception to my Dixie trophy nonchalance lays in Mississippi. Mississippi is the poster child for the Quality Deer Management move-

Aggressive quality deer management has transformed Mississippi into one of the hottest trophy whitetail states in all the Deep South.

It's no secret that Kansas produces quality whitetails. What is lesser known is that public "Walk-In" areas are available.

ment. The Magnolia State has become number one in 3½-year-old buck production, at 70 percent. Mississippi now produces the biggest bucks in all of the Deep South, with most of these residing in western Old Miss. All of the Mississippians that I know are hunt-club members, but Mississippi is well interspersed with public lands, including abundant national forests like the Delta near Vicksburg or Homochitto east of Natchez. There are also national wildlife refuges and wildlife management areas – 52 to be exact, available for an additional $15 fee. Archery season runs October through mid-November and again in late January. While Mississippi doesn't give permits away, they can be had over the counter.

Find out more by visiting www.mdwfp.com.

Going For Gold

Kansas Walk-In Wanderlust

The Sunflower State has become expensive for nonresidents whitetail hunters, but this is what the market will bear given the state's track record—including the third through sixth spots annually in the quantity of Pope & Young entries, and a No. 6 all-time spot in Boone & Crockett records. If you wish to participate you'll need to submit an early application for lottery tags by late April, though draw odds are nearly assured. Tag quotas were recently increased to placate farming and insurance interests, so seasons are generous and crossbows are allowed.

Kansas is comprised almost exclusively of private lands, so demand for trophy bucks leads to everything in sight being leased, leaving DIYers standing on the outside looking in. Luckily the DIY archer can take advantage of the Kansas Department of Wildlife & Park's 420,000 acres of Public Wildlife Areas that are leased private grounds open to public hunting on a walk-in-only basis. I count more than 80 of these areas scattered across the state. These aren't scrub properties either. I've witnessed some darn nice bucks on these properties in two different regions—missing a 150-inch 5x5 with my recurve on one of them. And no, I won't tell you which one. You'll have to do your own research.

Find out more by visiting www.kdwpt.state.ks.us.

The Iowa Conundrum

Ask the average whitetail hunter to name a single state that they would most love to win a lifetime deer hunting license for and most will automatically name Iowa. This might have something to do with a handful of high-profile

The author took this white-tailed buck in Iowa. Iowa private lands are some of the best in the nation, but public areas are available.

Illinois has remained a trophy hotbed for decades due to bucks like this Pike County gagger.

big-buck hunters residing there, but there is no way around the fact that Iowa produces monster bucks and lots of them. An almost ideal combination of rich farmlands providing unlimited, high-protein groceries set beside ample cover, top-tier genetics, extremely curtailed firearms hunting – especially during critical rut dates – and conservative harvest quotas creates a model for what many other states could be given similar management programs.

From the nonresident's perspective things are a little less rosy. It's easy to get the idea that Iowans are greedy and want it all for themselves. Nonresident tags are difficult to draw, license fees are some of the highest in the Midwest at $544 and out-of-state hunters are restricted from hunting certain parts of the state. As a whole, only 266,000 acres (less than 1 percent) of the state is comprised of public lands—though I've hunted these areas and was quite impressed with the quality of the hunting and lack of hunting pressure. It's almost as if residents have enough private ground tied up they don't need these public areas, save the occasional bird hunter.

Learn more by visiting www.iowadnr.gov.

Illinois Or Bust

Illinois comes up in serious whitetail discussions for one reason alone. The Land of Lincoln stands as a solid No. 2 in Boone & Crockett production and generally makes any top-five P&Y list. Illinois also has a reasonable amount of public land, especially in the south where national forests are common, just not in the state's most renowned trophy areas like Pike and Brown counties. You'll hear many Illinois hunters lamenting days gone by, insisting the state isn't what it once was. Of course, that could be said about just about any whitetail state in the Union. Deer herds peak and trough and the nation's whitetail herds are currently climbing out of a trough nearly everywhere.

Illinois whitetail tags are issued on a first-come-first-serve basis during a limited application period and are reasonably priced. When quotas are filled no more tags are issued. So Illinois requires advanced planning and paying attention to your calendar around mid-June. Illinois public lands have witnessed increased hunting pressure as more hunters who once plied private lands have been pushed out by outfitters and leases. But relatively low-pressure hunting can be found in the southern portion of the state, and along the Mississippi River farther from large population centers.

Find out more by visiting www.dnr.illinois.gov.

Texas is dominated by private land, but the price of admission is worth every penny due to bucks such as this one taken by Steven Tisdale.

South Texas Pay To Play

The Lone Star State has the lowest incidence of public lands for a state its size. Wildlife management areas are scattered throughout the state; all accessed only through a lottery drawing, though some of the most remote can have even to shoe-in odds. These public hunting areas, some better than others, amount to some 1.6 million acres and are worth investigating. Limited drawings assure they don't become overly crowded and quality hunting remains.

Visiting deer hunters are likely better served by paying a daily fee to bowhunt private ranches. Fees are based on trophy quality mostly, but also facilities provided—some ranches provide bunkhouse lodging, others allowing primitive camping—and how many hunters are hosted per season. Bowhunting-only properties are obviously the most appealing. Daily rates run from $150 to $300 per diem. While this may sound cost prohibitive, understand that 60 percent of all harvested Texas bucks are at least 3½ years old, the state supporting an average of 5.8 bucks per square mile.

Start by contacting a chamber of commerce in an area you'd like to hunt to inquire about landowners willing to host bowhunters. Follow up by interviewing potential hosts, then separate fact from bovine excrement, request references and contact past clients. Be sure to request references that were both successful and unsuccessful. The guy who failed to get his prize but says he would happily return is reference gold.

Learn more by visiting tpwd.texas.gov.

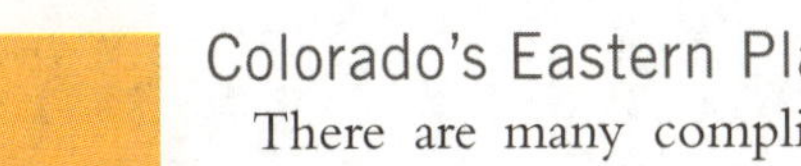

Colorado's Eastern Plains

There are many complications involved in bowhunting Colorado's world-class Eastern Plains whitetails. There is the matter of an early application deadline normally around April 1, draw odds decreasing in direct proportion to the amount of public lands available in a particular unit, and prime private-land "Ranching For Wildlife" hunts that require many years of accumulated preference points. Once a tag is drawn you'll be limited to spotty pieces of public lands, or be left scrambling to find a landowner free of outfitter or lease commitments

QUICK GUIDE TO KNOCKING ON FARMHOUSE DOORS

If politics reveal anything of importance it's that rural America marches to the beat of a different drummer. Gaining permission to whitetail ground is trickier than it once was, but still feasible given the right settings and approach.

Firstly, the odds of gaining hunting permission increases exponentially the farther from large population centers you travel. Sadly, this hinges on the fact that landowners closer to major cities are more likely to have suffered a tire-rutted field, littered driveway or loose cows resulting from a gate left open.

Finally, when approaching landowners it's always important to put your best foot forward. Basic manners, "Yes sir" and "No sir," for instance, are still appreciated in farm country. Tuck your shirt in, comb your hair, take off your hat and be willing to chat awhile. If the opportunity arises, offer to help with chores—mend a fence, split firewood, pitch hay to the horses.

In short, make an effort to present yourself as an upstanding, polite citizen who can be trusted to not do something stupid and make a landowner's life more difficult.

Colorado's Eastern Plains seem like an unlikely destination for monster whitetails, but regularly produces record-book bucks such as this.

– Ranching For Wildlife hunts the exception. Best case scenario on private ground involves a flat kill fee following a successful hunt, with others demanding money up front. Another unique aspect of hunting the Plains is while you might have the run of 70,000 acres or more, typically less than 10 percent of that landmass will represent productive habitat, meaning creek bottoms, patches of rough CRP or pastureland.

Is it worth it? I've bowhunted eastern Colorado three times. Those hunts resulted in whitetail bucks grossing 148 and 157 inches, and a mule deer scoring 185. Friends who hunt there more often tag bucks that make mine look silly.

Find out more by visiting cpw.state.co.us.

Ohio Buckeye Bucks

Ohio offers world-class whitetail hunting on a blue-collar budget. The Buckeye State offers OTC tags and 40 percent of the state's deer are harvested by bowhunters, including crossbows—Ohio one of the first to include crossbows in general archery seasons. The state hosts around 2.1 bucks per square mile and has long held a top-five spot in Pope & Young records. As would be expected, many of the state's best bucks come from exclusive private ground, but the state is well interspersed with wildlife management areas, Bureau of Reclamation administered properties and national forests, especially in the southeastern tier of the state. Travel off the beaten track and you're also more likely to find private property made available for nothing more than a polite knock on a farmhouse door.

Ohio has been on trophy hunters' radars for decades because of bucks like this one, taken by Bob Humphrey.

I especially like the looks of the Ohio River corridor between Parkersburg and Huntington, Kentucky, and the outlying Wayne National Forest areas just north of this valley. Plus, Ohio relinquishes some of the best suburban whitetail hunting in the nation.

Visit www.dnr.state.oh.us for more information.

The efficient bowhunting rig consists of many parts working together. The accessories chosen depend upon the game and conditions faced.

CHAPTER 11

MATCHING THE RIG TO THE GIG

THERE'S A LOT TO BE SAID for assembling, becoming intimately familiar with and extensively shooting a single bow setup. The old saying of, "Beware of the man who owns only one gun" is as true in archery as rifle marksmanship. "Auto-pilot" mode is often the only thing separating a successful season from failure, especially when season-making trophies are involved and nerves become frazzled. As someone who makes a living in the bowhunting trade, I often approach a single season with eight to 10 assembled and tuned, ready-to-roll bow outfits, so I know that switching bows regularly requires keeping things tightly wrapped.

Be that as it may, if you find yourself directing the vast majority of your bowhunting efforts toward a single species, or are contemplating a special bowhunt with conditions that are quite explicit or out of the ordinary, a species-specific bowhunting rig is always a good idea. Not all big-game animals or the country they inhabit are created equal. Some big game has thin skin and light bones, others have thick hides and heavy bones. There are many variations in between. While a subjective term, some animals are simply tougher than others; some die easy, others cling to life like a desert shrub in a summer drought. The country an animal occupies sometimes determines how difficult recovery becomes, an inadvertently gut-shot pronghorn on wide-open plains, for instance, is much easier to keep track of and recover than a whitetail in big-woods second-growth where walking erect is a challenge. Some animals bleed, others do not—a thin-haired, lean early-season Western deer verses a thickly furred, fat-laden northern black bear for example. Ultimately terrain and vegetation also dictate the kinds of shots you will receive—point-blank, average or long. Finally, bowhunting scenarios can vary as widely as sitting motionless for hours on a freezing stand and shooting with cold and stiff muscles, to shoots preceded by hot, sweaty scrambles up steep mountainsides that assure you're loose and limber.

It is absolutely true that you can assemble a single rig and successfully address every single one of these situations. Heck, I did it for years out of economic necessity. But it is also true that a species- or terrain-specific rig can give you a decided advantage under very specific conditions, an edge that

Every bowhunter has individual equipment tastes, but some gear makes more sense in particular settings than others.

can mean the difference between squeaking out bowhunting success and going home frustrated and empty handed after a highly challenging hunt. That is what we will be talking about here.

The Whitetail Bow

Easily 70 percent of North American bowhunters pursue white-tailed deer to the exclusion of nearly all other game. Mostly this includes treestands or ground blinds, and long sits in chilly to down-right cold weather while wearing heavy, restricting insulated duds. All of these stipulations point to an ultra-smooth-drawing, super-forgiving, whisper-quiet bow. This further translates into cam systems that allow hitting the anchor point without grunting or tugging through 17 inches of peak draw weight, and draw cycles free of a distracting, bumpy rollover. The bow's design should include a brace height and geometry forgiving of minor shooting form flaws created by cramped, twisted treestand or pop-up shooting scenarios, and the aforementioned cold and muscle stiffness. Most of all, whitetail bows should be uncompromisingly quiet.

Yet, despite the actual needs of 70 percent of the nation's bowhunters', the vast majority of the industry's flagship compounds—often entire line-ups—prove to be exactly the opposite.

This is most often linked to the speed trap—advertising hype and bowhunters believing that speed equals more success. Creating the fastest arrow speeds calls for radical cam systems, which create more challenging draw cycles that build into peak quickly, pull through peak longer—making bows feel heavier—and then drop into let-off quickly. This also equates to bows with brace heights in the neighborhood of 5 inches instead of 7 inches, which means that arrows remain on the string longer following the release, providing more time to

Stand hunting has different requirements than spot-and-stalk hunting, so assemble your hunting outfit accordingly.

introduce human error.

Granted, the "speed bow" label has been blurred by recent technology, but certain aspects remain. One of the most important new developments is longer risers combined with short, parallel limbs. This spreads bow mass across a wider axis for added stability and forgiveness. In general, you'll always find longer axle-to-axle dimensions make a bow easier to shoot well under pressure, though a bow that is too long can interfere with surrounding vegetation or blind roofs. In my opinion, 33 to 36 inches seems an ideal happy medium, the former best for shorter shooters, the later for taller archers. I also generally avoid the lightest bows while on stand, and prefer the steadiness of something that comes out of the box at slightly more than 4 pounds.

Accuracy enhancement and forgiveness also come through riser-to-limb-pocket alignment. Limb-pocket designs that spread limb contact over wider or two-point geometry effectively shift limb-pivot points backward, ideally in line with the bow-grip throat. This allows reflex (lower brace heights) without a loss of aiming and shooting stability. Add this to newer flexible cable guards that eliminate riser torque at full draw by pulling inward when drawn then snapping back outward on release to allow the fletchings to pass untouched, and you have a bow that is automatically easier to shoot well.

Manufacturers have also introduced new technologies that conquer shot noise and vibrations. String stops are perhaps the most important, and also contribute to accuracy by promoting more consistent nock separation following the release. Most string stops provide ample shot silence right out of the box, but I add string silencers to every hunting bow – especially those set up for whitetails – because there's no such thing as a bow that's too quiet. Parallel limbs also tame shot noise since limbs moving in equal and opposite directions on release cancel vibrations and shot noise while transferring maximum energy. Rubber modules added to limbs and risers at the factory also result in quieter shots.

So in quick review, the ideal whitetail bow in-

Season timing also dictates equipment set-up; hunting during cold seasons indicating a need to drop in bow weight, for instance.

cludes parallel limbs, a string stop and added factory silencing accessories for silence. In general the shortest axle-to-axle dimensions—at least in my opinion—should be avoided. Also, an overall geometry including a long riser paired with short limbs and limb pivot points aligning with the grip. Brace heights from 6.5 to 7.5 inches and a slim grip that accommodates shooting while wearing gloves in chilly to cold weather are also pluses.

With whitetails, silence is golden. Whitetails are chronic string jumpers, so quiet equipment is the key to success.

Ultimately, your whitetail bow should feel good to you; a bow that sits up straight at full draw without torque-inducing manipulation, including a comfortable grip allowing a lose, cradling grip, and a cam system promoting planting a pin on target and pulling straight into your anchor point slowly and smoothly (this can also be a factor of draw weight, as I normally drop draw weight 10 pounds before cold whitetail seasons) without struggling or dislodging the arrow from the rest, and especially free of attention-grabbing movement.

"Ideal" is always a risky label, but when it comes to whitetails it all boils down to a bow you can shoot well under pressure and that remains whisper quiet on release. A personal ideal is part technology, part dimensions, part feel, but if this also means sacrificing 25 or 30 fps—a speedy 325 to 345 fps bow instead of a barn-burning 350 to 370 fps model—I'll happily live with it. You can't kill what you can't hit, and though whitetails are generally shot at ranges of less than 35 yards, conditions are such that these can represent some of the most challenging shots of the season.

Accessories also factor into all of this. In arrows I want something that absorbs more of a bow's released energy to help make it quiet and up to the task of blasting through bone if I'm slightly off my mark or a deer jumps the string. Due to the predominantly short ranges involved with whitetails, I prefer heavy to middle-ground weight carbon arrows, perfectly willing to give up some speed for shots that go unnoticed by jumpy deer.

With regards to arrow rests, I want something that holds my shaft in place while waiting or drawing, but drops out of the way on release for added forgiveness. This design normally includes a deeply forked launcher topped by a "corral gate," or rotating launcher arms that drop or spin out of the way on release. They keep arrows in place and ready for the shot while drawing, but contact the shaft for 50 to 70 percent less time after the release—less time to introduce human error. Quality Archery Designs UltraRest is the original in this rest class and a perfect example.

With all other accessories for a whitetail-specific rig I live by the K.I.S.S. principle. This includes super-bright but uncluttered one- to three-pin sights, short and lightweight vibration-squelching stabilizers and a tightly woven wrist sling that allows a loose, cradling grip without fear of dropping my bow, but also unimpeded access while wearing gloves during fleeting shot opportunities. I prefer a back quiver that is easily hung from a handy branch, like Rancho Safari's Catquiver Mini, though many hunters opt for quick-detach bow quivers. I want my bow to sit comfortably in my lap and at the ready, and attached bow quivers make this difficult.

Bowhunting open-country pronghorn comes with opposite requirements than whitetail hunting—a premium is placed on longer shots.

The Open-Country Rig

My attitude takes a complete 180 when contemplating wide-open terrain and long-range game such as pronghorns, inherently spooky Coues whitetails, plains mule deer and even tundra caribou. For the most part these are animals that are relatively "soft," or at least own vitals easily breached with moderate energy, average draw weights and terminal tackle. These are also active hunts where warm early seasons and aggressive stalks mean that I'm typically warmed up and my muscles are limber. The emphasis is on all the speed that I can handle accurately, flattened arrow trajectory and long-range proficiency.

This starts with a performance-driven bow design, models built for bragging-rights arrow speeds via lower brace heights and more radical cam systems. I will also choose a higher draw weight than that wielded on the average whitetail stand; for me 70 pounds instead of 60. This points to today's flagship models, and while manufactures might advertise speeds of 350 to 360 fps, when you add a peep sight and string loop, nock and maybe even string silencers, and shoot even a light hunting-weight arrow, you're still looking at solid arrow speeds in excess of 325 to 330 fps. Understand that these bows and the speeds they generate require finer tuning and more solid shooting form for reliable accuracy – all subjects that we will address in detail in upcoming chapters.

Speed leads to forgiveness in one important area: judging range. When pushing the limits of archery capabilities and stretching yardage well past the 25- to 35-yard comfort zone of the average whitetail hunter, tiny discrepancies in yardage can lead to large misses. Of course, the modern bowhunter doesn't—nor shouldn't—leave home without a quality laser rangefinder. No bowhunter has any business taking a shot past 40 yards without first employing a laser rangefinder, ever, period. Still, even space-age technology isn't perfect. Sometimes high grass or brush prevents getting a laser reading directly off of animal hide, which may lead to the laser reading off of objects in the general vicinity and best-guess compensation. A single grass stem, unseen by the bowhunter, can lead to a misreading of four to six yards—or enough to completely miss with a slower bow rig. A faster arrow traveling at a flatter trajectory gives you a wider margin for error.

A lot of this is achieved through terminal tackle, namely lighter arrows. Light broadheads are also available, but I prefer to keep Front of Center (F.O.C.) balance high to counteract things like bad releases, crosswinds or small deflections such as grass stems or twigs. The 100-grain standard is ideal for the industry's lightest arrows—details of which I'll cover in an upcoming part of this book called

Bowhunters have no business taking longer shots if they don't know the range. A quality laser rangefinder is imperative.

The author received but a fleeting opportunity at this B&C-quality Coues whitetail. A lightweight, fast arrow saved the day.

Terminal Tackle. In the past this might have meant sacrificing durability and reliability, but today's space-age carbon shafts are much tougher than Super Lite aluminums of the past.

I try to build as much forgiveness into these speed rigs as possible by adding a full drop-away rest—preferably a fast-acting limb-driven design—and long active stabilizer in the 10- to 12-inch class that steadies every shot and sucks noise and vibration out of the riser. Every bow I shoot wears a wrist sling to promote a loose, cradling bow grip, but with my long-range rigs I adjust them so they actually support the bow if I completely release my grip. I typically wear a back quiver during open-country hunts, as compound bows were engineered to shoot best sans bow quivers, especially when even a slight breeze buffets arrow fletching while attempting to aim fine. The one exception is when backpacking, as the extra back quiver becomes more difficult to carry.

Precision long-range shooting also depends on the right kind of sight. A single-pin mover is an excellent choice here, allowing the shooter to dial the exact range down to a half-yard at any range from 20 to just about as far as you wish to shoot—including 100-plus yards used for off-season, long-range practice. Some hunters prefer fixed-pin sights, fearing they will forget to make adjustments to the mover in the heat of the moment. A five-pin sight gets you to 60 yards, 70 if you set your top pin for 30 yards, while seven-pin models take you out to 80 or 90 yards. You may not wish to shoot at healthy animals at 80 to 100 yards, but with quality practice an unintentionally gut-shot animal that pauses at such ranges allows you to punch another hole in it somewhere and increase your chances of a speedy recovery. Just sayin'.

The Heavyweight Rig

There are certain animals that are simply sturdier and sometimes tougher than run-of-the-mill deer. Elk come to mind as the most regularly bowhunted of these species, though others include moose, bison and many species of African plains game such as eland. The heaviest dangerous game is in a class all its own. Killing the big beasties with regularity is all about penetration and reliability should you encounter substantial bone. Certainly elk and moose have been killed by petite women toting low-energy outfits, but regular success on the biggest big game during the most demanding bowhunts sometimes means taking shots that aren't exactly textbook broadside through the ribs and point-blank close. With the right equipment setup the bowhunter can take longer shots at elk in open alpine habitat, for instance, heavily quartering shots with confidence of reaching vitals, or seeing accidental bone hits end positively instead of representing major catastrophes.

I'm generally not an advocate of bumping bow poundage to address a single hunt or species and al-

When it comes to big game such as elk, sturdy broadheads and heavy arrows can make the difference for dependable penetration.

ways prefer that an archer shoot a comfortable draw weight to promote maximum accuracy. In order to kill them you must first hit them in the right place. Additional draw weight doesn't turn bad hits into dead animals, no more than shooting a .338 Win Mag kills any faster than a .243 Winchester when bad hits are made with both. That being said, when bowhunting elk, moose or Africa's largest antelopes, I pull all the draw weight I can comfortably handle. When I'm bowhunting fall whitetails that draw-weight maximum might be 60 to 65 pounds. On elk I'm more likely to be pulling 70-plus pounds.

Since nearly all of my elk hunting involves active pursuit and warm muscles, or slam-dunk ranges over water, I generally don't mind a radical bow with a relatively low brace height, challenging cams or feathery mass. In fact, those super-light carbon-riser models with a starting mass of less than 4 pounds and fitted with the lightest carbon accessories available, are welcomed when tearing up and down steep mountains chasing bugling bulls or hiking long miles.

With the largest game much depends on the arrow and the broadhead it carries. This is always a delicate balancing act, especially when bowhunting elk. I want an arrow that's capable of pile-driving deep into burly bull elk, but also something with reasonably flat trajectory for longer shots or those through tight overhanging brush common in forested habitat. If I were hunting from stands over water or wallows with few shots taken at more than 30 yards, I might be inclined to choose the heaviest carbon arrows possible. But what happens if I must jump out of that stand and go running-and-gunning on a bugling herd bull passing me by? As high-performance bows become faster and faster I've continued to adopt heavier and heavier arrows, now to the tune of around 15 grains per pound of draw weight, or finished arrows weighing from 450 to 460 grains. This seems a good balance between penetration potential and acceptable trajectory. I also prefer the newest super-slim, G-nock diameter carbons, as they're highly aerodynamic, effectively buck crosswinds, are tough as a coffin nail, and slip through hide, flesh and bone quite efficiently for deep penetration.

Big wild boars can prove to be real arrow stoppers. A cut-on-contact broadhead and heavy arrow make short work of even the heaviest hogs.

When gearing up for an African safari and targets like this 400-pound hartebeest, the author chose efficient broadheads and heavy arrows.

I'm also pretty fussy about what I screw into the end of my arrows while bowhunting the big stuff. I won't hunt elk or any larger game with mechanical broadheads. This is a personal choice, as I certainly know highly successful bowhunters who do, including names you would likely recognize. My attitude stems from 23 years of guiding elk hunters and witnessing too many worst case scenarios. I've also had rugged cut-on-contact designs save my butt on a few occasions—including at least two bulls I would have cried to lose. Today I want a fixed three- or four-blade head with an all-steel ferrule, or high-tech cut-on-contact model with beefy blades—both with conservative cutting diameters of 1-1/16 to 1-1/8 inches, and uncompromising blade-locking systems or one-piece design. Off the top of my head, Muzzy's Trocar and Phantom SC, New Archery Products HellRazor, G5 Striker, Slick Trick ViperTrick, Wac'Em's three- and four-blade and Steel Force's Phathead are heads I'd confidently choose while pursuing elk.

For accessories, I start with a lightweight but indestructible fixed seven-pin sight, preferably

Cut-on-contact broadheads are best when deep penetration is paramount, because they slip through hide and bone more efficiently.

something including overall carbon construction or head, a drop-in "caged" drop-away arrow rest, 10-inch stabilizer that's relatively light but includes outboard weight for stabilizing efficiency like a feathery carbon-tube body with rubber-suspended weight at its end, and a braided wrist sling. My elk bows generally wear a quick-detach sling system, like those from Game Plan Gear with rubber mounting studs that double as silencers. When I begin with a lightweight carbon bow chosen for carrying ease, I'm more aware of the weight of any accessories added, as there's no point in starting with an easy toting 3.5-pound bow, only to match the weight of a standard aluminum-riser bow by adding heavy accessories.

Low-Energy Setups

Today more women and youth are enjoying bowhunting, while many old-time bowhunters are growing older and finding it difficult to pull the poundage they once did. Interestingly, many of the same rules that apply to bowhunting the largest game also apply to low-energy shooters pursuing average-size game. Intuition has long worked against the kinetically challenged, including those with short draw lengths of less than 27 inches, and pulling less than 50 pounds. The general inclination has long been to pair low-energy rigs with the lightest arrows possible and broadheads weighing less than standard. This appears sound on the surface, but can actually further handicap these archers.

Forget about speed. The key to killing animals cleanly with archery gear is ample penetration, and when limited energy is available this happens only through momentum. This means choosing a heavy-for-deflection, skinny-profile shaft and a standard-weight broadhead of 100 grains with sleek cutting tip or true cut-on-contact design, and conservative

Youth and women bowhunters are at a disadvantage with low draw weights and short draw lengths. Highly efficient broadheads and heavy-for-spine arrows are important to success.

cutting diameter. Some speed will be sacrificed with this combination, but when an animal is hit the desired pass-through results are more likely to occur.

Going Traditional

Traditional bows also qualify for the low-energy moniker, even those shot by strong adult men. Traditional archery is experiencing a renaissance as more bowhunters each season take a step back from technology and choose traditional equipment for bowhunting. Many of these archers want to return to the roots of bowhunting, emulating archery icons such as Fred Bear, Maurice Thompson, Saxton Pope and Arthur Young (of Pope & Young Club fame), others simply seek fresh challenges after decades of successful bowhunting, as traditional gear generally shortens effective range and calls for getting closer to game before shooting. Others simply want a simpler overall approach in these times of contrived living and technological overload. I choose traditional gear as an extension of my bowhunting enjoyment, another facet of archery in addition to compound bows, hunting with a traditional bow one week, compound the next. Despite what certain bowhunting factions seem to believe, one does not exclude the other.

No matter the reason, traditional bowhunters face many of the same problems that low-energy shooters do, as these primitive bows simply do not generate the same levels of energy as modern compounds. This doesn't make them any less deadly or attractive, they just require a different approach to lethality.

The biggest decision to be made in traditional archery is the choice between longbows or recurves. Archers of old, such as Howard Hill and Pope and Young, made the simple longbow famous, a graceful and simple weapon that's essentially no more than a bent stick with a string attached to each end.

Hannah Tisdale tagged this pretty Texas whitetail by choosing a streamlined fixed-blade broadhead to maximize penetration.

Tavis Rogers took this gorgeous Northwest Territories Dall sheep with a longbow and heavy cut-on-contact broadhead.

The string doesn't touch the face of the limbs of a classic longbow while at rest – not true of reflex-deflexed longbow models – making longbows extremely quiet in hunting situations. Recurves, made iconic by venerable archers such as Fred Bear and Ben Pearson, aren't exactly "modern" in a historical sense and were used as early as the 8th century B.C., composite versions used by civilizations as varied as the early Persians, Turks and Mongols. Recurves are characterized by limb tips that point away from the shooter and the bowstring contacts the limb curves while at rest, requiring padding at these slap points to make them hunting silent. Recurves generally store more energy and shoot a little faster arrow than longbows. Whichever you choose really has as much to do with personal preference as anything, since some archers prefer the raw simplicity of a longbow and its point-and-shoot dynamics, while others prefer the more defined pistol grip of the recurve and its improved performance and ability to use a more deliberate form of instinctive shooting.

The one big mistake that uninformed archers make when making the switch from compound to traditional bow is purchasing or ordering a bow with too much draw weight. You may be able to comfortably draw and shoot a 70-pound compound, but a recurve or longbow of that weight would likely prove unmanageable. The difference is let-off, or more accurately, traditional bows' lack of let-off. While modern compounds lose 65 to 85 percent of their peak draw weight at full draw, traditional bows actually gain 3 to 4 pounds for every inch added to draw length. So the standard weight measurement of 28 inches, as in 55 pounds at 28 inches, or 55#@28", could pull 61 to 63 pounds at 30 inches and heavier than anticipated, or only 47 to 49 pounds at 26 inches and lighter than the shooter desired. On average, adult male archers will want to start with a traditional bow pulling 45 to 50 pounds at their respective draw length, women

Recurve bows come in anything from 52 to 64 inches; the needed length is based on each archer's physical dimensions and draw length.

35 to 40 pounds at their draw length, and slowly graduate to a bit more weight as they become stronger—though there's no sin in sticking to a beginning draw weight. Until the late 1970s most recurves were delivered at 45#@28", and much game was killed with them. For most shooters a midlength bow is best; meaning 56 to 60 inches in recurves (slightly longer for those with the longest draw lengths) and 63 to 67 inches in longbows.

The other major difference between compounds and traditional gear is the later are shot with fingers and generally you aim without sights – meaning you shoot instinctively. This requires much more practice than compound shooting, reinforcing hand-eye coordination and muscle memory without technological crutches. With time and practice shots at game taken with traditional bows requires little thought, other than remembering to pick a spot in the pursuit of "aim small, miss small" ideals. Traditional shots invariably come off much more fluidly, which also makes them deadly on running targets at reasonable ranges with amble practice. It's akin to throwing a baseball in that you can't really explain how you hit anything, it just happens—but only after plenty of repetition.

The strict traditionalist uses a classic longbow or recurve made of natural wood backed with fiberglass, wood arrows and one-piece, hand-sharpened broadheads. This is as sound an approach as any, and classic traditional bow designs are pleasing to look at in a way that compounds never will be. Wood arrows—Port Orford cedar is the most popular for straightness and consistency, Sitka fir is a tad more durable but slightly lighter, birch and bamboo for added weight and durability—are fun to make and obviously effective. The ends of wood arrows are tapered to accept glue-on nocks and broadheads with 5-degree tapers. Crowning (a bright color cap), cresting (distinctive stripes once used as identification, today for aesthetics) and fletching a dozen wooden arrows can enter the realm of arts and crafts, another part of the allure of traditional archery. Many traditional archers make their own gear, including leather "Robin Hood" back quivers, arm guards or bracers (to protect the forearm from painful bowstring sting) and tabs or finger gloves (to protect fingers from bowstring abrasion while shooting).

Traditional broadheads aren't primitive for the sake of aesthetics, but simple, sleek designs made to maximize penetration. Classic heads like the Zwickey (founded in 1939) are one-piece welded designs that are not only super rugged and require hand sharpening with file and whetstone, but their cutting tip and knife edges penetrate like crazy, assuring ample penetration on game with inherently low-energy longbows and recurves. An average compound bow outfit now generates around 70 to 80 foot pounds of Kinetic Energy. A hunting-weight longbow or recurve produces about 45 to 50 pounds of KE.

More recently a modern age of traditional—maybe more accurately, single-string shooting—has arrived. This includes takedown longbows and recurves designed with machined-aluminum risers, limb laminates and handle designs including space-age carbon, plus carbon arrows and broadheads owning classic lines but constructed and manufactured with space-age materials and manufacturing technology. There's absolutely nothing wrong with this approach, or the mix-and-match approach I use – shooting classic recurves with modern carbon arrows and broadheads. There are no rules, no matter what some self-appointed keepers of the gate like to believe. If shooting a compound-risered recurve holding an elevated rest and carbon arrows makes you happy, go for it. I've successfully bowhunted with a number of aluminum-riser recurves and carbon arrows and view them as no less pure than a primitive bow free of man-made materials shooting wooden arrows and homemade broadheads.

When using modern carbon arrows in traditional bows—which I do as a matter of course due to more reliable penetration on game—it's important to understand that many carbon-arrow selection charts are of little use for choosing a traditional shaft because they are designed for compound bows. Compounds whip arrows forward as cams unroll, but traditional bows push them steadily as limbs spring forward. Traditional bows generally require a much "softer" spine than compounds, even when com-

The author used "modern traditional gear" to tag this tremendous desert muley, including a milled-aluminum-riser recurve.

paring apples-to-apples draw weights. For instance, I normally shoot .500- to .400-inch deflection arrows from my traditional bows, the latter only with heavy heads that weigh 175 to 200 grains.

The other caveat to using carbon arrows for traditional bows is finding models that are heavy for spine, preferably something in the 10 to 12 grains per inch range. I've used lighter, standard-issue compound carbons in appropriate deflections and added plastic 5 to 8 gpi weight tubes to increase mass—with great results on anything from 3-D shooting to big-game hunting. But now I prefer heavy-for-spine carbon arrows. Carbon Express' wood-grain Heritage (10.11 gpi in 150 with .495-inch deflection) or X-Nock Easton Axis Traditional (9.8 gpi in 400, with 75/100-grain brass break-off inserts) are perfect examples and longtime favorites.

Traditional bows kill with momentum, not the kinetic energy that modern, speed-obsessed bowhunters find so fascinating. This means that to increase penetration traditional shooters must increase arrow mass and shoot very efficient cut-on-contact broadheads without exception. So, while you might successfully bowhunt with a compound and 350- to 400-grain finished arrows carrying 100-grain tips, experienced traditional bowhunters normally shoot something finishing at 500 to 600 grains, including a 150- to 200-grain broadhead to boost Front of Center balance (F.O.C.). Extensive tests performed by Ed Ashby (on dead African dangerous game and Australian Asiatic buffalo—animals larger than African Cape buff) have shown extreme F.O.C. in the 20-plus percentages offer a penetration advantage, literally dragging trailing arrows through flesh and especially bone. I'll discuss F.O.C. in more detail in the section on Terminal Tackle. For the time being, let's just say that in traditional archery the higher the F.O.C. the better performance you'll get in the field.

True one-piece broadheads that are milled from tool or stainless steel are now all the rage with modern traditional bowhunters, or at least designs with heavy blades anchored in milled-steel or aircraft-aluminum ferrules with steel set screws. These models can prove alarmingly expensive, like $25 or $35 each! If you can afford them, by all means use them. They're bulletproof and deadly effective. I assemble heavy traditional heads using classic one-piece-welded heads like Zwickey's No Mercy or more modern glue-ons like STOS, combined with long 45-grain aluminum or 75-grain steel broadhead adaptors (Precision Designed Products makes the best), according to the finished weight needed. These heads blast through heavy bone unscathed and even survive clattering impacts with rocks after a miss.

Gearing up correctly to assure we get the job done should be our first priority. The animals we pursue deserve no less. A large part of this is hitting them where it counts, but just as importantly is assembling bowhunting outfits that make the best of available technologies to meet the conditions at hand.

Traditional arrows need heavy cut-on-contact broadheads and high F.O.C. balance to assure ample penetration with limited energy.

The author chooses accessories based on the conditions and the type of shooting he expects to encounter on each hunt.

CHAPTER 12

EFFICIENT ACCESSORIZING – IT'S ALL IN THE DETAILS

DURING TWO PERIODS IN MY life I've worked retail in archery departments. For 23 years I guided 20 to 30 big-game hunters annually. I've also spent an inordinate amount of time in hunting camps across North America and Africa, a proclivity that kept me destitute for decades—and led to the above-mentioned, temporary vocations. Having been deeply immersed in the archery industry for more than 28 years, with bowhunting dictating the course of my life for more than 35 years, I've always been fascinated by the equipment that people are shooting and why they choose it.

As an archery technician I've serviced 25-year-old bows I wouldn't have wished on enemies. I've been asked to refletch arrows that were obviously crooked and damaged. Many of those customers were operating under dire financial limitations. Just as often they simply possessed an over-developed sense of "If it ain't broke, it don't need fixin'" – compounded by acute tightwad tendencies. Those were quirks that I could actually wrap my brain around.

What I've always found more baffling was exactly why some customers and guided clients chose the accessories attached to their hunting rigs. You'd ask these fellows why they chose a particular arrow rest or release aid and they couldn't articulate a coherent reason. It was as if accessory choices were made by throwing darts at an archery equipment catalog or playing Pin the Tail on the Donkey while standing in front of a wall of archery merchandise.

I actually do believe that you can make even outdated bows better by adding new-model accessories. I also believe that choosing the right accessories for the conditions a bowhunter regularly faces can make them more efficient and productive. Some of those details we discussed in the previous section under Matching the Rig to the Gig, but here I intend to answer some common questions that arise while making accessory choices.

Arrow Rests: Total-Containment Versus Drop-Away

This is a question that might be viewed in the same light as the tired Chevy versus Ford debate; in other words a personal choice based on unquantifiable calculus or preconceived notions. In truth, whether you attach a total-containment or drop-away arrow rest to your bow is a little more objective, as it directly affects how well you perform in

Total-containment arrow rests, like this TRUGLO Storm, are popular because they keep arrows under control.

the field under very specific conditions. To begin, let's investigate some innate pros and cons.

Total Containment Pros: Bowhunters generally choose full-containment rests for control. The original in this area, the Whisker Biscuit, includes encircling bristles with an open circle in the center to accommodate an arrow, and a side drop-in slot. Stiff bristles hold the arrow from all sides, so once an arrow is dropped in the bow can be twisted to any angle without dislodging the shaft. More recent incarnations are created by a bottom launcher and two support arms coming in at 10 and 2 o'clock to hold the arrow in place. The retaining arms are adjustable for arrow diameter, the most advanced including plunging supports with adjustable tension. Three-point containment rests allow fletchings to pass through the rest arms untouched, eliminating fletching wear and perhaps providing a slight reduction in arrow drag.

A loaded bow can be hung in heavy wind or bumped before the shot without dislodging the arrow. For shooters who have a difficult time keeping arrows on an open arrow rest during the draw cycle, or when nerves make hands flutter, such designs assure that arrows will stay in place and allow uninterrupted shots. They're essentially foolproof in terms of keeping the arrow ready for action before and during the shot, while a lack of moving parts assures they're also extremely reliable.

Drop-away arrow rests support the arrow while drawing, but fall from beneath the shaft before fletchings arrive.

Drop-Away Pros: Drop-away rests solved a reoccurring problem with early launcher rests—fletching contact and its effect on accuracy. The standard-issue launcher rest used by release shooters before the advent of drop-aways used twin, width-adjustable rest arms on a spring-loaded base that gave away to downward pressure, but greatly restricted the amount of fletching helical that could be applied to the arrow, especially after thinner carbon shafts appeared. The cock vane (off-colored fletching) pointed downward to pass between the launcher arms, and the hen vanes (two matched colors) passed over the launchers. Adding too much helical resulted in contact with one or more of the launcher arms, creating arrow bobbles or kicks away from the contact. This became especially pronounced as bows became faster and arrows lighter. The solution was to reduce fletching-helical spin, which resulted in trickier tuning while shooting fixed-blade broadheads – the reason mechanicals took such a quick foothold.

Enter the drop-away rest. Here was a way to completely eliminate fletching contact, since the launcher arms dropped from beneath the arrow after release to allow fletching to pass untouched. This allowed the application of aggressive helical or larger fletchings to create more stabilizing spin and drag for better control of fixed-blade broadheads. More importantly, drop-away launchers contact the arrow for 50 to 70 percent less time during launch, giving the shooter less opportunity to introduce human error through nervous wobbles, or after dropping the bow arm on release to watch the arrow fly – a bad habit called "peeking."

Total-Containment Cons: Total-containment rests would prove automatic winners in all bowhunting situations if it weren't for a single fact: since the design contacts every inch of the arrow from tip to nock following the release, accuracy is maintained only through rock-solid follow-through. Steady follow-through is important to pinpoint accuracy no matter your equipment choice, but absolutely imperative for consistency while shooting a full-containment rest.

This presents two glaring issues. First, total-containment rests are commonly installed on beginner or entry-level bows since a lack of moving parts makes them affordable, at least in their most basic forms. But, lack of experience makes it less likely an archer will employ consistent and steady follow-through. Second, as a hunting rest, how likely is it that the average bowhunter will remember to execute unfailing follow-through during a stressful shot at a coveted animal?

The problem boils down to follow-through, or lack of, and the influence the shooter has on the final arrow destination. Small movements during the release are magnified with each yard added to total range. On short-range game like whitetails from treestands, for instance, and to assemble 6-inch groups at a maximum effective range (the vital area of a white-tailed deer measures about 8 inches) the total-containment rest proves aptly sufficient and thus continues to be popular. For precise 3-D or target shooting, or for game taken at ranges exceeding 35 to 40 yards (admittedly a subjective number), they might not make an ideal choice; eroding accuracy enough to cause frustrations and missed game.

Drop-Away Cons: The modern drop-away arrow rest is a precise instrument that requires proper installation, and sometimes tuning to individual bow and arrow setups. There are exceptions, like self-contained designs that require no tuning, but they still require proper installation. Many archers just don't possess the confidence or mechanical acumen to properly install and tune a drop-away rest. I've found that if I read installation instructions carefully, following the steps to the letter, I'll encounter few problems. But I've also been tinkering with bows for 30-plus years. Sure, a bowhunter can hand this job over to a pro-shop professional, but what happens should you encounter a problem in the field during an important hunt far from home—something as simple as a screw working loose and falling out or an activation cord snagging on brush and pulling loose? Will you be able to remedy the problem yourself and get back into action quickly?

Drop-away rests also require regular maintenance, or at least careful vigilance. They have moving parts, after all, and today's high-performance compound bows unleash unprecedented energy levels. Activa-

Full-containment and drop-away arrow rests offer equal accuracy potential, though much depends on shooter experience and skills.

Drop-away rests come in two basic styles; limb driven (left, Vapor Trail Pro-V) and buss-cable/ spring activated (right, Trophy Ridge HX).

tion cords regularly stretch, for instance, and are also vulnerable to snagging while fighting thick brush or derricking a bow into a treestand on a pull-up rope. At the very least, bowhunters must conduct regular inspections to assure that nothing works loose (I use Loc-Tite on all key parts to reduce the chance of this occurring). Today's drop-away rests are exceptionally reliable—a fact that wasn't always true—and I haven't suffered a problem in more than a decade. But any time you install a gizmo with multiple parts, many moving, failure is possible.

Which rest style you choose depends largely on the degree of accuracy you demand and at what ranges, overall shooting experience and how confident you are working on your own equipment. One style isn't intrinsically superior to another, but each style has its own strengths and weaknesses based on the conditions you face in the field.

Best Of Both Worlds

Self-contained containment/drop-away arrow rests have become all the rage, and with good reason. Quality Archery Designs' UltraRest and Ripcord are two originals in this arena, though others have joined the race. The basic design includes a deeply forked launcher topped by a retaining bar closing the launcher opening when engaged. The drop mechanism is triggered by a factory-adjusted, internal inertia trigger, the launcher engaged manually or via an activation cord attached to the downward buss cable. Newer versions allow letting down without disengaging the launcher, an important feature if game is still present and a shot eminent. Once loaded, the arrow is 100 percent contained by the felt-lined launcher and top retaining bar, so it is always ready for action no matter how nervous the shooter becomes. Upon release, the launcher drops to allow fletchings to pass unimpeded.

If this style of arrow rest has a single drawback it is that loading an arrow takes slightly longer. The arrow is nocked and centered on the arrow shelf, a thumb wheel or lever is activated to tip/lock the launcher into place and capture the arrow. To unload an arrow, the launcher must be triggered manually. The rest launcher can also be activated by drawing the bow and allowing the activation cord to do its work, but this approach requires an arrow cradle to assure the arrow is positioned correctly for pickup.

Another drop-away design offering trouble-free use is the caged launcher with limb or buss-cable activation. This style of drop-away includes an extra-wide launcher spanning the entire width of a containment cage. The arrow is nocked and dropped through a slot (some with spring-loaded or rubber containment gate) and forgotten. Felt, rubber or fleece lining assures no rattling inside the containment cage. When the bow is drawn the launcher automatically scoops up the arrow and positions it for the shot. This design is highly accurate and likely allows slightly faster follow-up shots.

Drop Activation Systems

As a quick aside, let's address the question of buss-cable versus limb-driven drop-away systems. Standard buss-cable activation includes spring(s) pulling the launcher continually downward. The activation cord, which remains loose while at rest, is pulled tight during the draw cycle by the downward buss cable to defeat that spring and raise the launcher into the shooting position. Springs alone pull the launcher from beneath the arrow as the downward pressure of the buss cable is released. Limb-driven activation involves a launcher spring that pulls continually upward while the activation cord is pulled tightly to disengage the launcher and is anchored to a limb. Tension on the taut, limb-mounted activation cord is released as limbs are pulled together during the draw cycle, allowing the launcher to lift into place and lift the arrow into place. Upon release, the limbs snap back into place—away from one another—pulling the launcher from beneath the arrow. Buss-cable activated designs work quite well and are an excellent choice for the vast majority of archers. Limb-activated designs generally allow more precise drop-rate tuning, namely to maximize how much time the arrow spends on the launcher before fletchings arrive and increasing arrow stability and accuracy slightly. Since the launcher is free floating for a blink after the release, a smidge of forgiveness for launch flaws is also introduced. Though none of these accuracy

One popular drop-away rest design includes deep arrow forks for control combined with fall-away action for fletching clearance.

advantages will likely be noticed by anyone but world-class, professional-level target shooters.

Finger-Shooting Rests

Releasing the bowstring with your God-given fingers has largely gone out of favor in the past couple decades, but many bowhunters still prefer the added control that it lends to the shooting sequence, especially in fluid bowhunting situations. Finger shooting also requires a different arrow rest design than for arrows launched with release aids.

The reason is that the bowstring rolls around the finger tips during the release, which pushes the arrow nock out of center, and as the bowstring pushes forward and works to center itself again—so-called archer's paradox—universal equal-and-opposite physics push the arrow's nock end into the bow. This side pressure must be absorbed by a horizontal-situated rest (release rests move vertically). A rest arm holds the arrow at the correct height and the side plate or pressure button absorbs the horizontal movement of the arrow as it passes.

One old-time favorite that is just as viable today, is a spring-loaded pressure button—once called a Berger button—mounted through the riser, combined with a spring-loaded flipper-arm rest for arrow support. The pressure button absorbs arrow paradox as the shaft passes and the flipper arm gives way to passing vanes or feathers. Other designs include literal side springs – the arrow arm created by a tail of that spring, or dual leaf springs situated horizontally and vertically to hold the arrow side and bottom.

Traditional shooters approach things more simply—which also means a complete dependence on natural feathers that collapse laterally after encountering hard objects. Longbows and recurves include an arrow shelf and side pressure plate carved into the riser. The arrow shelf is covered with something

The finger-shooting rest includes side pressure to absorb arrow paradox and forgiving bottom support.

soft, quiet and preferably springy to hush the draw cycle (like Bear Archery's "Rug Rest"), a small wedge of leather or adhesive-backed fleece added to the sight window to protect bow finish and quiet the shot from passing shafts and feathers. Side-plate thickness can also be varied to help tune for specific arrow and point combinations. Some traditional archers – usually gap shooters who use the tip of their arrow as a primitive sight pin – prefer a slightly elevated rest, like something made from a multitude of parallel, parabolic feather sections. But strict instinctive shooters normally prefer arrows to sit as tightly to the bow hand as possible—as long as fletchings aren't contacting the hand web – which can actually create painful cuts.

Which Release Is Best For You?

The vast majority of bowhunters today choose a wrist-strap, index-finger release because of the obvious advantages provided. Attaching the release to your wrist means it's always with you and available for instant response to shot opportunities. Also, since most of us have at least passing experience with firearms, if not an extensive rifle-hunting past, index-finger triggering is highly intuitive. For most bowhunters the discussion ends there.

Yet there is more to the wrist-strap, index-finger release than this. Most germane to bowhunting efficiency and accuracy is the choice between caliper or open-sear engagement mechanisms. Most bowhunters choose caliper releases because that's what they've always used. Unfortunately, this long-time standard may not always be the best choice,

Wrist-strap, index-finger-triggered releases remain popular with bowhunters due to their intuitive nature, especially those who have shot firearms.

The wrist-strap release is always with the hunter and ready for action, a design that makes it bowhunting's most popular.

depending on how you set up your bow.

The venerable caliper release is best used for direct bowstring-serving hookup. This means adding a brass nocking point or two above the arrow nock, a rubber eliminator button below to eliminate nock wear from hard release jaws and nock pinch that can dislodge the shaft after letting down without shooting. Smart bowhunters who choose this approach add an extra layer of neatly wrapped string serving below the eliminator button. This allows the release jaws to wear on this layer and leave the protective string serving beneath unscathed. The system allows instant hook-up without taking your eyes off the target – like an approaching buck. Conversely, using a caliper release in conjunction with popular string loops requires taking your eyes off the target to fish the jaws into place, and generally more fumbling when shooting under pressure.

The string loop has become increasingly popular, in fact, it seems more bowhunters now shoot a string loop than not. It offers an accuracy advantage due to square nock engagement, results in less serving wear and lessens the possibility of dislodged arrows after let-down. The best release option while shooting a string loop is an open-sear release design, sometimes referred to as a hook- or claw-style release. To hook up with an open-sear release and string loop, the open-sear post is pinched into place between index finger and thumb, a maneuver that requires minimal practice to master even by feel.

The T-handle, thumb-trigger release has long been popular with serious target shooters, and is now quickly gaining favor with serious bowhunters looking for an accuracy advantage or working to extinguish target-panic symptoms. One of the major problems with index-finger triggering is its inherent familiarity. Those who grew up slapping shotgun triggers or incorrectly snatching at rifle triggers while directing fire at back-40 cottontails are inclined to do the same with archery releases. The slow, steady trigger squeeze resulting in a surprise release is as rare as the perfectly squeezed rifle trigger. Index-finger releases lead many archers to the first stages of target panic—trigger punching. The archer fights to get their pin settled on the

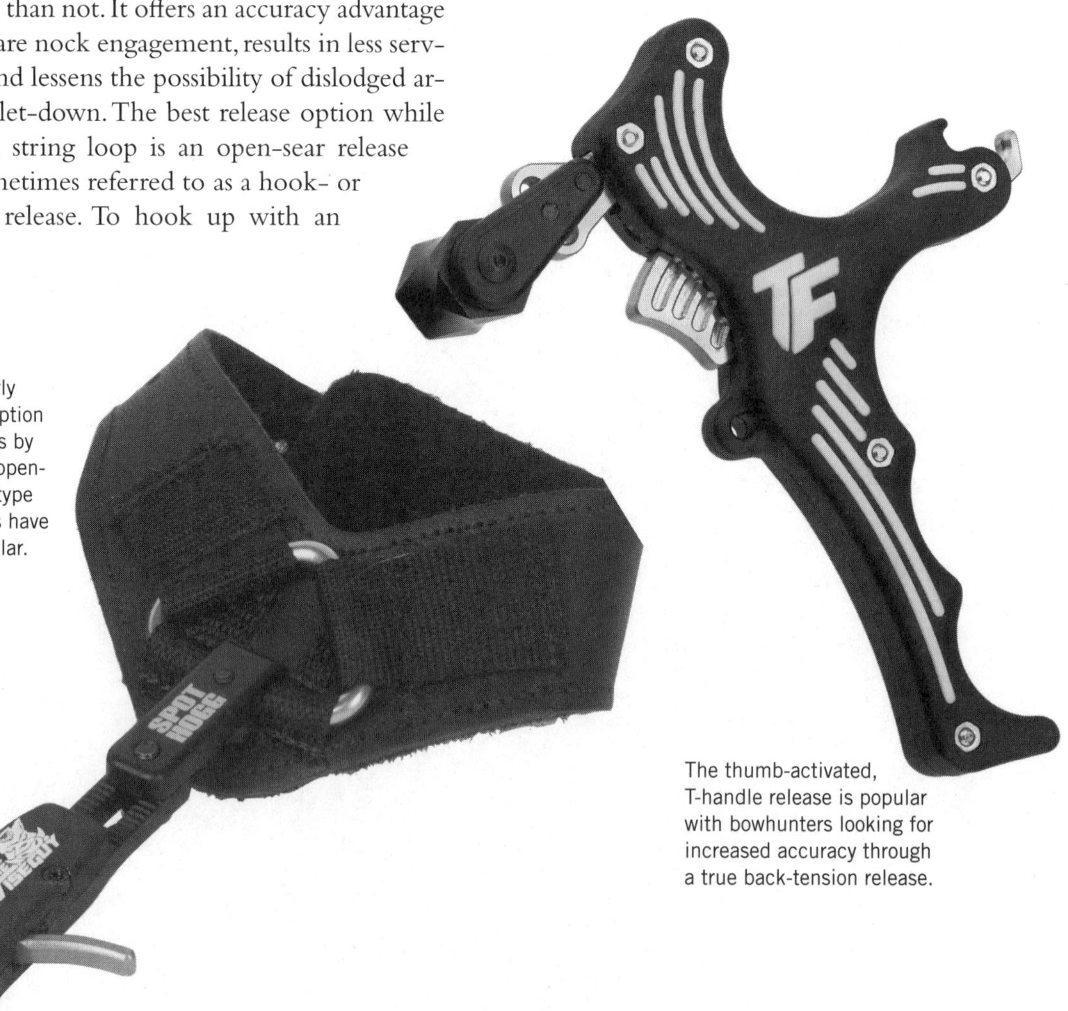

With the nearly universal adoption of string loops by bowhunters, open-sear or hook-type release heads have become popular.

The thumb-activated, T-handle release is popular with bowhunters looking for increased accuracy through a true back-tension release.

bull's-eye, becoming increasingly anxious and or impatient, the index finger poised over the trigger like a coiled snake. The proper pin finally sweeps over the bull's-eye and the mind screams NOW! and the snake strikes, jerking the trigger. This is hardly conducive to top-notch accuracy. Even if the archer attempts to slowly squeeze the trigger, the hyper-sensitive index finger allows precise anticipation of when the shot will break.

The T-handle short-circuits that anticipation by using a less sensitive digit. Thumb triggering is less intuitive, but when done properly, need not include real muscle movement. A T-handle release allows true back-tension triggering, which I'll cover in the chapter on shooting fundamentals later in this book. In short, I'll just say that T-handle, thumb-activated releases are an easy fix for ridding yourself of trigger-punching habits and circumventing or expelling debilitating target panic symptoms—which includes a multitude of mental glitches that prevent you from shooting your best.

I use identical four-finger, T-handle models, one with closed and another with open sear. I use both with string loops, the closed sear while bowhunting from stands or blinds and the open for run-and-gun stalking forays. The closed-sear release is clipped onto the string loop and left hanging, allowing grab-and-shoot response to sudden appearances of game. The open sear allows me to hook up without taking my eyes off game or on the fly. I've also drilled the pinkie end of the stalking T-handle and inserted a length of stout cord to allow hanging the release around my neck. I experiment with lanyard lengths to assure it's not so long it gets in the way of shooting, but long enough to address any possible shooting scenario.

Finger shooters have two basic choices: finger glove or tab. Both protect the fingers from string abrasion, though a tab promotes more even bowstring and finger separation. The shooting glove is preferred by many for instant grab-and-shoot capabilities, and because it stays in place more reliably. The shooting tab can slow the shot sequence slightly, but generally results in superior accuracy. Olympic archers shoot tabs, for instance.

Stabilizers – Boon Or Bane?

The bow stabilizer was once an accessory used exclusively by paper-punching target archers, so in certain bowhunting circles they're still viewed with disdain. That has largely changed, though many archers use stabilizers that aren't providing maximum utility, which includes actually stabilizing the shot. The active-stabilizer design has confused the situation somewhat. "Active" refers to stabilizer designs that actively absorb vibration and noise from bow risers. This is accomplished through rubber "hinges," shifting silicone fill, heavy parts suspended in elastic polymers or simple, shock-absorbing rubber

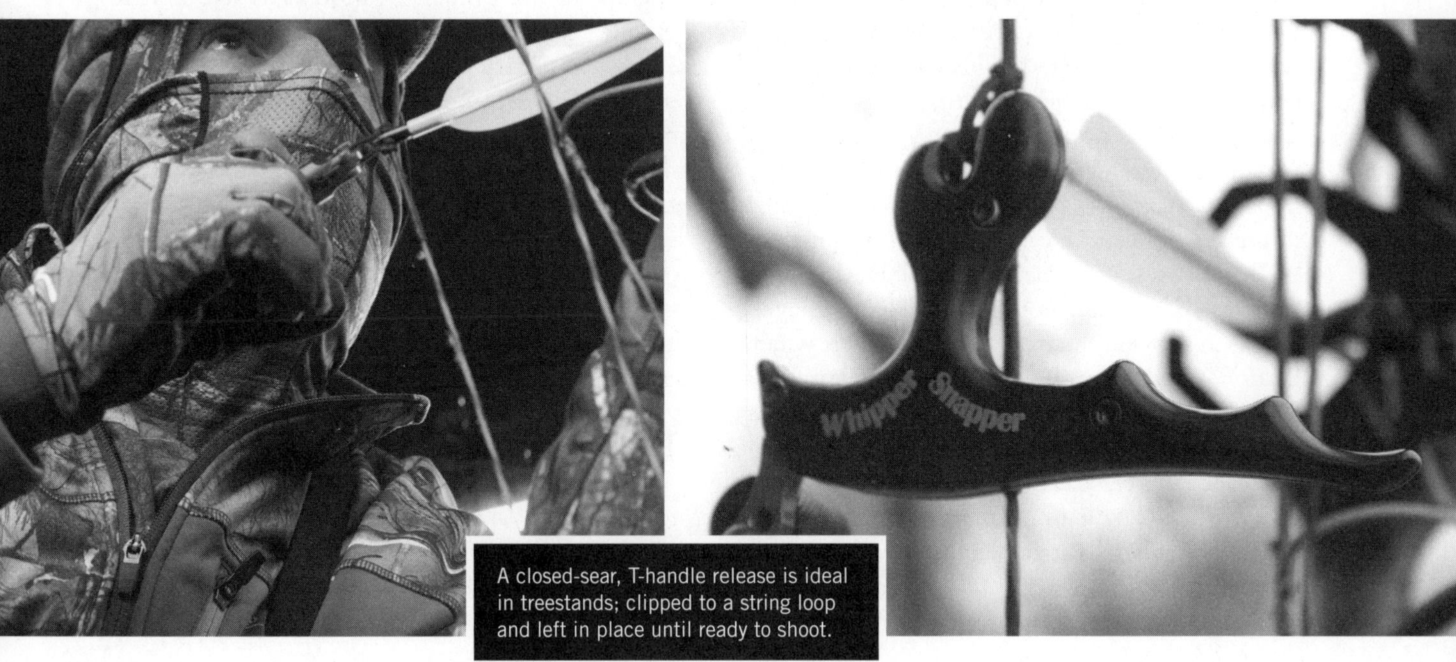

A closed-sear, T-handle release is ideal in treestands; clipped to a string loop and left in place until ready to shoot.

Many bowhunters avoid stabilizers, claiming they get in the way while shooting. But stabilizers steady and quiet every shot.

coverings or parts. An active stabilizer doesn't need to be very long to provide silencing benefits. And in bowhunting silence is golden.

In other cases the stabilizer provides nothing more than balancing weight. Even back in the days of solid-steel stabilizers I used them to help a bow sit up straight in my hand so I could concentrate on aiming and not manipulating my bow's attitude at full draw. This is normally a matter of trial and error, auditioning a good number of models, applied front and back when possible, or even offset models, to create perfect balance. A bow that sits plumb in the hand at rest and especially at full draw is much easier to shoot well. Another stabilizer advantage.

But, to provide the true benefits of added stabilization—steadier shots, finer aiming abilities—stabilizers must be long and heavy enough to actually provide true benefits. Think of this in terms of the tightrope walker's balance pole. That pole, like an effective stabilizer, must minimize the bow-torque effects of nervous twitches and even wind. For the average whitetail hunter shooting at reasonable ranges, this benefit is discovered at about 7 to 8 inches, minimum. For long-range shooters or precision target shooters, that effect comes into play at about 10 to 12 inches.

Balance and stabilization also depends on weight, so some stabilizer models feature adjustable weight systems that can be moved up and down their length, and particularly weight that can be added or subtracted to the end. Some stabilizer models also include offset bars mounted to standard stabilizer mounts but situated next to the riser to counteract the torque caused by side-mounted accessories such as loaded bow quivers. Experimentation allows you to settle on the best feel.

So are stabilizers worth the extra weight and confusion? I'll just say that I haven't shot a bow without an active 8- to 12-inch stabilizer in decades.

Quivers East & West

If you shoot a bow you'll need something to store and carry arrows with. In the beginning and up until the days of Howard Hill and Ben Pearson, bowhunters carried arrows in simple leather tubes strapped over their backs or at the hip. These facilitated quick backup shots, but also allowed arrows to rattle together noisily and damage broadheads. Fred Bear is generally credited with inventing the first commercial bow quiver around the mid-1950s. Today's bowhunters have an endless supply of options and the opportunity to choose a model to best serve their individual needs.

Detachable arrow quivers remain popular because they're easily removed on stand, and hold arrows while walking.

Bow-mounted quivers have emerged as the most popular means of toting arrows into the field because of their obvious convenience and handiness. With the popularity of the white-tailed deer and the resulting stationary pursuit, quick-detach bow quivers are likely the most prevalent today. The detachable quiver varies from flimsy models suited only to storing arrows, to those solid enough to leave in place while running-and-gunning elk hunting. Flimsy units might actually allow arrow fletchings to rattle together if left in place while shooting, or worse, allow arrows to fall out after just a few shots. If you're using a quiver solely to tote arrows into a stand or blind and removing it as soon as you're situated, this isn't really a problem, and they are quite affordable. But if you want to leave your detachable quiver attached to the bow while shooting, a sturdier model is called for, one that includes rigid milled-aluminum parts and carbon support rods, for example, and lateral and vertical adjustment for optimized bow balance. Too, if you plan to remove your detachable quiver after climbing into a stand, a system allowing you to mount it to the tree or stand and keep it instantly accessible is an excellent feature. A solid detachable quiver is also a boon for bowhunters who travel often and must remove their quiver to store their bow in a case.

Western bowhunters who regularly engage in proactive spot-and-stalk ploys are better served by a fixed, two-piece quiver design. Such designs attach to the riser ends top and bottom (usually via integrated mounting receptacles), moving the arrow gripper closer to fletchings and eliminating the potential for rattling, and spreading the weight of the loaded quiver over a wider, two-point axis. These are unlike detachable quivers, which mount to a single point, usually atop sight brackets that push them farther outside the center axis. Two-piece arrow quivers generally hold shafts closer to the riser. Overall, two-piece quivers offer superior bow balance and silence for those who invariably shoot with a quiver attached. Their only drawback is that they normally require tools to remove as needed. With traditional bows, a two-piece, solidly attached quiver can actually increase stability by adding steadying weight—without negatively effecting balance due to the canted position most instinctive shooters adopt to open the sight picture and get their eyes over the shaft.

There's also a lot to be said for a separate back or hip

quiver. Most importantly, compound bows generally aren't engineered to balance perfectly while wearing a quiver, though Hoyt has finally started offsetting stabilizer mounts to compensate for a loaded quiver on flagship models. Shooting in even a slight breeze can also present problems, since vanes and feathers will act like weather vanes and move the bow about while aiming. I've experimented with hip quivers and found them troublesome while hiking or stalking, especially while fighting thick brush, where they will get caught and hang up frequently. They also allow fletchings to wave like a flag while stalking. But they are wonderful in stand and blind situations.

Two-piece, non-removable quivers are largely a Western concern, as they normally prove quieter and more stable.

This leaves a modern back quiver, the best of these the St. Charles style named after Pope & Young Club founder Glenn St. Charles. Rancho Safari perfected this design with its Catquiver models. The Catquiver includes a top fletching hood and bottom broadhead cradle, each molded from rugged ABS plastic, connected with a length-adjustable single bar (Mini) or twin aluminum tubes (original), everything covered in silencing fleece. Larger models also solve the problem of organizing and carrying gear into the field and two-pillar Catquivers include attached pockets and lashing straps, second-generation Catquiver Minis are available attached to full-blown daypacks of various sizes, from streamlined fannies to packs large enough to bailiwick several days. They represent a sleek, highly practical system to keep arrows handy but off the bow, and all the necessary gear on your back. The system also hides bright fletchings, protects feathers from weather, and will not deploy mechanical broadhead blades accidently or dull fixed-blade heads from constant inserting and removal from dirty foam hood liners.

Silencing Needs

I've said it before, and I'll say it again—there's no such thing as a hunting bow that's too quiet, especially when white-tailed deer are involved. There was a time when the bowhunter had to work hard to ferret out and eliminate bow twangs, buzzes, rattles and pops. That is less of an issue today, as manufactures began putting as much emphasis on engineering quiet bows as cranking out raw speed. The archery world is now chock-full of silencing accessories, names like LimbSaver and BowJax leading the way. While the average compound bow is quieter out of the box than ever, many bows can be made even quieter by addressing specific points and applying aftermarket silencing accessories.

The first priority should be the bowstring, since it represents the most blatant noisemaker. This has largely been addressed with string stops that are found on just about every decent compound model today. String stops largely eliminate string twang, but I've found that adding standard string silencers calms string noise to a dull thump. CatWhiskers (Rancho Safari still makes the originals) are still my favorites after all these years, as they are water and burr proof, and don't interfere with peep sight rotation like solid silencers slipped between string strands can, plus they don't require pressing the bow like when installing slip-over silencers. Just tie an overhand knot, pull it tight, add a drop of superglue to prevent slippage and cut with

Rancho Safari's Catquiver allows shooting a better-balanced, quiver-free bow while keeping arrows and gear handy.

scissors to separate the individual strands. Don't forget buss cables, as they are strung tighter than ever and can produce small pings of their own. I usually add a half of a CatWhisker to each cable.

The next most important area of the average compound is its limbs. Many companies now install limb silencers at the factory. Many do not. I've largely abandoned clamp-on split-limb silencers, though there is absolutely nothing wrong with them, they simply require more tools for installation. Instead I prefer one-piece rubber models that wedge tightly into place between split limbs, or adhesive-backed models for solid limbs. I've also found that limb silencers boost the accuracy of split-limb model bows, tying them together so they work as a single unit.

Now, you can address the remainder of your bow. I often use existing rubber silencing products to wedge into riser and accessory cut-outs. Wedge-fit limb silencers, for instance, can often be installed into riser cut-outs to help an active stabilizer further squelch vibrations, especially beneath limb pockets where the most potential for vibration and noise exist. Wedging smaller parts of rubber silencers like single BowJax arms cut from limb silencers, for instance, into arrow rest or sight cut-outs is extremely effective for eliminating small tuning-fork hums or annoying buzzes. Rubber disks and stars are also offered to slide tightly over cable slides and string-stop support rods.

Never forget the arrow shelf and sight window, places where an errant arrow can click against unprotected metal. I carefully trace and cut out adhesive-backed foam or fleece and apply to the entire arrow shelf and sight window—as well as the underside of sight apertures, arrow-rest cage interiors or uncovered launchers. If arrow contact is possible, cover it in fleece, including the insides of quiver hoods and quiver support rods. For those shooting traditional recurves, use top-quality adhesive-backed fleece or thin buckskin leather and fletching cement to pad the bowstring contact grooves on limb curves and eliminate loud string slap against hard fiberglass.

As you can see, choosing the right accessories is a little more involved than grabbing random merchandise from store display racks and shelves. Choose your gear wisely and you'll become a more efficient and productive bowhunter.

After a car accident caused an extensive shoulder injury, Atsko's Mike Jordan used crossbows to continue bowhunting.

CHAPTER 13

CROSSBOW INSIGHTS

CONTROVERSY AND CROSSBOWS ARE OLD friends, even eight centuries after Pope Innocent II wrote "...the deadly art, hated by God, of cross-bowmen..." At its root this actually had more to do with common foot soldiers using crossbows to fell noble knights than anything on God's mind, as if any mortal man might presume to guess His likes and dislikes. Later in history, an article in England's Magna Carta actually called for the banishment of "crossbow men" – a weapon of choice for the era's dreaded mercenaries.

Crossbow phobia remains today with certain segments of the bowhunting community, despite the crossbow's widespread acceptance and legalization during general archery seasons in more states every season. Crossbows have undoubtedly attracted an entirely new segment of hunters; proponents say these new converts will use crossbows as a stepping stone into more conventional archery equipment, while opponents claim these are only gun-hunting usurpers taking advantage of our more desirable seasons. No matter which side of this argument you take, the fact remains that crossbows are now the fastest-growing segment of the archery industry. They are also here to stay.

This is largely the result of increased crossbow opportunities, a lobbying effort making the 1990s in-line muzzleloader push appear amateurish by comparison. There is also no denying that the age of the average bowhunter is slowly increasing. Of the several demographic surveys I've observed recently, those born in the mid-1960s now constitute bowhunter's national average. Bowhunting needs new recruits if it is to survive, since if we vanish game managers will happily hand our seasons to others for the sake of "maximizing opportunity," which in bureaucratic speak means keeping license revenue flowing. Crossbows provide the obvious bridge, allowing youngsters and other interested people lacking the strength to pull a hunting-weight bow an opportunity to begin their bowhunting journey. Existing bowhunters are also growing older – meaning very soon many of us will find it difficult to draw a compound or traditional bow suited to hunting. We can hardly be expected to sit the bench spinning yarns of our glory days. No, we'll be shooting crossbows.

I never really saw myself shooting a crossbow. But when I took a nosedive from a high tree, which resulted in major shoulder damage, extensive rotator-cuff surgery and the slow and arduous process

Crossbows also allow youth and women hunters that might be unable to pull heavyweight bows to enjoy archery seasons.

of rehabilitation, my options quickly narrowed. My choices remained a spring without hunting since I wasn't allowed to shoot a gun either, or a crossbow (a doctor's approval and special permit are required in my home state of Idaho). No-brainer. At this writing I've tagged three spring gobblers and a black bear with a crossbow, with a Texas hog hunt in the works. Much more than proving "better than nothing," crossbows have actually offered much fun and excitement. I'll be bowhunting with vertical bows again by September (God willing), but crossbows will forever remain in my bowhunting arsenal, a complimentarily option, like traditional bows are to my compound bows.

If you're anything like me and have discovered a newfound interest in crossbows, or are contemplating a crossbow purchase as a first step into the bowhunting sport, you'll want to read on. This is your crash course in everything crossbow related.

X-Bow Mechanics

The first real difference you'll notice in basic crossbow configuration is compound, or wheeled/cam-driven, versus recurve-limb designs. Performance-wise, at least when top-end wares are involved, there isn't one bit of difference in delivered speed or performance. Top-end recurve-limb crossbows—meaning Excalibur nearly exclusively—usually include slightly heavier draw weights to produce the same speeds as comparable compound models, but other than that the difference is largely aesthetic, though an argument could be made in favor of simplicity. That heavier draw weight could mean additional struggle while cocking for those of us with bad shoulders or weak arms, but today's "winch-style" cocking mechanisms largely negate this argument. The story changes considerably with budget-priced crossbow models, where compound models have a definite edge in performance.

Hunting crossbows—not toy models—vary widely in price; from economy models setting you back only $350 to $400, to flagship models priced at 1K or considerably more. All are offered with shoot-ready packages. What you're buying for that extra money is performance, a discrepancy gap much wider than that found between flagship and mid- to budget-price vertical-bow models. Whereas $1,000-plus might buy 350 to 360 fps ATA speeds in top compound-bow models, paying half that only results in a loss of 25 or 30 fps. Those gaps widen considerably with crossbows – $1,000 or more gives you crossbow speeds of 370 to 400 fps, and half of that money gives 70 to 100 fps less. Does this really matter to the average hunter? It really depends on the conditions faced in the field and the animals being pursued.

Last spring I acquired two similarly priced crossbows weeks before turkey season, and sighted them in to be ready for opening day. The first of those, Carbon Express' Intercept Axion LT, pushes bolts to around 360 fps with 175 pounds of pull and a 13.5-inch power stroke. I shot a feeding, quartering-to gobbler with it at 25 yards and the bolt—tipped with an aggressive mechanical broadhead—broke his wing butt and passed through to travel another 15 or 20 yards. That tom never knew what hit him and traveled exactly three steps before falling on his face. My other crossbow, a Stryker by Bowtech Katana, launches bolts to 385 fps via 155 pounds of pull and a 13-inch power stroke. I shot a mature, strutting gobbler with it at 30 yards, the aggressive mechanical broadhead and bolt blasted through, skipped off the ground and lodged solidly in a cedar post 20 yards beyond. That gobbler ran 30 yards and expired right beneath my pop-up-blind shooting port. Two turkeys, two shots, two dead birds.

Now, did that 25 fps of added velocity make one bit of difference in the results on those turkeys? Not one bit—the gobbler hit with the "slower" x-bow actually expired faster. Did the faster model accomplish anything the slower model could not? Obviously not. Though these were only turkeys, I can't imagine the results would differ substantially on white-tailed deer shot from treestands at less than 30 yards. The Katana might penetrate slightly more dirt on the opposite side of the animal, but both crossbows would result in venison in the freezer.

Now, that being said, where I began to notice a difference in performance after continued experimentation was when I began stepping back from the target. At 35 or 40 yards the two models remained essentially equal, at least in my ability to hit fist-size spots offhand. At maybe 60 yards the difference slowly revealed itself, the "slower" crossbow dropping farther down the target face while shooting the same bolt.

Would this mean anything to the average Eastern bowhunter plying thronged woodlots? Very likely

A major advantage of a crossbow is it doesn't have to be drawn in the presence of game, which makes shot timing much easier.

not, as shots at whitetails seldom exceed 35 yards. Out West, or while guarding the edge of expansive agricultural fields, that difference in performance might become more noticeable. Too, if circumstances are such that I'm still limited to shooting a crossbow come September while chasing bugling elk, I would automatically choose the more powerful weapon for even the slightest boost in penetration potential. Stuff, as they say, happens and I want every ounce of insurance I can muster. Still, remove the Stryker from the equation and I would confidently hunt elk with the Carbon Express.

Speaking of carrying – understand that crossbows are innately heavy and highly unwieldy. Just the thought of charging around at high altitude and through grabbing brush while dogging bugling bulls and toting a crossbow makes my shoulder ache. A crossbow might only weigh 3 or 4 pounds more than a compound bow, but they are also less streamlined and just don't include the convenient "handles" of conventional bows. A sling or pack-lashing arrangement allowing you to carry the x-bow flat to your back, with limbs sitting behind the shoulders, will go a long ways toward eliminating frustrations.

Crossbow Considerations

So which crossbow should you choose? Budget is likely the largest determining factor for most. To my mind the best approach is to invest in thorough research, determine which crossbow model provides the most bang for the buck within the budget you have established, in respects to raw speed

After major shoulder surgery, the author was faced with either no hunting or hunting with a crossbow. He chose crossbows and enjoyed a productive spring season.

(which translates into delivered energy) and carrying weight. Safety features such as anti-dry-fire mechanisms, forehand guard (you do not want fingers anywhere near the shooting rail while squeezing the trigger) and safeties that engage automatically during cocking are all big positives. For the average blue-collar bowhunter this model likely rests somewhere in the middle of the price-point spectrum, which means something around $450 to $500. Some companies offer better deals than others, but all offer perfectly acceptable performance models at a price that won't break the budget.

For common turkey and deer hunting I'd shop for something producing a minimum 300 fps from around 150 pounds and owning at least a 10- to 11-inch power stroke. Of course, this is somewhat subjective, as some models are more efficient than others. For instance, one Bear-X (a division of Bear Archery) model produces speeds of 375 fps from only 135 pounds due to an extra-long, 17.5-inch power stroke created by a reverse draw system that also shifts balance between the hands. The unit also costs around $1,000.

After perusing Cabela's extensive line of crossbows, I found a Parker model pushing 300 fps from 160 pounds for less than $450, a Wicked Ridge model producing 320 fps from 155 pounds at the same price, and a PSE Archery unit producing 350 fps from 155 pounds for less than $350—just to toss out some highly-random examples. By spending slightly more I see a $600 Barnett producing 360 fps from 165 pounds and a 14-inch power stroke. At

Hunt-ready crossbows come in price points from $350 packages to those costing in excess of a $1,000.

those prices these models also come equipped with complete, ready-to-shoot packages. Any of these crossbows, and many others in their class, would serve the Eastern whitetail hunter very well, without busting the bank.

The tipping point seems to arrive around 360 fps or more, when crossbow models begin to push the $1,000 mark. One thousand bucks buys you the aforementioned 385 fps from 155 pounds and a 13-inch power stroke of the Stryker Katana, 360-plus fps from 175 pounds and 13.5-inch power stroke of the Carbon Express Intercept Axion LT, or 375 fps from only 135 pounds and a 17.5-inch power stroke of the Bear-X Fisix FFL. Horton provides a 370 fps model powered by 165 pounds for the same $1,000. Prices in excess of $1,000 (up to nearly $2,000) provide 360 to 364 fps from 165 pounds in deluxe TenPoint packages, or 380 to 400 fps from 260 to 280 pounds and 13.1- to 14-inch power strokes in Excalibur recurve-limb models. Other 400-plus fps units with premium price tags include Mission Archery's MXB-400, PSE's RDX, Barnett's Ghost 415 Revenant and Darton's Toxin, for those who insist on the most cutting-edge performance available. Remember that these are only examples and I'm sure I've missed some obvious highlights.

Top-end performance results from designs with improved efficiency – like Stryker's Katana or Bear-X's Fisix FFL, including better limb materials and design, reverse-draw technologies and more radical cams, aspects that are difficult to glean from a specification sheet alone. A greater indicator of what you can generally expect from a crossbow is revealed through its power stroke. The longer the power stroke, the more time the bowstring has to push the bolt on its way and the more energy generated. The shortest power stroke I see from a "performance" crossbow—again the Stryker Katana—is 13 inches. Bear-X's 17.5-inch Fisix FFL power stroke is the longest. So to my mind a high ratio of speed to power stroke and draw weight is a good indication of a highly efficient design. Add price to the calculus to determine which crossbow gives you the most performance within your target price.

Before laying down hard cash for a new crossbow you really need to audition the overall fit and feel of any potential purchase. AR-style, collapsible stocks are an excellent feature, as they allow a wide variety of shooters, from young kids to women to grown men, to shoot a single model. Many x-bows are equipped with adjustable check pieces, allowing you to customize height in relation to a specific sighting system. Others include fixed stock dimensions like those found on hunting rifles. If a crossbow doesn't fit acceptably, or forces you into an uncomfortable shooting position to enable looking through its scope, you'll never shoot at its full potential, and shots at game will never come off fluidly.

Sighting Systems

The very first modern crossbows that I shot 20 years ago held solid-pin sights. Those days are finished, kaput. In fact, scouring both Cabela's and Bass Pro Shops' extensive mail order websites I can

The author used a top-end Carbon Express crossbow pushing bolts to 360 fps to tag this spring bear with a single shot.

find not a single pin-sight option.

The modern crossbow is sighted via a magnified or red-dot scope system including multiple aiming points correlating to various distances. Package deals included with most crossbows include a scope regulated to that very model, including separate crosshairs, hash marks or aiming dots for ranges from 20 to 50 or 60 yards. Others, like the scope included with my Stryker Katana, include multiple aiming hash marks, yardage spaces manipulated via a variable-speed ring mirroring the variable-power adjustment ring of standard rifle scopes. The shooter fires his crossbow and bolt combination through a chronograph to receive an accurate speed and then dials the scope to the appropriate setting, automatically setting gaps between various range-aiming points. Sans chronograph, the shooter can work in trial-and-error fashion until longer aiming points correlate to each measured range.

Many crosshair crossbow scopes also include an illuminated reticle with adjustable intensity settings for low-light shooting or those with especially poor eyesight. Several multi-dot "lighted-dot" systems are also offered, generally with fewer range options, say 20, 30 and 40, instead of five like most optical crossbow scopes. For the average whitetail hunter this shouldn't present an issue. If you do choose a scope system with battery-powered illumination, read your state's hunting regulations thoroughly to assure they are legal where you hunt.

Another ingenious option is HHA Sports' Optimizer Speed Dial, a Picatinny-style mounting rail with adjustable attitude and a knurled range wheel to dial the mounted scope to a desired range. This arrangement allows choosing a single-point red-dot or standard crosshair optical scope, sighting in for a middle-range yardage and dialing the rail up or down according to each different range. This eliminates clutter and allows using a top-quality, low-power rifle scope with exceptional light-gathering efficiency.

Speaking from experience, optics makes precise aiming with a crossbow nearly effortless. It also requires minimal practice for pinpoint shot placement. When I'm shooting spring gobblers with vertical bow, I pick a tiny spot and hope my arrow

Modern crossbows are sighted with scopes. The shooter can choose between dot and crosshair models, both with illumination.

hits close enough to result in a quick kill. With the turkeys I shot with a scoped crossbow, I was able to place my shots exactly where I wanted them.

Cocking Considerations

With the purchase of any crossbow, no matter its price point or model, you'll receive a rope-cocking device. These are fast and easy to use, including a stout rope holding two roller-equipped bowstring hooks and comfortable pull handles that look like the starting handles on lawnmowers or outboard motors. The rear of the crossbow stock includes a rope groove; the string hooks are attached to the bowstring on opposite sides of the bolt rail; the cord is pulled into the rear stock groove; the handles are pulled until the string clicks into the sear. The rope-cocking device is small and easy to stash in a pocket or fanny pack, can be hooked up and employed in seconds – plus it assures balanced alignment of the string on the sears to promote maximum accuracy, though it does require a certain degree of muscle. Someone with a shoulder injury, youth or small-statured shooters, and older hunters might find it difficult or impossible to cock their high-performance crossbows while using only this basic option.

These x-bow shooters will want to purchase a crank-style cocking device. These are reminiscent of the hand winches found on boat trailers – but much smaller and including dual spools. They hold geared spools that store excess rope attached to pulley-equipped string hooks that are attached to the bowstring. Then these ride on each side of the bolt rail during take-up. A crank handle allows easy operation and click-lock mechanisms eliminate backlash during the cocking process to make them extremely safe. The best crossbow "windlasses" include silent mechanisms so they won't spook nearby game, and help reduce cocking effort by 70 to 90 percent, allowing even youngsters, small-statured and older hunters to cock the stoutest crossbow models. Without a mechanical cocker for each of my crossbows I wouldn't have been able to hunt while my wrecked shoulder was still healing. Generally, each crossbow manufacturer produces a brand-specific mechanical cocker as every stock configuration is slightly different.

The mechanical cocker for my Carbon Express crossbow, for instance, plugs into the rear of the cheek piece via an X-like cross section to prevent twisting. It comes on and off instantly and includes an ambidextrous handle that can be removed while unstowing line so that it isn't spinning in your face or otherwise interfering, while also allowing compact storage in its own zipper-topped neoprene bag. The Stryker includes a clamp-on cocking winch that slides into a top stock slot, a rear knurled knob tightened to lock it in place, the rigid handle spinning freely while pulling the line, hook and pulleys to the bowstring. Both must be removed and set aside before shooting.

The draw weights of modern crossbows require a cocking device—including anything from simple rope cockers to winch devises.

Other companies like TenPoint and Browning integrate winch-cocking mechanisms into the stock, eliminating the need to dig it out of a pocket or pack when needed. TenPoint's ACUdraw is bolted right to the stock side, for instance, a streamlined system that doesn't get in the way of aiming or shooting.

Crossbow Accessorizing

Crossbow accessories differ from those for conventional bows, but just like those, they are designed to make life easier and increase efficiency in the field. Many companies offer crossbow-mounted bolt quivers, usually quick-detach models meant to be removed once on stand or inside a blind. The biggest drawback here is since they must be mounted beneath the limbs, or on and parallel to the stock itself, laying your weapon on the ground can lead to crushed fletchings or nocks clogged with debris. One exception is Rancho Safari's BC Xbow Quiver, which is based on the Catquiver design with a covered hood and broadhead cradle. Mounted beneath the limbs using the limb-pocket riser as a base, the two-piece system allows resting your crossbow on the ground atop the quiver without crushing fletchings or exposing nocks to potential clogging.

Of course, a handy back or hip quiver is always a bolt-storage option, and the approach that I prefer,

Regularly waxing your crossbow string and cables assures longer life and fewer maintenance issues.

Just like compounds, crossbow quivers come in detachable and fixed models. The best one is dependent on how you hunt.

Crossbows must be de-cocked after every hunt. The easiest way to do this is to shoot it, and a discharge bolt is the best solution.

as the average crossbow is already unwieldy enough without adding additional clutter. Rancho Safari's Catquiver Crossbow or Mini Crossbow are shortened versions of the original, made to fit 18- to 24-inch bolts. I prefer this approach as it allows me to hang bolts within easy reach while occupying elevated stands, lean it in the corner of pop-up blinds, or sling it across my back while hiking or stalking. Bolts are instantly accessible, without adding imbalance to my weapon.

Every crossbow deserves a case, either a zippered soft case to protect it from hard knocks while lashed to an ATV rack or riding in a pickup bed, or a hinged hard case if you intend to travel far by land, sea or especially air. To assure bowstrings last longer, a tube or stick of rail lube or wax is imperative. Before every hunt apply lube or wax generously to strings, cables and rail to minimize friction and serving wear. As I've already hinted, crossbows aren't exactly a joy to carry any distance at all. This calls for a sling. All crossbows are equipped with sling studs front and rear, some with multiple hookups that permit classic across-the-back carrying, or riding up front commando style. Choose something wide and preferably padded and you'll remain much happier. Another accessory worth considering, especially when hunting from stationary positions, is a steadying shooting stick. Shooting with my bum shoulder in the very beginning of recovery, shooting sticks allowed me to shoot fist-size groups with my crossbows at any reasonable range – even while standing.

Crossbows have introduced many different folks to bowhunting, and those introductions can lead to future vertical-bow hunters.

Due to the extreme draw weights of crossbows, de-cocking your weapon after the hunt can prove troublesome. I simply install a sturdy small-game blunt to one of my standard arrows and keep it on hand to shoot into a soft patch of ground after the hunt. Several companies, like Parker RED HOT Crossbow Accessories and Carbon Express, offer special discharge bolts made of tougher materials to absorb the abuse of being shot into hard ground, and a dish-faced blunt to prevent them from burying in soft soil or penetrating tree roots resulting in difficult extraction. They're worth the investment, as discharging your weapon follows every crossbow hunt.

Finally, consider an aftermarket trigger assembly like those offered by TriggerTech. Like aftermarket target-rifle triggers, these are drop-in replacements providing smoother, lighter trigger pulls and crisper breaks than those supplied by many—but not all—factory triggers. The roller-sear design allows precise trigger pulls down to 2.5 pounds like those found on custom target or varmint rifles. They aren't cheap, around $200, but can greatly improve downrange groups. They're made for a wide variety of crossbow brands and models.

Whether using crossbows as a door into bowhunting seasons, or due to temporary or ancient injuries, or to outfit a child or petite adult, crossbows offer a solution for those unable to shoot hunting-weight vertical bows. They aren't especially difficult to master, and allow more archers the opportunity to successfully hunt big game that were previously out of reach.

When bowhunting, the broadhead does the actual killing, the arrow is the delivery system. Buy the best you can afford.

CHAPTER 14

TERMINAL TACKLE

IN BOWHUNTING, MUCH DEPENDS ON terminal tackle—the broadhead that actually inflicts lethal hemorrhaging and the arrow carrying that broadhead to the mark. Without a straight arrow and sharp, true-flying broadhead you'll never hit your target, penetrate vital organs or create the massive hemorrhaging required for fast recovery. This makes arrows and broadheads two of the most important equipment choices you'll make while compiling an overall bowhunting outfit. I guess this is why I find it so fascinating to see that some archers choose arrows and broadheads so indiscriminately. I dealt with this frequently while working retail. I see it in hunting camps around the globe. Much of this is pure ignorance, believing one arrow is much the same as another, but as often money enters the equation.

"I drew an elk tag and need some arrows and broadheads," declares a retail customer. "Which ones are the cheapest?"

Really?

Of all the miscellaneous expenses involved in modern bowhunting, including precious vacation time away from work, the cost of top-quality arrows and broadheads constitutes the least of your worries. Buy cheap arrows and points for shooting small game or stump shooting, but when important big-game hunts are involved, for goodness sake buy the best you can possibly afford. You have a lot invested in perhaps a single shot at game. Why take that shot with subpar terminal tackle? Your quarry also deserves nothing but your best shot.

Arrows, like various rifle cartridges, and broadheads, like the bullets those cartridges are loaded with, work best when matched to the job at hand. This is based on factors such as expected range, animal size and equipment capabilities. We brushed over some of the basics of arrow and broadhead selection in an earlier chapter, "Matching the Rig to the Gig." Here we'll investigate the finer points of arrow construction, specifications and classes as they best serve your bowhunting needs.

The "Perfect" Arrow

Deeming any single piece of archery equipment "perfect" is wading into dangerous waters. Bowhunting is so multifaceted, individual shooters' preferences so wide-flung, one man's perfection can prove another's poison. Since my opinions generally appear on public forums, I'm regularly taken to task for my equipment preferences, especially as they pertain to terminal tackle. For example, I prefer fast, light-for-spine arrows when bowhunting open country and light-framed game, while others have pointed out that heavier arrows carry energy better over the long haul. I prefer heavy-for-spine arrows for whitetails because they're quieter, whereas others point out lighter, faster arrows minimize the effects of string jumping by arriving on target quicker. I believe small-diameter, streamlined broadheads are best for the biggest big game; also believing these heads kill just as fast as wide-cutting heads, while others argue that aggressive mechanicals always result in quicker kills, even without pass-through penetration.

None of these people are wrong—though it seems many argue for the sake of arguing, especially when afforded the anonymity of online response forums, due to some form of disillusioned self-aggrandizement. We certainly don't have to agree on every point. If something works for you, by all means stick with it. That being said, experience counts for something, and my 35-plus years of bowhunting experience, hundreds of bow-tagged big-game animals and 23 years of successfully guiding bowhunters has demonstrated, sometimes painfully, what consistently works and what does not.

Material Concerns

The hard-core traditionalist may choose wood arrows, and there's certainly nothing wrong with that, or aluminum as a nouveau classic – another perfectly acceptable choice. But in the world of modern archery carbon is where it's at. Carbon is stronger, surviving impacts with rocks or wood or bone that would instantly throttle any wood or aluminum that came before. Carbon recovers from harmonic oscillations much faster than any other material, "settling" or recovering from archer's paradox (the flex imparted during launch) in a shorter distance to create more stable flight. This also translates into deeper penetration, as "impact paradox" is also minimized, the shaft more closely tracking broadheads through wound canals and minimizing slapping against wound-channel sides that sheds energy. The best modern carbons have also begun to match aluminum for straightness tolerances – the best are normally +/- .001-inch. In general terms, carbon is also quieter whether in flight, when tapped against unguarded accessories and when pulled across arrow-rest launchers.

One excellent exception to the all-carbon rule are carbon and aluminum composite shafts like Easton's A/C/C for instance, which offer the harmonic recovery and ruggedness of carbon, combined with the straightness advantage of aluminum.

Once internal-component carbons took hold with the first Beman ICS and Gold Tip shafts, standard inside diameters of .245 inch became the rule, accommodating readily available, direct-fit Easton Super or Bohning Signature Nocks. More recently, carbon shafts have begun to grow thinner, from .224 inch (direct-fit H-Nock) to .204 inch (Easton X-Nock, Bohning A-Nock) to ultra-slim .168 inch (direct-fit G/A Nocks, Easton/Bohning). Thinner shafts minimize wind drift and generally promote deeper penetration than similar-weight shafts through reduced surface-area friction. Skinny arrows typically include thicker walls to produce the proper spine stiffness, often making them heavier – 10 to 11 grains per inch (gpi) – though there are exceptions. Thicker walls also make them nail tough, and many include proprietary insert/outsert systems to protect leading edges from damage. These are offered in 32 threads-per-inch standard-thread outserts or newer 40 t.p.i. Deep Six H.I.T. inserts. If you regularly bowhunt in stiff winds, skinny arrows give you an edge, and hunters seeking maximum penetration on the biggest game or from low-energy bows would do well to choose a heavier, skinnier arrow.

Other interesting developments include tapered carbon (Carbon Tech Panther, Alaska Bowhunting Supply GrizzlyStiks and Quest Archery Products Power Punch) and Carbon Express' Dual Spine Weight Forward and RED Zone technology. Tapered carbon provides more spine latitude, faster recovery from launch and impact paradox and an automatic boost in F.O.C. Carbon Express proprietary technologies include melding various carbon materials to create different densities and dynamic

spine along its length for better broadhead control. Maxima RED technology (found on Maxima RED and BLU RZ), for instance, includes stiffer ends and a "softer" RED Zone middle to manage flex and oscillation, placing the steering fletchings and leading broadhead on stiffer platforms to minimize wind planing. These technologies cost more, of course, but are worth the investment if pinpoint accuracy while shooting fixed-blade broadheads is important to you. They're also more forgiving of imperfect bow tuning or shooting form.

Arrow specs are a common source of confusion. Straightness tolerances from +/- .001 inch (near perfect) to .006 or .008 (budget-price shafts) are common. Such specs essentially say no single arrow of that model will fall outside of those straightness tolerances—some companies actually guarantee it. The straightest arrows cost more because straightness is a result of careful sorting, not manufacturing process, as fewer of them make the cut and demand remains high. They instill confidence, but the average archer likely won't notice any difference between top-grade shafts and anything exhibiting specs of less than, .003 to .004 inch. Anything outside those specs I generally avoid for big-game hunting, though they're fine for stump shooting or small-game hunting with blunts and Judo Points. Likely more important to overall accuracy is matched weight—.5

Carbon is the arrow material of choice. Carbon arrows now feature tight tolerances that match those of aluminum.

Carbon arrows are accurate and penetrate deeply because they recover from launch oscillations faster than aluminum.

to 2 grains per dozen is good—and overall spine consistency around a 360-degree axis. The latter is impossible to determine without very sophisticated equipment, so the best advice is to stick with major brands with solid reputations.

Arrow Balance

Front of Center, a.k.a. F.O.C., is an often neglected, but highly important, factor effecting arrow tuning ease, flight characteristics, forgiveness and penetration potential. Put in the simplest terms possible, this constitutes the percentage of an arrow's weight made up by its front half, dictated largely by construction and especially insert and or point weight. F.O.C. effects tuning ease for the same reason a barroom dart is heavily weighted at its front. An arrow with insufficient forward weight results in unstable flight, and the rear tries to overtake the front. More weight up front, or less in the rear, increases in-flight stability because the tip essentially "drags" the arrow along its path. As an interesting bit of physics, when an arrow is launched, violently whipped

F.O.C., or Front Of Center, is the percentage of an arrow's weight situated in front of its center, and it affects arrow flight.

forward by the bowstring, released and sent into flight, all of that imparted energy quickly travels up the shaft like an electrical current, for lack of a better analogy. By the time the arrow moves three to five feet from the riser, 100 percent of the available energy has traveled to the front of the arrow and is being carried by the point. The higher the F.O.C. percentage, the more efficiently that energy is carried, translating into flatter trajectory and increased downrange energy on target. High F.O.C. also makes arrows more forgiving to imperfect releases, and especially in-flight obstacles such as encountered branches. In other words, high F.O.C. is less likely to result in wild deflections due to seemingly insignificant twigs, leaves or grass stems on the way to the target. As discussed in the section on traditional gear, higher F.O.C. can also result in deeper penetration, the same stabilizing effect enjoyed in flight actually dragging the shaft through bone and the wound canal.

Compound shooters consider 9 to 12 percent F.O.C. minimum for reliable fixed-blade broadhead flight and 7 to 9 percent for field points or streamlined mechanical broadheads. This is generally provided automatically via average-weight carbon arrows and standard 100-grain points. Where more attention must be paid is when shooting the heaviest carbon arrow models, or aluminum shafts, or with draw lengths and finished arrows exceeding about 30 inches. Traditional shooters seeking maximum penetration consider 12 to 15 percent F.O.C. minimum. These numbers are always offered as minimums because of our continued obsession with speed, tight pin gaps and flattened trajectory.

Bumping those numbers higher isn't a sin and provides more of the advantages discussed above, but only to a point. Switching from a new-industry-standard 100-grain to a 125-grain old-industry-standard, for instance, makes a lot of sense in many bowhunting applications like short-range whitetails from stands in brushy terrain or while pursuing bull elk, and makes boosting F.O.C. no more difficult than re-zeroing your sights. Replacing standard aluminum inserts with those made of brass or stainless steel is another instant solution—an approach many manufacturers have begun to offer as stock accessories. On the other hand, installing a traditional head weighing 200 grains to an average-weight carbon arrow would result in excessive F.O.C. and diving arrow flight. I normally shoot for 15 to 17 percent on compound arrows and up to 18 to 20-plus percent on traditional arrows. One quick note of caution: boosting tip weight can alter spine needs and often requires a stiffer arrow.

To determine F.O.C. carefully measure your arrow from the cut-off point or just behind the glue-on point on wood arrows to the nock throat, then determine the exact mathematical center and mark it with a pencil or felt-tipped pen. Next, set that same arrow, with point installed, on a sharp edge and mark its precise balance point. Measure the distance between these marked points and divide that by the overall length of the arrow. Move the decimal point two points right to receive a percentage.

Long-Range Speed Arrows

The all-around, do-it-all bowhunting rig is as sound an approach as any, but when I have a special bowhunt planned with very specific conditions I enter that foray with more confidence knowing I've assembled a rig specifically suited to the conditions most likely to be encountered.

The long-range speed rig is perhaps the most pointed in this discussion and in regards to F.O.C., the only time I worry about maintaining minimal F.O.C. percentages, as this normally translates into weight, and weight translates into speed erosion to the tune of 5 to 7 fps per 25 grains of arrow mass

The author took this spot-and-stalk pronghorn at 73 yards with a lightweight arrow and streamlined mechanical broadhead.

added – all other factors remaining equal. If I anticipate a spot-and-stalk pronghorn hunt, as an example, when I know shots will stretch well beyond average range, and especially when I go after those frustrating, wildly paranoid, elfin whitetails of the Coues persuasion, I set up for all-out speed. Lighter arrows provide an instant velocity jump. Here we're talking carbon shafts in the 6.5 to 8.5 gpi class in the 400 to 330/340/350 deflections/spines holding 100-grain heads that are the most useful to average bowhunters with draw lengths around 29 inches and shooting about 65 pounds.

Such shafts are currently represented by wares like Carbon Tech's Cheetah (6.5 gpi in 400 spine); Victory Archery's .205-inch-diameter RIPVX (6.4 gpi in 350), RIP (8.2 gpi in 350) or .168-inch-diameter VAP (8.2 gpi in 350); Black Eagle Arrow's Carnivore (7.5 gpi in 350) or .224-inch-diameter Spartan (8 gpi in 350); Easton's .224-inch-diamter The Hexx or .205-inch-diameter Da' Torch (both 7.9 gpi in 330); Gold Tip's Velocity Pro (8.2 gpi in 340) or .168-inch-diameter Pierce (8.3 gpi in 340); and Carbon Express' Maxima BLU RZ (8.5 gpi in 350) or Whitetail (7.9 gpi in 350). The lightest carbon arrow I'm aware of is the High Country Archery/Carbon Revolution Speed Pro Max, at 5.5 gpi, an arrow so light (around 300 grains finished weight) that its use actually voids the warranty on many compound bows.

Paired with a streamlined mechanical broadhead – or low-profile fixed blade in states like Idaho or Oregon where mechanicals aren't legal – and short, high-profile and stiff vanes like Bohning's Blazer-style designs, you're set up for a high degree of accuracy at long ranges and a built-in margin for error if your range judging proves slightly off.

Heavyweight Punch

Deep penetration on the biggest game is a matter of applying momentum and not high levels of kinetic energy. I find kinetic energy of little use for determining the penetration potential of bowhunting arrows, providing little more than apples-to-apples comparisons of performance. KE is a rifle-hunting concern, a formula determining delivered energy via shock; though despite speed being dou-

When deep penetration is needed, slim, heavyweight arrows provide a performance edge, like this Carbon Express PileDriver PTX.

bled in the KE formula (Speed^2 x Arrow Mass ÷ 450,240), if you run the numbers on a test group of arrows, light to heavy, you'll discover that heavier arrows always produce higher KE numbers. Still, arrows and broadheads kill by hemorrhaging, not shock, so pushing that broadhead deeper to produce more tissue damage is the name of the game.

Other advantages provided by heavier arrows include generally improved durability and reliability following hard impacts with bone or rocky ground while stump shooting or small-game hunting, or after a miss, and much quieter shots. Heavier shafts simply absorb more of a bow's available energy, resulting in less escape energies that translate into vibrations and resulting shot noise. So, if you spend a good deal of time pursuing rabbits or squirrels in punishing terrain, a heavy arrow will save you money in the long run by resulting in fewer broken shafts. If you take nothing but short-range shots at white-tailed deer from stands or blinds, a heavier arrow will result in quieter shots and fewer string-jumping animals.

Many will argue that last point, believing they can beat a white-tailed deer to the jump by shooting a faster arrow. In a vacuum this might prove true, but understand that the speed of sound is around 1,126 fps. To put it simply, that's more than three times faster than the fastest compound bow. A wound-up whitetail's reaction time is measured in milliseconds. Tests have shown even a human can jerk an 8-inch target out of the path of a speeding arrow from 25 yards away based on auditory clues alone. So, yes, you might reduce the effects of a string-jumping deer by a couple inches by shooting a faster arrow, but the better approach is to give them nothing at all to react to. This is most easily accomplished by shooting a heavier arrow.

When addressing thick-skinned, heavy-boned game, cut-on-contact broadheads like this New Archery Products HellRazor are ideal.

Be that as it may, where heavy arrows really shine is shooting big animals, seeking maximum penetration on less-than-ideal angles and blasting

Presented with a quartering-to shot the author depended on a tough broadhead and heavy arrow to breach the shoulder blade.

through bone like shoulder blades while staying in one piece. "Heavy" is subjective to draw weight and length, but for the average bowhunter shooting 65 pounds at 29 inches (several manufacturers have told me they sell more bows at these specs than all others), this means something weighing about 10 or 12 gpi in a 330/340/350 spine. Something like Easton's .168-inch-diameter Injexion Carbon or A/C (10.3 and 10.5 gpi in 330, respectively), .205-inch-diameter Full Metal Jacket (11.3 gpi in 340) or .168-inch-diameter Deep Six 4mm FMJ (11 gpi in 330); Carbon Express' .205-inch-diameter PileDriver Pass Through Extreme (10.32 gpi in 350) or .245-inch-diameter PileDriver Hunter (11.3 gpi in 350); Alaska Bowhunting Supply's tapered GrizzlyStik TDT (about 450 grains total without point, a thin, tapered-carbon design accommodating draw weights from 55 to 70 pounds); Carbon Tech's .245-inch-diameter Rhino (10 gpi in 45/70, 11.5 in 55/80 deflections); and Bloodsport's .168-inch-diameter Evidence (10.2 gpi in 350). For the quietest short-range shots possible, maximum ruggedness and penetration potential at any range, especially on the largest game, heavy arrows offer the answer.

Down The Middle

For average bowhunters plying average conditions and game—or those wanting to keep things as simple as possible and assemble a single rig for all bowhunting pursuits—choosing arrows somewhere between the extremes makes a lot of sense. A middle-of-the-road arrow might drop slightly more than a lighter one at longer ranges, penetrate slightly less on the largest game and maybe result in slightly elevated decibel levels on release, but it will get the job done in a wide variety of bowhunting situations. These are the SUVs of the bowhunting world—not supplying the raw speed of a sports car, or the hauling capacity of a big-block pickup, but taking you where you need to go with proper caution and applied skill.

Since most of us are just average guys enjoying bowhunting average-size big game at average distances, the industry delivers the goods with a wide variety of options. This is why arrows weighing between the heavy end of 8 and just shy of 10 gpi are the industry's most common options.

This could be anything from Easton's popular all-carbon, .205-inch-diameter Axis (9.5 gpi in 340 spine) to Carbon Express' standard-diameter Maxima Hunter (8.9 gpi in 350), standard Maxima RED (9.07 gpi in 350) and standard Mayhem Hunter (9.8 gpi in 350); to Beman's ICS Precision Hunter (9.3 gpi in 340) or ICS Whiteout (8.8 gpi in 340); Victory's .168-inch-diameter VAP TKO (9.1 gpi in 350), VAP Camo (8.6 gpi in 350), .204-inch-diameter RIP Camo (9 gpi in 350) or VForce (8.7 gpi in 350); Gold Tip's XT (.003 inch straightness), Pro (.001 inch) or Hunter (8.9 gpi in 340); to Black Eagle Arrows' Renegade (8.7 gpi in 350)—or any other carbon arrow in this class.

It's easy to look on this dizzying array of arrow specs and decide that 7.5 gpi to 9 gpi to 10.5 gpi makes little difference to your bowhunting efforts. But when multiplied by the overall length of your arrow these numbers can add up to spell 42 to

For the average bowhunter, namely whitetail hunters, a middleweight carbon arrow offers an ideal combination.

120 grains of additional or subtracted mass. These are substantial numbers and affect everything from trajectory to penetration potential. If you change nothing about your bow and the accessories it holds, you're still able to control the goals you wish to achieve with the arrows and broadheads you choose.

Bolt Dynamics

There is a little more to modern crossbow bolts than chopping down vertical-bow arrows to length. Crossbow bolts must by necessity include a larger diameter to safely ride atop the bolt rail, and be stiff enough to withstand the incredible amounts of energy unleashed by today's high-performance crossbows—some pushing 400 fps or more. Bolts must also be heavy for spine, as 18 to 24 inches isn't a lot of shaft to carry all that energy downrange with enough authority to push through big-game vitals. They also hold special flat-backed or half-moon nocks that act as platforms for the bowstring to push against during launch. Regarding these styles, I suppose you can get into campfire arguments over such details, but I find no difference in accuracy between the two. Ultimately, defer to each manufacturer's recommendations.

I'm surprised to see many popular x-bow bolts holding aluminum inserts, as such short projectiles really call for a high degree of F.O.C. to assure reliable broadhead flight. Certainly, this forward weight can be created by heavier broadheads, starting at 145 grains and moving up to 175 grains, but if you've bowhunted in the past you no doubt already own a supply of 100- or 125-grain broadheads. In this case 75- to 100-grain brass inserts make more sense. They're automatically tougher, and also shift concentrated mass to the front of the bolt where it's needed most—especially at the highest grains-per-inch ratings.

In hunting-weight bolts offered by major arrow manufactures, 278 to 300 grains finished weight, without point, in 20- to 22-inch bolts (or around 8.5 to 9 gpi) appears to be the bottom-end mass. For turkey and deer-size game shot at ranges of less than 30 yards, this should be all the bolt you'll ever need, especially if using a more efficient fixed blade broadhead – or mechanical head for turkeys.

Crossbow bolts come in 18- to 24-inch lengths and many weights. Follow each crossbow manufacturer's recommendations.

Yet, I always err to the side of caution, in this case meaning higher gpi ratings and heavy brass inserts – though, again, a heavier broadhead easily makes up the difference.

The lightest, fastest x-bow bolts suited for turkey and small to average deer include Easton's Bloodline Crossbow Bolt (10.5 gpi); Beman's White Box Bolts (400 grains finished, including 100-grain point) and ICS Crossbow Hunter (10.5 gpi); Black Eagle's Executioner (9 gpi); BloodSport Hunter and Witness Bolts (300 to 325 finished); and especially Gold Tip's Swift (7.3 gpi) and Ballistic (8.5 gpi). These last two are the lightest bolts offered for hunting that I'm aware of.

Midweight bolts, perhaps better suited to heavier deer, the biggest hogs and similar-size game, include Easton's 11.3 gpi Bowfire and Victory's 325-grain finished, brass-inserted XBolt.

If I were to tackle elk or moose with a crossbow, or simply wanted to take longer shots at any game of say 50 or 60-plus yards, I'd look to the heaviest bolt models, represented by Easton's Full Metal Jacket Crossbow (13.7 gpi); Gold Tip's Nitro (13.9 gpi); and nearly all of Carbon Express' x-bolt models, including the 380- to 403-grain finished-weight Maxima Hunter (20 and 22 inches respectively), 420- to 449-grain Mayhem, 442- to 479-grain PileDriver and 430- to 479-grain Whitetail Crossbolts. One unique exception is Victory's VAP VooDoo Bolts, 20-, 22- and 24-inch versions weighing only 320, 340 and 345 grains. But they also include three-section, super-slim shaft connected by two milled-aluminum Rail Rider Technology couplers, creating only two points of contact on the rail and resulting in faster launch speeds and deeper penetration led by a Penetrator Broadhead Adaptor. Aluminum remains viable in crossbow bolts since it generally offers heavy payloads at affordable prices, including the Easton Magnum 2219 in 7075-T9 alloy (13.8 gpi) and Carbon Express GameSlayer T6 Aluminum Crossbolt (457 to 494 grains in 20- and 22-inch lengths).

Length isn't as critical, and a too-long bolt shoots perfectly fine, though a too-short bolt is best avoided. Basic bolt lengths include 18, 20, 22 and the rare 24 inches, the first is best suited to crossbows with power strokes of 10 or 11 inches, 20-inch bolts to 12 to 13, 22-inch bolts to 14 to 15 inches and the latter to crossbows owning the longest power strokes of generally 16 inches or more. A longer bolt also carries more weight, so can also be used in a crossbow with shorter power stroke to increase delivered energy through added mass.

Most modern bolts hold 2-inch broadhead vanes such as Bohning's Blazer, though others hold 3-inch vanes. Two-inch vanes are likely best suited to mechanical broadheads, 3-inch to fixed-blade broadheads used on sturdier game such as elk—or in states where mechanicals are not legal for big game.

Basic Arrowsmithing

The serious bowhunter really should learn to assemble their own arrows, if for no other reason than to quickly address issues as they arise during the season. Basic measuring is an easy task that can be performed at home to assure the proper cut-off length. I prefer to draw my bow with an uncut arrow and have my wife or a friend mark the proper cut-off point with a felt-tipped marker—generally ¼ to ½ inch in front of the riser when snugged into my anchor point to prevent broadhead interference with the riser or rest. It is perfectly acceptable

Fletching your own arrows allows you to build the arrows you want, including custom colors and special fletching types.

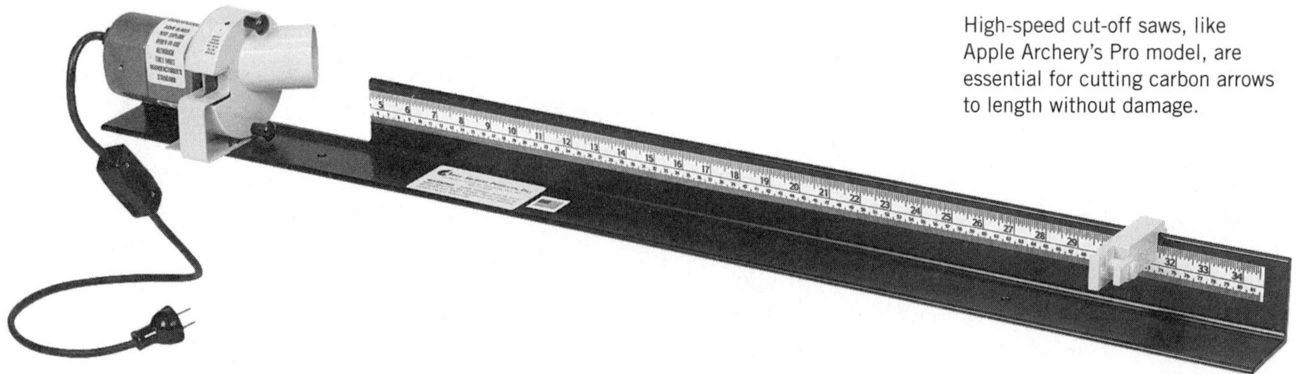

High-speed cut-off saws, like Apple Archery's Pro model, are essential for cutting carbon arrows to length without damage.

for the broadhead to be drawn inside the arrow shelf, if for example the shaft must be cut shorter to stiffen spine and aid in tuning, as most drop-away rests create an overdraw situation and deep launchers prevent broadheads from straying outside the shelf area and inflicting injury to the shooter. Like the old carpenter's maxim says, measure twice, cut once. Err to the side of caution and cut slightly long if you're uncertain. You can always cut excess arrow away—you can't put it back.

Today's high-modulus carbon fiber demands a high-speed cut-off saw for clean cuts free of splintering. Even a fine-toothed hacksaw won't suffice. Friends have used thin cut-off blades and high-speed Dremel tools for this work, but if you go through a lot of arrows a commercial cut-off saw is a smart investment. Quality arrow cut-off saws retail for $100 to $150, but pay for themselves quickly by eliminating trips to pro shops and resulting fees.

Being an accuracy stickler, I carefully prep all arrow-shaft ends before installing components. G5 Outdoors' Arrow Squaring Device (A.S.D.) or Burt Coyote/Lumenok's FAST Fletched Arrow Squaring Tool are both sound investments, used to precisely square the ends of shafts before installing inserts and nocks, assuring precision component alignment. I also find standard inserts supplied with certain arrow brands highly suspect, so toss them and replace them with top-quality, American-made inserts from Precision Designed Products, which also offers brass inserts of various weights for those looking to boost F.O.C.

Cyanoacrylate (super) glues are popular for installing inserts into carbon shafts. I use this type of adhesive regularly, as it's fast and extremely reliable. The only problem is it bonds too quickly. A small bead of glue is applied to the insert and the inserts jammed home quickly, excess glue whipped on a paper towel. Hesitate during this process and you can end up with an insert that's not fully seated. This instant setting is convenient when fixing a small-game or stump-shooting arrow in the field, but doesn't allow precision alignment of broadheads for bowhunting. For this reason I prefer two-part epoxy, or a Bohning product called Insert Iron, which is also heat reversible. Both allow time to manipulate inserts within the shaft before bonding.

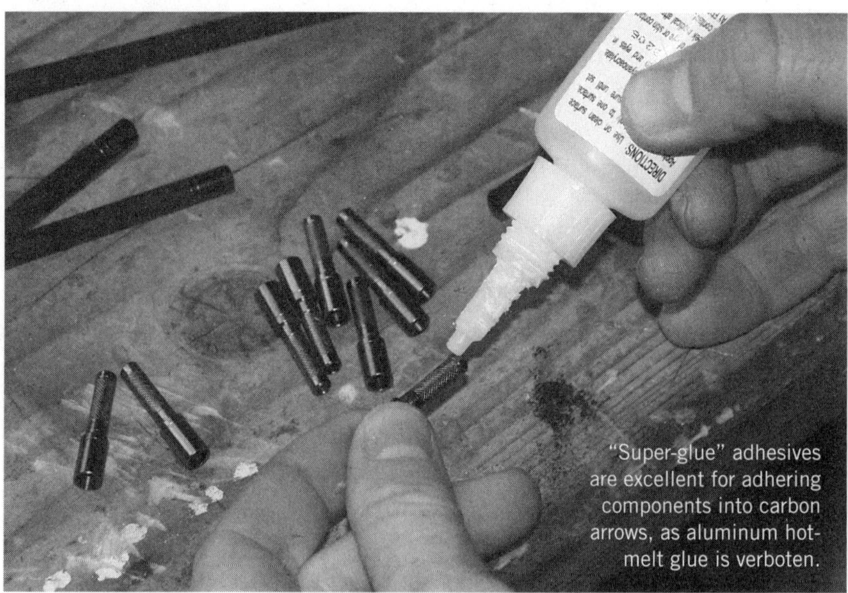

"Super-glue" adhesives are excellent for adhering components into carbon arrows, as aluminum hot-melt glue is verboten.

Building your own arrows assures unsurpassed quality control for better bowhunting accuracy and lasting performance.

This allows, for instance, installing broadheads into inserts, adhering them to the shaft, and checking for perfect alignment by spinning assembled arrows on an inspector with twin, bearing-equipped rollers and a horizontal cradle. Any alignment deviation is revealed by slight point wobbles. Slow-cure adhesives allow tweaking insert attitude and correcting slight inconsistencies—small deviations that can affect overall broadhead accuracy.

Rolling Your Own

Fletching your own arrows saves money, makes you more independent of archery pro shops and allows you to produce not only prettier arrows suiting your tastes and exact needs, but assuring top-notch accuracy sometimes lacking in mass-produced wares. Fletching arrows is simpler than you might believe, requiring minimal mechanical aptitude and practice. The only real requirements are proper tools, adhesive and a supply of preferred fletchings.

A fletching jig does nothing more than hold individual (sometimes multiple) fletchings in place on the shaft while the adhesive sets. This is usually accomplished through a removable clamp held in place by powerful magnets or pressure fit. Many fletching jigs include set fletching attitudes, better units allow a high degree of adjustability for fletching offset or helical. Offset fletching involves a straight clamp set at an angle to the shaft to induce shaft spin when subjected to passing air. Helical clamps include built-in spin and adjustments allow you to add more or less spin to the shaft, within the bounds of the shaft diameter. Both approaches work as well as the other for stabilizing fixed-blade broadheads. Offset, or helical twist, is applied either right- or left-wing, or clockwise and counterclockwise, respectively.

This wing business is a holdover from the days when all arrows held natural feathers—still viable, even necessary for traditional shooters—and which side, or wing, those feathers were taken from on the actual bird. Right-wing seems to have emerged as the industry "standard" (high-tech "lipped" vanes like New Archery Products' QuikSpin, for instance, a few "air-foil" bladed broadheads, are or require right-wing fletching attitude). Right-wing fletching also works to tighten broadhead threads in flight and on impact, left to loosen. Regarding traditional bows shot off the shelf – I've heard arguments of right- verses left-hand helical and shelf clearance, but have shot both from the same bow within the same minute with identical impacts.

Fletching jigs come in basic models with no adjustment capabilities – not necessarily a bad thing, budget models made of plastic (also not a bad thing) that allow a full range of adjustment, and pricier units constructed of aluminum that permit adjusting clamp positions clear off the arrow shaft. I own and use all such models, and all do a fine job of applying fletchings to all manner of arrow shafts. But I must also say that my three all-metal Bitzenburger Dial-O-Fletch (in left- and right-hand helical) have been with me 30-plus years without a single problem or worn part, and allow me to apply nearly wrap-around helical on my traditional arrows to help steer large cut-on-contact broadheads.

The author fletched these arrows with New Archery Products' heat-shrink fletching sleeves and killed this black bear just hours later.

Another factor of fletching arrows is reliable adhesion via the correct adhesive choice. Some plastic vanes include glue activator compatible with cyanoacrylate, or super-glue, adhesives, creating quicker and more reliable bonding. Other plastic vanes require thorough cleaning with something like acetone, then the cyanoacrylate adhesives offer quick adhesion. Slow-cure (5 to 10 minutes), air-dry fletching cements are generally the most reliable with feather fletchings, though most modern versions also work just as well with plastic vanes after cleaning. Scrubbing the shaft's fletching area with an abrasive cleanser, like Bon Ami, rinsing and allowing them to dry thoroughly also goes a long way toward assuring long-lasting, reliable fletching adhesion. If you find arrows are shedding fletchings regularly, it's normally a cleaning-preparation issue.

Modern bowhunters also have the alternative of instantly replaceable, one-piece fletching cartridges as heat-shrink or modular units. I admit I was skeptical at first. I first tried them because I received some arrows that I wanted badly to try just as I was on my way out the door for a bowhunt. So with a loaded truck waiting I cut those arrows to length, installed inserts and used hot water to heat-shrink some New Archery Products QuikFletch sleeves into place, all within 20 minutes. I shot those arrows upon arrival in camp to check my sights, and tagged a gorgeous black bear with them before nightfall—a complete pass-through, fletchings unscathed. That's the biggest selling point of one-piece fletching options—they're absolute timesavers.

Feathers Versus Vanes

The choice between natural feathers and plastic vanes is a balancing act of compromises involving actual steerage, forgiveness, durability, weatherproof qualities and sometimes equipment choices. Feathers have remained a staple since man first bent a stick and tied a piece of vine to each end, and remain as viable today as ever. For traditional bowhunters shooting off the shelf they represent an absolute ne-

Natural feathers are standard when shooting traditional gear, but also welcomed on arrows shot from compound bows.

cessity, as the lateral give, or ability to collapse completely flat and spring right back into shape, makes shooting in that manner possible at all. Compound shooters also benefit from this lateral give, feathers proving more forgiving when contacting a rest arm or launcher, shot through total-containment rests, and even small obstacles encountered along its flight path. But while feathers exhibit exceptional lateral give, they remain stiff when pushed from the side, meaning they provide exceptional steerage and arrow stability, especially with attached broadheads. The primary feathers from which fletchings are fashioned are truly a wonder of nature, something man with all his technology has been unable to reproduce.

Feathers are also much lighter, a 4-inch feather, for instance, weighs about 7 grains, while a single plastic vane of the same length can weigh more than triple that. Fletching with lighter feathers automatically results in improved F.O.C. balance by removing weight from the rear of the arrow, and faster launch speeds.

The problem with feathers is that they aren't very durable, can prove noisy when brushed against clothing or vegetation and are completely worthless when they become wet. Normal shooting eventually frays and tatters natural feathers, meaning they must be replaced more often—and they cost three to four times more than plastic vanes. Feathers are also easily crushed or damaged by pushing them against the grain. Here's a quick tip: mussed feathers can often be popped back into shape by waving or twirling them over steady steam for a few minutes. When brushed against objects during a stalk or while on stand feathers can create noise that alerts game. Finally, in wet weather feathers become problematic. If they become wet they flatten and offer zero arrow steerage. Waterproofing compounds are available but normally provide only temporary fixes in persistent rain. Feathers must be purchased either left- or right-wing, while a single vane can be fletched either way.

Plastic vanes are nearly the opposite of feathers structurally, providing little lateral compromise and a high degree of side-pressure give. Push a vane from the edge and it remains rigid. Push it from the side and it bends easily. This means that a vane that contacts any part of the bow or accessories, or an obstacle in flight, will not yield and it will push the arrow off course or cause arrow kicks and bobbles. It also means they don't provide the same degree of stability in flight, requiring more precise tuning for equal accuracy.

But vanes remain highly popular because they're extremely durable and resistant to damage, extremely affordable and stand up to any type of weather including downpours with zero effects. Vanes are also more aerodynamic than feathers, their thin edges and smooth surfaces sliding through the atmosphere with less friction. This means that although they are three times heavier than natural feathers, resulting in slower launch speeds, they overtake feather-fletched arrows of the same weight and launched from the same bow within 45 to 50 yards, thereafter surpassing them in speed. For long-range shooting, vanes are superior. Generally, vanes are also easier to work with during fletching.

Broadhead Style & Function

The same random arrow selection hinted at earlier can really get you into trouble when it comes to broadheads. This is normally a function of grabbing a head that is too aggressive for your bow setup, in terms of draw weight and length, or the game you're hunting—though the opposite can also prove true. Let's say you're limited to 50 pounds of draw weight due to injury, size or age, or pull a draw length less than 27 inches. You choose a popular, wide-cutting mechanical broadhead because all your friends use them, or they appeared devastating on the latest episode of your favorite outdoor television show, or maybe they were just on sale. The heads are said to be the most deadly broadhead on the market because they have three blades cutting 2 inches wide and a special tip that stretches the hide before entry to create exaggerated entrance holes. I've just described a head that, in my opinion, would require a dead minimum of a 65-pound bow drawn to 28 or 29 inches. Your 50-pound bow and sub-27-inch drawn length will undoubtedly result in disastrously insufficient penetration. Your equipment just doesn't produce the energy needed to push all of that broadhead through tough hide and ribs and completely perforate vital organs.

Conversely, spring turkey season is quickly approaching and you stop by your local X-Mart to pick up some broadheads in preparation. But all they have on hand are fixed-blade heads left over

Broadhead style affects performance goals, including (left to right) aggressive mechanicals, standard mechanicals and fixed-blades (which breached this whitetail shoulder blade).

from last fall, with a conservative 1-1/8-inch cutting diameter. These are great heads for sturdier elk, but for turkeys and their baseball-size vitals, they don't offer any margin for error. Also, even if such a head should center the vitals, its conservative cutting diameter would give that gobbler plenty of time to take wing or scoot into thick brush and possibly be lost. The aggressive mechanical mentioned in the first scenario includes the possibility of turning a marginal hit into a dead bird, and imparting some shock on impact to discombobulate the bird and allow hemorrhaging to do its work.

In still another example, those conservative heads you found at the X-Mart might prove the ideal head come elk season, providing excellent flight from high-performance bows and assuring the deep penetration needed for the largest big-game animals. They would also serve the first bowhunter well when directed at deer-size game from a low-energy bow setup.

As you can see there is a little more to broadhead selection than availability, price and popularity.

Assignment Specific

In very general terms, long-range bowhunters' first concern should be unsurpassed flight characteristics. Since most long-range game also comes with thin hide and light bones—like pronghorns—a streamlined mechanical broadhead is normally the best choice. How aggressive this head should be is dictated by bow capabilities, as light arrows and increased range also mean less energy available on target. The most aggressive mechanical designs, including the widest cutting diameters and deployed blade angles that chop instead of slice, demand 65- to 70-pound bows pushing 315 to 330 fps real-world speeds – not inflated advertised ATA speeds. Those shooting less energy, like 60 pounds or less with draw lengths shorter than 29 inches, should look into a less aggressive, more efficient mechanical design, say one with rear-deploy blades, cutting diameters of 1½ inches or less, and blades that slice instead of chop when fully deployed. Two blades generally penetrate better than three or four; each blade added requires more energy to shove through a given medium.

A wide-cutting mechanical, like Wac'Em's Expandable, produces wider blood trails for easier tracking after the hit.

Compact mini fixed-blade heads are also useful as long-range ammo, especially in states where mechanical heads aren't allowed. Raw speed, and your abilities to tame this speed through precise tuning to harmonize all associated parts, absolutely dictates broadhead choice. This is because lots of exposed blade set along longer ferrules, especially one-piece cut-on-contacts with the appearance of airplane wings, catch more passing wind than streamlined or small-profile heads.

When bowhunting the very biggest game—whether North American elk or moose, or African dangerous game—a highly efficient broadhead design can make all the difference, especially if your arrow finds heavy bone. This approach also applies to those on the low end of the energy spectrum—archers pulling compounds with less than 55 pounds of draw weight and/or less than 27 inches of draw length, and traditional archers shooting any recurve or longbow. With heavy gear and long draw lengths, say 65 to 70 pounds or more, and any draw length of more than 28 inches, a sturdy fixed-blade head is sufficient for elk- or moose-size game. Anyone wielding equipment below those numbers should be looking into more efficient cutting-tip or true cut-on-contact broadhead designs.

I use the term "sufficient" purposefully, as I tend to be a pessimist who always thinks in terms of worst-case scenarios. When gearing up for annual elk hunts, for instance, I always choose the most sturdy, indestructible broadhead available that also allows me to maintain the degree of accuracy I demand. This normally includes a conservative cutting diameter (1⅛ inch) held on an all-steel ferrule with blades at least .036 inch thick and anchored by a reliable retention system to assure the blades aren't shed if heavy bone is encountered. My last elk, for example, was shot through the shoulder blade, the arrow exiting intact behind the last rib on the opposite flank.

Somewhere in the middle sits the average whitetail hunter, North America's most numerous bowhunting demographic. The knee-jerk reaction to losing just a single buck, even dealing with an especially challenging blood trail, is usually to seek something cutting bigger holes and spilling more blood. The mechanical broadhead was born largely in this quest – and because compound-bow performance began to outpace the average bowhunter's knowledge to fine-tune fixed-blade broadheads that were designed for slower arrow speeds.

The mechanical idea is nothing new, appearing as early as the 1950s, though it took another four

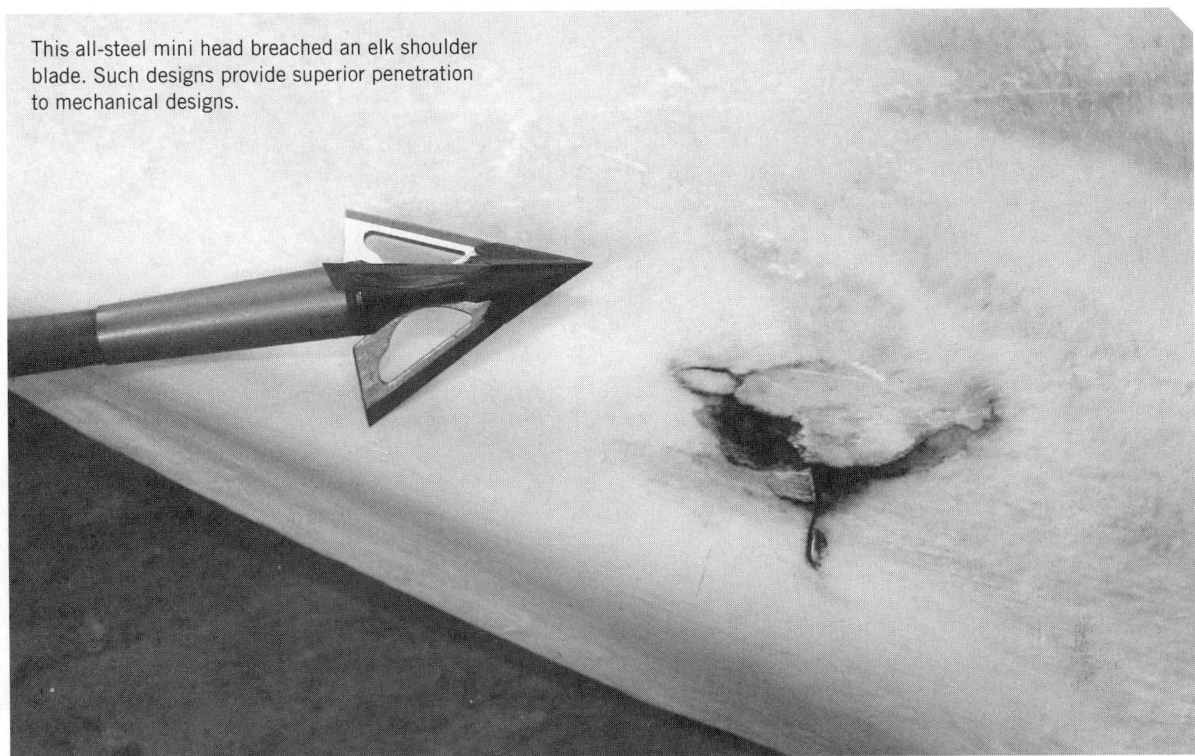
This all-steel mini head breached an elk shoulder blade. Such designs provide superior penetration to mechanical designs.

decades, better engineering and space-age materials to perfect the design. They can prove deadly—given enough energy. But it's always important to remember that no matter the broadhead design, that two holes—entrance and exit—are always better than one, especially when shooting from elevated stands where low exits are necessary to spill tracking blood. You can shove a 2-inch-wide mechanical into an animal from above, kill him cleanly and quickly, but without a low exit hole to spill blood, recovery—especially in wet conditions or thick brush—can prove time consuming. This becomes more pointed with marginal-but-lethal hits where an animal might travel 200 or 300 yards. There's no bucking physics – moving parts, wide cutting diameters and blades that chop instead of slice always result in less penetration – all other factors remaining equal.

Is your current broadhead achieving pass-through penetration most of the time? If not you should seek a more efficient design. This could mean a mechanical with less cutting diameter like 1½ inch instead of 1¾ or 2 inches, one wearing a cut-on-contact tip for more efficient penetration, or rear-deploy blades instead of those that must flip 180 degrees on impact. A 1-3/16- to 1¼-inch fixed-blade cutting diameter, like that of the venerable Thunderhead 100 and original MX-series Muzzys, remain in play because they provide a good balance between true flight and blood-letting cutting diameter at typical whitetail yardages.

But do wide-cutting mechanical heads automatically translate into faster recovery of game than narrower fixed-blade heads? Intuition would automatically say yes. Using an aggressive mechanical to slash a 2-inch hole through lung tissue should cause almost twice as much hemorrhaging as a 1⅛-inch-wide fixed-blade mini head, and result in death in half the time, right?

I've certainly seen deer shot with aggressive mechanicals drop within 10 yards of the hit. But what about all of the animals I've shot with sleek, low-profile cut-on-contact heads that also dropped inside that distance?

Any broadhead breaching both lungs eliminates negative pressure created after exhaling, making it impossible to draw another breath, massive hemorrhaging quickly filling the lungs with blood and causing quick death. But how an animal reacts immediately after release is a matter of imparted shock. Shoot an animal with an aggressive mechanical and you'll generally receive an audible queue signaling a successful hit – a punching-bag "thunk" or sharp

Fletching size is dictated by broadhead type – smaller sizes for mechanicals, larger for fixed-blade heads.

"thwack" as massive energy is transferred from your projectile to that animal. The animal becomes understandably alarmed when something slams into its side so dramatically. Natural instincts take over, adrenaline flows and they attempt to distance themselves from the perceived threat, even when dead on their feet. A trained male athlete might cover 100 yards in 10 seconds, and I wouldn't bet on him in a race against a panicked whitetail.

I've had whitetail bucks travel 200 yards after being shot through the heart with a 2-inch three-blade mechanical—while also leaving little blood behind. I've also witnessed bucks travel only 10 or 15 yards after taking a conservative fixed-blade broadhead through the heart, never seeming to know what hit them.

To gain a better perspective into this energy transfer take a tough piece of carpet and nail it securely between a couple of 4-inch by 4-inch posts laying on the ground. Then attach an aggressive mechanical to an arrow and attempt to push it through that carpet. Breaching the material will likely require some effort. Now replace the mechanical head with a cutting-tip broadhead and perform the same test. It will slip through nearly effortlessly.

I'm certainly not advocating abandoning mechanical heads. If they work for you there's absolutely no need to change. But when bowhunting in states where mechanicals aren't allowed, or when shooting low-energy equipment precluding an aggressive mechanical, there's no reason to feel handicapped or fear losing a badly hit animal because you've sacrificed a certain amount of cutting diameter—because wider heads don't automatically equal faster kills.

Assuring Straight Flight

It doesn't matter if you use a mechanical, a replaceable-blade or fixed cut-on-contact design, but it does matter what kind of fletchings you pair that broadhead with. Fletchings create drag on the rear of the arrow to assure the broadhead stays out front where it belongs. It is important that your broadhead not outmatch the trailing fletchings, which leads to wandering arrows and poor accuracy, and especially erratic broadhead flight. As a general rule, fletching surface area should exceed exposed broadhead-blade surface area by four or five to one. This makes new-

The arrow-broadhead combination you choose should ultimately depend on animal size and equipment capabilities.

er 2-inch high-profile vanes, such as the Bohning Blazer or equivalents, ideal for all mechanical and mini fixed-blade heads on the market today. When using the once-standard 1-3/16- to 1¼-inch fixed-blade design, old-standard 4-inch vanes or feathers become a safer option. Full-size one-piece, cut-on-contact heads used by the average traditional bowhunter are usually paired with three 5-inch feathers, sometimes four 3-inch feathers. The idea is not to push the minimum-ratio envelope, but to provide all the stabilization a broadhead could possibly need and then some, providing a margin for error in real-world situations and not the target range.

Factors such as shooting fingers can also mean bumping up to the next-largest fletching option, choosing a 4-inch instead of a 2-inch fletching, for instance, to help arrows recover faster from finger roll-over.

Since I'm the anal type, but also because I see real results, I normally assemble hunting arrows separately from everyday practice and target arrows. The major departure here is waiting to install inserts until individual broadheads are screwed home. This not only allows me to double-check alignment on a spinning arrow inspector (as discussed earlier), but align fixed blades with fletchings before the adhesive sets. Or in the case of two-blade cut-on-contacts with or without bleeders – align all exactly alike with the main blades sitting vertically or parallel to the nock throat. I find by aligning every broadhead exactly alike—instead of the random seating provided by mounting broadheads after insert installation—I receive tighter broadhead groups with each broadhead and arrow combo working on the same dynamic during launch and flight. It's generally only a matter of inches, but in bowhunting situations I want every possible advantage. This instills confidence—a priceless commodity anytime you draw a bow on coveted game.

Hopefully the next time you step into an archery shop to prepare for your next bowhunt and purchase new arrows and broadheads for a coming season, you'll remember this advice and put more thought into how those choices will affect efficiency and the goals you wish to accomplish. Modern bowhunters have a world of options at their disposal and should take advantage of that variety to better outfit each foray and assure regular success.

Shooting a bow requires combining several disparate actions, which then requires deeply engraining practiced routines.

CHAPTER 15

SHOOTING YOUR BOW

SHOOTING A BOW IS AN inherently difficult endeavor, and much like golf, casting a fly rod or certain video games it requires a good deal of hand-eye coordination and long repetitive practice. You are asking yourself to perform many disparate tasks simultaneously—engaging muscles to pull and hold a bowstring at bay, while other muscle groups remain completely relaxed, ultimately putting the process above the end while also striving to meet that end. Executing a technically perfect shot must become first priority, no matter the end result, while also trying mightily to hit a finite spot. In bow shooting we are also balancing the needs of making a physical action deeply cerebral. The problem is that most archers believe bow-shooting proficiency is a destination, a place you arrive at with enough shooting practice and concerted effort. In truth, shooting a bow well is a continual path toward proficiency without a final destination. Like golf or casting fly rods, you really never master shooting a bow, you simply travel toward different levels of proficiency. Sometimes you're moving backwards, always striving to be better—to shoot tighter groups or shoot better under pressure, to shoot farther or become proficient with more challenging equipment like a recurve instead of a compound, for instance.

This is a particular challenge for Americans. As a society we are so goal oriented, so driven to succeed, to meet some Calvinistic ideal, we too often put the cart before the ox. In archery we concentrate so intently on hitting a target, centering the bull's-eye, we forget that executing a technically perfect shot is first more important than where our arrows land. There is also the element of instant gratification involved, many convinced if they cannot pick up archery with minimal effort they're not naturally inclined, making it easy to give up.

There are many important parts to this perfection and before we address bull's-eyes at all we really should be instilling these important fundamentals. This starts with basic equipment fit, and then deeply engraining proper shooting form so that it permanently sticks, seeing us through a lifetime of bow shooting. This is actually easier if you've never touched a bow, beginning the journey with a clean slate. Self-taught archers with many years behind them normally face the herculean task of undoing bad habits before replacing them with good—just as it's easier to teach a person to fly cast who has never touched a spinning rod.

For this reason alone, whether starting anew, or starting over, I recommend removing the target from the equation altogether. Like tai-chi, the successful archer goes through the motions repeatedly and exhaustively, deeply embedding certain movements, feelings and foundations before they are ready for the big fight—or actually sending an arrow into a target, and especially before directing an arrow at another living creature. This is also the fastest way to undo bad habits, starting from the very beginning and removing result-driven feedback.

Most bow-shooting problems stem from focusing too intensely on results, instead of first instilling solid fundamentals.

This is what makes archery so fascinating, so addicting for so many. It never becomes stale and seldom proves boring—it is never truly mastered. You are on a continual path to self improvement and relaxation in the face of self-imposed pressures. I like to believe that shooting a bow makes anyone a more patient, self-aware and ultimately better person. But interestingly enough, when you do find that balance between skill, mental confidence and calm—when you've learned to make executing a technically perfect shot more important than where your arrow arrives after release—your arrow will find the mark, you will become better at hitting your mark, and bowhunting success will automatically follow.

FIRST THINGS FIRST – PROPER BOW FIT

To shoot at your best you must first find a bow that fits your physique. In modern terms this means a bow that fits your specific draw length, but in traditional archery this indicates a basic compatibility to your physical stature *and* draw length.

There are no hard-and-fast rules here, because any traditional bow can be shot at any draw length by any archer short or tall. Yet, enjoying maximum performance from a traditional bow comes by matching general physical measurements to general draw lengths. A short recurve or longbow (52 to 56 inches in recurves, 60 to 62 in longbows) loads best and produces optimum arrow speeds at draw lengths from, 26 to 28 inches of draw length, any draw length more than 28 inches resulting in overstressing the limbs. Conversely, the longest recurves or longbows (62 to 64 inches in recurves and 70 to 73 inches in longbows) don't produce top performance when drawn less than 28 inches, 30-inch or more draw lengths providing the power stroke necessary to properly load longer limbs and produce top performance. Hand in hand, a 52- to 56-inch bow length results in painful finger pinch, the bowstring wrapping around fingers at too-acute of an angle, for any archer pulling such a bow more than, say, 28 or 29 inches. Too, a 5-foot, 4-inch tall archer would likely find a 62-inch recurve or 70-inch longbow unwieldy, while a 6-foot, 5-inch archer might find a 56-inch bow rather unstable, even if you were able to completely eliminate the aforementioned finger pinch. This is all rather subjective, as at 6 feet, 5 inches tall, I've killed game with my 52-inch Cascade Archery takedown recurve, it's just that when I shoot 3-D competition—and not turkeys or deer while sitting flat on my rear in tight brush—I'll invariably shoot higher scores while shooting a 62- to 64-inch recurve.

This overall length issue is somewhat true of compounds as well, but to a lesser extent, especially since the vast majority of compound shooters now employ releases (eliminating finger pinch with shorter bows). Compound finger shooters require a bit longer axle-to-axle length compound for comfort and shootability – some prefer up to even 40 inches. In today's marketplace a 40-inch bow can prove difficult to find, many companies not including a bow with such dimensions in their lineup at all. Such bows, if available at all, are generally target models often lacking performance – though that's not necessarily a bad thing, as "slow" bows have killed plenty of animals. I've certainly shot the shortest compounds successfully with releases, but am normally most comfortably shooting something at least 33 inches axle-to-axle, 34 to 36 inches even better. A shorter person would likely find their comfort zone in more compact axle-to-axle models. Though many modern designs have blurred any generalization I might make, including long risers combined with short limbs and cam designs that swing well out to effectively open bowstring angle at full draw and make a shorter bow feel up to 3½ inches longer. What you shoot best generally comes down to feel. With bow fit – if it feels good, go with it.

The subject of actual draw length becomes most important when shopping for a compound, due to let-off and draw-length-specific rear walls created by string or limb-draw stops. Shooting a compound with a draw length that is too short results in "hunching" into the shot or the need to bend the bow arm and engage muscles at full draw. A draw length that is even slightly too long requires the shooter to stretch into the shot, overextending the anchor point, holding muscles and creating possible bowstring contact with the face. There is

Even simple traditional bows require the right fit to shoot well. This hinges on draw length and overall bow length.

no "good enough" with compound draw weight—only Goldilocks' just right.

Determining Draw Length

There are two reliable ways to mathematically determine draw length, each based on actual body measurements. You can also simply draw a non-draw-length-specific bow and mark how far back it is pulled, but this is best accomplished with professional assistance to assure proper shooting form is applied. Of the most reliable mathematical methods, wingspan measurement is maybe the easiest. This involves standing against a wall with arms spread 90 degrees to the torso with fingers extended, then allowing another person to measure from fingertip to fingertip with a tight tape. This number is then divided by 2.5. Another reliable method is to hold an uncut arrow between open hands, place the nock end to the center of the chest plate, extend both hands along the shaft out front and 90 degrees to the torso and mark the arrow at the extended finger tips. This is your draw length, give or take a ¼ to ½ inch.

Determining draw length by actually drawing a bow is best accomplished with a weakling recurve or longbow, or even a strung 5-foot length of 1-inch PVC tube, plus a commercial draw-length arrow with graduated marks and corresponding measurements.

Proper draw length should also be evident through visual clues while at full draw, especially the draw arm and elbow. At full draw the draw arm and extended elbow should create a straight line from the arrow tip, straight down the arm and to the rear-pointing elbow. A draw length that is too short will reveal itself through an elbow that's cocked away from the body, a draw length that's too long, pulled into or around the body. Another indication of a draw length that is too long is an archer who appears to be leaning backward at full

Proper draw length is important to good shooting. If your bow doesn't fit physically, you will never shoot your best.

Shooting a bow with a slightly shorter draw length can help you avoid bowstring contact while wearing heavily insulated duds.

draw, while leaning or craning the head forward is an indication of a draw length that is too short. The bow arm should remain straight and locked, not bent at the elbow. The archer should stand straight up, with shoulders sitting directly over the hips. Overall, final bow fit is best accomplished with the help of a professional, as this is a measurement you will return to for life.

One caveat to the exact draw-length rule applies to those shooting white-tailed deer in cold conditions while wearing puffy insulated clothing. Shortening draw length a half to full inch allows you to bend the bow-holding elbow outward slightly, opening a wider path for a released bowstring to pass—though, this does sacrifice a bit of power stroke, energy and aiming stability. It is always easier to slightly shorten your draw length than lengthen it. Adding a string loop can also call for a ½- to 1-inch shorter draw length to compensate for the additional backset of the D-loop itself.

Eye Dominance & Draw Weight

Two other important factors to assuring bow compatibility are eye dominance and draw weight. Everyone has a strong or dominate eye. This is your default eye for tasks such as looking through a camera viewfinder or spotting-scope lens. It is possible to, say, shoot right-handed while being left-eye dominate (as I have for 30-plus years), though you will pick up shooting, especially with sights, much faster if you start with your dominate eye. When I temporarily injured my right-hand bow-drawing fingers many years ago, my doctor asked that I not shoot for at least nine months, so I started shooting recurves left-handed. Within a month I was shooting traditional bows better than ever after starting with a clean slate and eliminating some bad habits.

Eye dominance is easy to determine. Pick a bright but finite object like a light fixture located across the room. Concentrate on it, and with both eyes open quickly encircle it by creating a circle with both hands, index finger to index finger and thumb to thumb, centering the object. Don't think about it, just do it. Now close one eye, and then the other. The eye that allows that object to remain centered is your dominate eye. Choose a bow, right- or left-handed, that corresponds. If you've been shooting cross-eye dominate for years but are experiencing debilitating problems such as target panic, start with a clean slate and make the switch during the off-season. In three to four months you'll be shooting as well as ever, within a year likely shooting better than you ever have.

Draw weight gets more bowhunters into trouble than any other equipment factor. Male egos are mostly to blame, masculinity and draw-weight bragging rights seen as one in the same. This is just silly, as I'm really more impressed by how well you can shoot or how many big-game animals you've tagged—not how much draw weight you can pull. I already delved into this subject in great detail, but it bears repeating. You should be able to plant a pin on a small spot and draw your compound bow straight back, smoothly and slowly, without that pin coming off the spot. You should also be able to sit

You'll generally shoot better with a bow correlating to your dominant eye—even if you're right-handed and must shoot left-handed.

flat on your rear, legs extended straight forward, and draw your bow between your legs, straight back and without lifting it even slightly. If you cannot perform these maneuvers, back your draw weight off until you can—unless there is a compelling reason not to, like maybe you're already on the lower end of legal draw-weight limits. Modern compounds, carbon arrows and efficient cutting-tip broadheads don't require a lot of draw weight for successful bowhunting. My wife shoots only 48 pounds at 25 inches but has shot right through two white-tailed deer and a black bear with her little compound bow, heavy-for-spine arrows and efficient broadheads.

All of these factors make ordering from a catalog a huge gamble when purchasing a first bow, or when getting back into archery after a long absence. Do yourself a favor if you're in this situation—visit a full-service archery pro shop and get professional assistance. You might pay slightly more, but that equipment is also backed by quality service before and after the sale. In other words, if you have a question about your new bow a month after purchase, the pro-shop employee will be there to answer those questions and help you sort out problems or tuning issues.

Shooting too much draw weight leads to poor shooting. Shoot a draw weight you can easily handle under all conditions.

SHOOTING FORM FOR LIFE

To shoot a bow with any amount of consistency a rock-solid and highly repeatable series of shooting-form protocols is imperative. Years after becoming proficient with your bow, even after tagging dozens of big-game animals, a re-examination of proper shooting form is how you shake off frustrating slumps. It is the simple things, for the most part, that normally short-circuit good shooting.

It's most common to find completely self-taught archers, those who didn't so much as consult a book or magazine article on the subject while beginning, are those who also most easily fall into shooting slumps. Having no real foundation in proper shooting form, having never had a seasoned mentor or professional coach show them the proper way to shoot a bow, they assembled their shooting form piecemeal through feel and guesswork, their brand of shooting form often allowing problems to creep in and ruin their best efforts.

Shooting Stance

Everything starts with stance. To begin, stand with shoulders 90 degrees to the target and feet spread to slightly more than shoulder width, the rear foot placed 90 degrees to the target, the front cocked slightly toward the target and weight distributed evenly on the balls of the feet. Many traditional archers bend their knees very slightly to accommodate the fluid nature of instinctive shooting, but the compound shooter should strive to center the shoulders over the hips and keep the back straight. Once this feel is established and repeated until it becomes subconscious, it is easier to shoot well in the sometimes contorted positions bowhunters find themselves facing regularly—whether caught in midstep during a stalk and forced to shoot with feet reversed, shooting steeply up or down hill, especially from an elevated position, and even while seated or on your knees from inside a pop-up blind or to clear overhanging brush.

At full draw the bow and draw arm, and torso, form a perfect T while addressing a target on flat ground. Now, to maintain that perfect form while shooting from a stand at targets situated well below, or shooting steeply up or down hill, the archer bends or swivels at the waist, maintaining the rigid T relationship between bow and draw arm and upper torso. The common mistake when shooting from elevated positions is to simply drop the bow arm to accommodate the shot angle, which shifts the anchor point, alters the sight picture and generally causes high misses. Think of your hips as a gyroscope of one of those dash-mounted automobile compasses, and your arms and torso as the north-pointing needle. This applies whether standing, on your knees or sitting. It even applies in extreme cases like shooting a traditional bow canted horizontal and 8 inches off the ground while sitting on your knees and bending at the waist to shoot beneath low horizontal branches.

All-Important Bow Arm

The bow hand and arm is vitally important to shooting consistency, as it is the one part of your body in contact with the bow during the entire shot. It must remain rigid but relaxed, and also in a comfortable position that is easily repeated. I start by pushing the heel of my hand into the grip, cocking my elbow slightly outward until pressure is applied with the bowstring, and then turning it downward to lock it into place. The idea is for the pressure of the bow's draw weight to push straight through the wrist, up the forearm ulna and radius bones and upper-arm humerus bone straight into the shoulder. This allows rigid bone, and not elastic muscle, to support bow mass and draw weight while at anchor, resulting in a much more stable base, more consistent follow-through and less fatigue while aiming—or when forced to remain at full draw long minutes while waiting for an animal to clear brush or look away. Any time you introduce muscle into the process of holding the bow at full draw and aiming you open the door to nervous twitches or natural muscle spasms. I've also found that flat or "low-wrist" grips best accommodate this approach, a trend now seen in the latest compounds, as "high-wrist" grips disengage

The bow arm is the base for every shot, so it is important to adopt a system that locks your shooting form in tight.

the wrist and break the straight-line use of rigid skeletal structure. I have even removed plastic or wood grips from the handle completely, shooting straight off the riser.

Get A Grip

The grip is also vitally important to accuracy because it is the actual contact point between you and the bow. An improper grip can easily introduce accuracy robbing torque. The tendency is to death grip the bow handle out of pure anxiety, knuckles turning white and tendons creating deep furrows in the skin. Others start with a loose grip but then grab at the bow handle upon release for fear of losing control or even dropping their bow. I actually prefer to avoid the term "grip" altogether in relation to supporting the bow, because the bow shouldn't be "gripped" at all. Instead the bow should be cradled. To accomplish this place all of your fingers together and hold them vertically (many archers seem to want to spread their fingers widely, the index finger often moving into the arrow shelf and posing potential risk from sharp broadheads). Now make a V or U with the thumb. Slide the bow grip into this V, like a shovel on a hardware-store rack, and allow gravity to hold the bow in place.

Today's compound bows are so recoil and vibration free upon release that you could likely do nothing more and maintain a perfect grip through every shot. But a wrist sling gives archers the security needed to alleviate the fear of dropping the bow. Adjust the sling so it actually supports the bow at rest, and concentrate on maintaining that relaxed, open-V or -U hand attitude during the shot and following the release. If you must, it is okay to lightly touch the index or middle finger and thumb at full draw, but only if you can successfully resist the urge to snatch at the bow handle during or after release.

The problem with grabbing or snatching at the bow at the moment of release is it is never performed evenly shot to shot, especially under pressure—whether it's that tournament-winning shot at a 3-D tourney or a season-making shot at game. This makes eliminating grip manipulation altogether the safest bet for repeatable accuracy.

Solidly Anchored

Another vital part of that steady quest for accuracy is a comfortably solid, dead-to-rights consistent and easily repeatable anchor point. The anchor refers to where you plant your fingers, knuckles, hand or release itself while at full draw. Your anchor es-

The term "grip" is misleading, as the bow handle shouldn't be gripped at all, but instead cradled loosely to avoid torque.

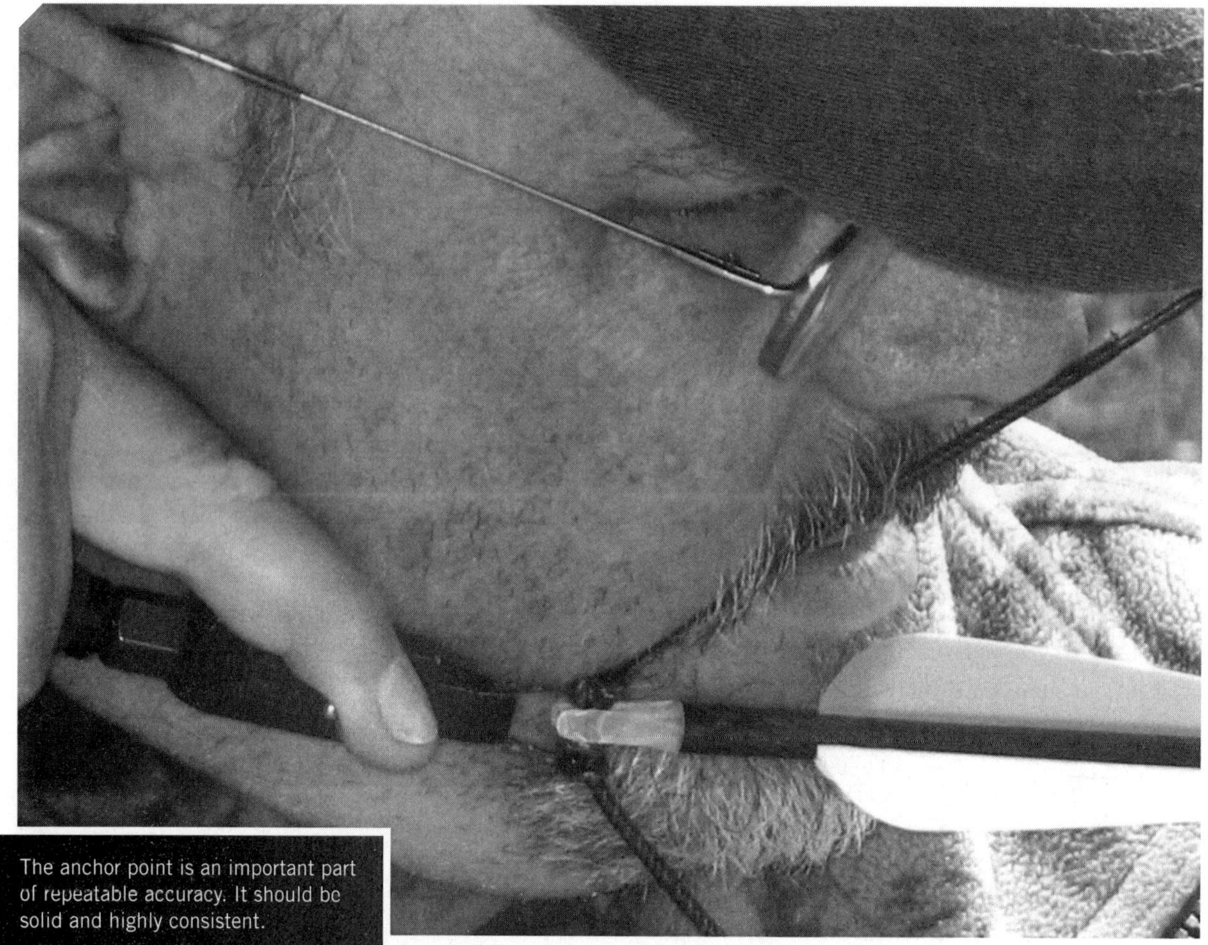

The anchor point is an important part of repeatable accuracy. It should be solid and highly consistent.

sentially creates the rear sight in your aiming system. Imagine trying to shoot an iron-sighted rifle with a rear sight that moves between shots. If you anchor at a different point for each shot, each shot will hit in a slightly different spot. Most importantly when establishing, or re-establishing, an anchor point is finding a place that feels completely natural. An anchor point that is forced will hardly prove reliable under pressure. Your anchor must feel right and feel natural. The anchor must also be based on an unmovable facial feature—preferably bone like a jaw, tooth or cheek—or an ear opening or your nose. Bones, your ear canal or nose, are anatomical features that do not move or give. In general, an anchor situated on the forward portion of your face is best to avoid bowstring contact with the face or hair.

I also like to use a double-point anchor to assure fail-safe repeatability. For instance, while shooting recurves I anchor at the corner of my mouth, pressing my index finger to an incisor tooth, wrapping my thumb beneath my jawline as a double-check anchor. Either one of these points would work by itself, but combined they give me a 100 percent infallible anchor. While shooting compounds and a T-handle release I press my index-finger knuckle into the hollow behind my ear hard against bone and wrap my thumb around the rear point of my jaw. I might substitute the ear opening to achieve the same effect. Or I might use a cheekbone and ear canal. Using two points of reference is foolproof insurance when shooting from the twisted or contorted shooting positions often encountered in the field, and especially from the confines of a treestand. Many archers use a kisser button, which is a small disk of plastic secured to the bowstring at a specific point, as their double-check anchor placed at the corner of the mouth or at a cheekbone. If your current anchor point isn't giving you the comfort and consistency you need to shoot your very best, it's never too late to change. Just be sure to give yourself a couple months to become accustomed to it before heading into the field to bowhunt.

Back Tension

For a more solid anchor and much steadier aiming while at full draw, it's also important to learn to use back tension while at full draw. The tendency with beginning or many self-taught archers is to use only arm muscles alone to power and hold the shot, while ignoring the power potential of the stronger back muscles. The muscles in your shoulders and back are much stronger than your arms alone, and from the standpoint of leverage, much better equipped to hold a powerful bow at bay while at full draw. To get a better feel for how your shoulder muscles can help give you more power and control during the shot, hold your elbows at your sides with arms bent and consciously pull your shoulder blades together, attempting to make them touch. Once you get the feel for how to engage your shoulder muscles you can use them to not only hold the shot, but help trigger the release (true back tension, which we'll get to shortly). Shoulder and back muscles are much larger and stronger than your arms will ever be. Use that power to your advantage.

Triple-A Aiming

Savvy archers strive to adopt shooting routines that help get them through bowhunting's most stressful moments – whether that involves a 3-D tournament shoot-off, or a shot at that big buck you've been waiting for all season. You might call these checklists, or maybe more accurately, checkpoints visited along the way to assure everything is done correctly during anxious moments. This is important, as the mind tends to lose an accurate sense of time when under pressure, causing bowhunters to hurry the shot or shortcut the shooting process. As a former big-game guide, one of the common mental mistakes that I witnessed all too frequently was failure to aim—or at least to aim properly.

The basic stumbling block is that most bowhunters view aiming and shooting a bow as a two-step process. They think all there is to it is placing the pin exactly where they want to hit and letting 'er rip. This is also the easy explanation of why so many easy misses occur given otherwise slam-dunk opportunities. These misses are most often a matter of short-cutting the process in the hurry to get a shot off and relieve the stress of that encounter.

Truth is there are three distinctive steps to aiming properly with a compound bow with sights and a peep. To make these three steps easier to remember I've assigned each step an A, as in AAA aiming. Admittedly, thinking of the aiming process in these terms can require a little time to absorb, but once established this three-step process becomes seamless and allows you to function flawlessly even under pressure. It will make big misses at big game much rarer.

The three A's are ACQUIRE, ALIGN and AIM. Let's run through one shot to get a better feel for how each step plays a part in an effective aiming approach.

AAA Step 1: ACQUIRE

You're standing before the target or addressing game after assuming the proper shooting stance and maintaining a loose, cradling grip. Step one in the actual aiming process starts by ACQUIRING the target. This is no more than the process of shifting all focus onto the target as a whole, or the general area you want to hit. While doing this you're also drawing your bow, moving your draw hand into the general vicinity of your anchor point and getting all of your pins into the general vicinity of the kill zone or bull's-eye. At this point you are not aiming

Aiming a bow with sights is a three-step process. The first step is to simply mentally acquire the target.

at all, only shifting focus onto the target and getting through the basic necessity of the draw cycle. In an actual bowhunting scenario this would also include timing the draw cycle so as not to alert or spook the animal you hope to shoot, or shot timing. That's it, nothing more.

AAA Step 2: ALIGN

Now that you've tugged your bow to full draw and moved all your pins onto the target or animal you wish to shoot, the second step is to ALIGN the shot and any part of your shooting form that is involved in executing a technically perfect shot. In general terms you're getting the appropriate pin into the overall kill zone. You are not yet aiming! Before the actual aiming process begins you have a few checkpoints to pass. You'll need to snug into your anchor tightly, double-checking consistency and alignment, assuring shooting form is true and consciously loosening your grip. While you're running through this quick checklist you're also aligning the peep and aperture-alignment ring solidly. The basic rule to remember at this juncture is that executing a technically perfect shot and assuring everything is aligned perfectly is more important than releasing an arrow. Don't allow yourself to move forward until everything is ALIGNED perfectly for the shot, no matter how important that shot or how impressive the antlers a buck is wearing are.

AAA Step 3: AIM

Finally, you get to AIM! But hold up one more heartbeat… true aiming is a little more involved than just hanging a pin where you want to hit and cutting the shot loose. As all mechanical parts of ALIGNING the shot are being finalized you should

The second step while aiming is to align, settling into solid shooting form and anchor point, and aligning peep and sights.

have picked a SPOT exactly where you want your arrow to arrive. The SPOT should consist of the smallest detail you're physically able to discern – a single hair, a burr a deer has picked up in his travels, a cowlick on his side, a wrinkle or shadow on its hide – according to how far the shot is and how acute your eyesight is. Obviously, this SPOT should correlate to vitals, or an angle required to breach vitals. As the actual aiming process begins you should shift every molecule of concentration onto that single, tiny spot, burning a hole through it, ignoring everything else. Never, but never, glance at the buck's antlers or split concentration on another animal following your target. Once committed to the shot, nothing else matters. Only the SPOT matters, as that's where you want your arrow to go.

Now an interesting transformation takes place. As you concentrate on that SPOT with all your existence you will find you don't need to consciously AIM at all. Your pin will have automatically moved to that SPOT, floating over it automatically. Don't fight it. Absolutely don't try to control it. Don't even think about it. Just continue burning a hole through that SPOT, allowing the proper pin to float into it, around it, in and out of it. And begin slowly squeezing the release trigger or allowing the bowstring to slip from your fingers, pulling shoulder blades together, allowing the pin to float until the shot explodes on its own. Even then, continue to aim, executing proper follow-through until the arrow sinks into the target.

If you will take the time to learn and instill these easy steps, heeding the three A's, I guarantee when that shot happens you'll soon be putting your tag on game. Sure, you might miss your SPOT, but I'll bet you don't miss it by much. Aim small, miss

Actual aiming comes last in the aiming process, which includes picking a spot, allowing the pin to float, and then the release to happen on its own.

small! You certainly won't be missing vitals. Instilling these distinct steps requires some patient mental reprogramming, but practicing these habits during the off-season also means your hit-to-miss ratio will soar this season.

Instinctive Shooting

The AAA program, slightly altered, also applies to instinctive shooting, though sights and peeps are obviously removed from the equation. Instinctive shooting, as we determined earlier, is a form of directing arrows to the target without mechanical reference points—though it can always be argued that the arrow tip becomes a sight, even if you aren't gap shooting and consciously referencing it. It is easy enough to determine how dependant on the point of your arrow as a reference point you are by shooting at a lit candle on a black-dark night – in a setting where it's safe, of course.

Be that as it may, the process of "aiming" a traditional bow involves the same basic steps, though they generally become a bit more streamlined because of the fluid nature of shooting traditional bows and to a lesser extent, due to the lack of let-off and the urgency of releasing before muscles give out. Shooting a compound without sights also proceeds in the same manner.

What changes most dramatically is the instinctive shooter begins the actual AIMING process from the moment the target is addressed. The degree of concentration required of successful instinctive shooting is so intense the traditional archer picks a SPOT and begins "burning a hole through it" before even drawing the bow. Picking a SPOT becomes part of the ACQUISITION process and continues through the Step-3 AIMING as a continuous or fluid process.

Due to the fluid, instinctive style of shooting and the highly demanding concentration invested into every single shot, ACQUIRING the target and AIMING include an interesting facet normally not employed while shooting with sights – that of mentally creating your SPOT. Certainly, the instinctive shooter is well served by picking an actual, visual SPOT and concentrating on that. But the intense concentration required of "aiming" without sights, the Zen-like mental state that must be entered to shoot a sight-free bow extremely well, means a much deeper state of mental involvement is necessary. The traditional archer must envision the entire shot process, see every inch of the arrow's path before drawing, mentally seeing the arrow hit the SPOT. To help the brain wrap itself around these intense mental exercises the instinctive archer also creates their own SPOT as a way of funneling this visualization and concentration on and off at will. I have seen it suggested that the instinctive shooter visualize something highly familiar to them, like a coin, button or key. I visualize a laser dot. I pick a spot, and then place my laser SPOT on top of that point and concentrate on hitting it with every ounce of concentration I can possibly muster.

While engaged in doing this I draw my bow, anchor tightly, double-check shooting form all around, slowly pull my shoulder blades together, feeling them burn and simply allowing the shot to happen, the string slipping away like a tree shed-

Shooting sans sights demands intense concentration – picking or creating an aiming point and ignoring everything else.

ding a leaf. Even during fleeting shot opportunities requiring a snap-shot response, or at moving game, I create my laser SPOT, concentrate on it while allowing the shot, even when lead-off angles are involved, to just happen.

Of course any kind of mental visualization requires practice, especially for those with analytical minds who do very little day-to-day creative work. Mental visualization is something I will cover in greater detail in a later section called "A Strong Mental Game."

Mastering The Release

Releasing a bowstring properly, especially with fingers, is a difficult maneuver to explain on paper, akin to attempting to explain to someone exactly when to allow a baseball to slip from your fingers while delivering a fastball or cutting off a runner stealing second base. It becomes easier to explain what not to do, or at least habits to avoid.

Let's start with fingers: The first dilemma is just how to grasp the bowstring. Some try to grab the bowstring way out on the finger tops, believing they'll enjoy a crisper release, but this sacrifices a good deal of control and can lead to physically "crooking" the fingers into the draw to maintain that control. Obviously you don't want to get too big a bite on the bowstring, as this makes it difficult to get rid of. Whether shooting split fingers (index finger over the nock, middle and ring finger under) or Apache style (three fingers under the nock), try to envision carrying a paint can by its wire handle. You hook your fingers to the first joint and allow it to hang, your hand remaining otherwise relaxed. This is how you should engage a bowstring with fingers, which also allows better control of the arrow, avoiding twisting it off the rest or arrow shelf. Allow your strong shoulder muscles to do the work of holding full draw weight, keeping the forearm and hand re-

The finger release can involve compounds with sights (top), a compound without sights (left) or shooting instinctively with traditional gear like Fred Bear once did (right).

An excellent description of a proper finger release is allowing the bowstring to slip away like snow falling from a pine bough.

laxed, the fingers just hooking the serving.

The maneuver to avoid is consciously flicking the bowstring and arrow away upon release like ridding your fingers of a sticky booger, or plucking it like a guitar string. Just let it slip away like snow dropping from a pine bough. You should also strive for a surprise release, allowing the shot to happen on its own accord. The "1, 2, 3, Now!" release is the worst possible approach and generally leads to target panic, dumping the string as the pin sweeps across the target or your brain screams that the instinctive sight picture is correct. This is part of proper aiming, concentrating on the SPOT, allowing the pin to float, or remaining patient while instinctive shooting and until everything feels right, and allowing the shot to simply happen, the string slipping away and following through thoroughly.

Mechanical Release

Using a mechanical release makes things a bit easier, the reason some 70 percent of bowhunters employ them today. Although they make for a more consistent release, mechanical aids still come with inherent problems. The biggest of these is trigger punching, which is largely a symptom of popular wrist-strap, index-finger-triggered releases. This is a symptom of anxiety and allowing your desire to hit the mark override the need to perform a technically perfect shot. The finger hovers over the trigger while at full draw like a coiled snake, your pin sweeps over the bull's-eye or SPOT, and the snake strikes—NOW!!! It's a horrendous habit that should be avoided at all costs.

One solution is to shorten the extension shank of your standard wrist-mounted release so the jaws or open sear just reach the base of the fingers at rest. What this accomplishes is bringing the release trigger deeper into the index finger at full draw, preferably into the first joint (minimum) or the middle pad. This moves the trigger away from the overly sensitive finger tip where the release cut is more easily anticipated. This also more easily allows you to move all of your fingers as a single unit—like squeezing an ATV brake lever. This adds trigger control and provides a close approximation to a true back-tension release, insofar as that is possible with an index-triggered design. This involves pulling the bow into the draw stops, anchoring tightly, gently wrapping a finger around the release trigger, and then slowly pulling your shoulder blades together and into the draw stops until the pressure of the increased draw length pulls the trigger into the static finger.

True back tension is more easily applied with a hand-held T-handle, thumb-activated release. The same process is involved: reach your anchor, wrap the thumb around the trigger barrel, then slowly pull into the draw stops by pulling the shoulder blades together, the thumb pulled into the trigger barrel and cutting the shot. Of course, the thumb-activated release can be triggered conventionally, by simply squeezing the trigger barrel to slowly increase tension on the mechanism until the shot cuts. Even when used in this manner, T-handles with a thumb trigger promote a steadier, more even triggering because the thumb isn't nearly as sensitive as the tip of the index finger, making it more difficult to anticipate the cut-away.

Shortening release extensions and triggering with the middle of the finger pad provides better index-trigger control.

All Depends On Follow-Through

On more than one occasion I've had a friend on a hunting trip, or an acquaintance in the middle of a 3-D tournament, complain of a streak of bad shooting. I normally offer one simple piece of advice to see immediate improvements to their shooting: Follow-through. Follow-through is a simple process of continuing to aim intensely and holding steady through the release, shot explosion, arrow flight and impact with the target. I like to pretend I can direct my arrow's path—will it into the center of my SPOT—if I concentrate hard enough, especially when that arrow is in flight. Another friend, a longtime Army Command Sergeant Major, says he envisions a launched arrow as a Vietnam War-era wire-guided missile, which required continuous manipulation while in flight to hit the mark.

These are only mind games, of course, as I don't possess ESP and an arrow is not a wire-guided missile, and once an arrow is on its way there's nothing we can do to influence its final destination. What such a mindset does accomplish, though, is assure you don't bobble the bow or drop your bow arm during launch, which does effect where your arrow ultimately arrives. Any movement while the arrow is still in contact with the bow rest will result in that arrow going somewhere other than where it was directed. These are forms of anxiety or lazy shooting form. In the first case, the archer is so worried about where his arrow is going he jerks the bow out of the way to watch his arrow fly—most commonly called "peeking." The problem is, when that anxiety becomes intense enough that the release and peeking occur simultaneously, arrow flight will be negatively influenced, normally manifested in scattergun arrow groups as no two "peeks" come off exactly alike. By lazy I mean allowing shooting form to collapse or fall apart before the shot is complete. Each shot is completed only when the arrow sinks into the target.

The funny thing about peeking is there really is no need. If the peeking archer would simply follow through thoroughly and continue aiming smartly, their arrow will arrive on the mark nearly instantly.

Rock-solid follow-through is the cornerstone of every perfectly executed shot. Don't quit aiming until the arrow drives home.

Sloppy shooting form really is a form of laziness. Don't slack off just because you've released a bowstring. Hang in there another half second and your shots will proceed more successfully.

Other forms of bow movement are a matter of poor release or target panic. Flicking the bowstring like something sticky you want rid of, or plucking it like a string instrument, are common forms of a poor release that send arrows on errant paths. I've seen others who jab their bow hand at the target upon release like the gangsters in movies who "punch" their victims with each shot of a fired gun. It's also common for those suffering from target panic (a mental block causing them to freeze below the SPOT, among other symptoms) to twitch the bow upward during release. They get pretty good at it, too, timing the release and twitch flawlessly so a certain degree of accuracy is enjoyed—until they must shoot at an animal they want badly under intense pressure, turning the twitch into a jerk, the arrow yanked completely over a trophy buck's back.

Amazingly, many archers suffering from the worst kinds of trigger-punching ills like peeking symptoms, shooting-form collapse or target-panic flinches either have no idea they are performing these shooting flaws, or simply refuse to believe they are. One of the most revealing ways to closely examine these sorts of shooting flaws, or basic failure to follow through, is to video the shooter making a few shots. Video your hunting partner, progeny or spouse and have them video you in turn. This will quickly reveal and put to rest any denials of shooting form, release or follow-through failures. This allows the shooter to work toward solutions. Seeing is believing, and most smartphones available today have video capability that's plenty good enough for the task.

Shooting form isn't a mysterious form of tai-chi or intricate series of dance moves. Good shooting form is fairly straightforward; some would say based in common sense. But it is also something that must be engrained to the point of penetrating the subconscious, so even under intense pressure, when pulses pound and hands flutter, good shooting form sticks with you and helps guide you through successful shots at game.

To quickly detect shooting flaws, try videoing yourself shooting three to five shots and then study the replay afterward.

The bow setup is comprised of many parts working together. If those parts don't work in harmony, overall accuracy suffers.

CHAPTER 16

BASIC BOW SET UP & TUNING

IT'S BEEN NEARLY 25 YEARS since I've lived close to a town of any appreciable size. The only kind of action I've ever required to be near is rutting whitetails or bugling elk, and I have absolutely no need for, as every New York City denizen offers as if by rote, Chinese food at 1:30 a.m. This is how I've designed my life, though there was a time when living in the boonies and experiencing a bow or arrow emergency required time-consuming trips into town and a pro shop visit.

Long ago I decided that if I was going to get serious about this bowhunting thing I needed to learn to work on my own equipment and assemble the tools necessary to make that possible. So started a slow trial-and-error education, but we're talking the mid- to late 1980s. Today we live in the Information Age. The answer to any bow and arrow question you could possibly conceive of is now found in the pages of a multitude of books or magazines, not to mention numerous Internet forums.

Even if you live only minutes from an archery pro shop, it really does pay to learn to set up and tune your own gear. I mean, what happens if you're in a hunting camp far from home and something goes awry with your equipment? Let's say you've been dropped in the Alaska bush for two weeks, or drop-camped aboard horses deep into trackless wilderness. Without a handful of basic tools and some bow-mechanics know-how a simple equipment breakdown can quickly turn your long-anticipated hunt into a miserable camping trip.

Aside from such contingencies, the serious archer really can gain the confidence and independence that comes from assembling and fine-tuning your own hunting outfit. No doubt most pro-shop experts are absolute wizards at their craft, but they're also frequently harried during the busy season, rushing through work with a "good-enough" attitude. I don't want good enough. I want perfection. I take whatever time is necessary to assure that this is the case before I enter the field. This lends confidence, something more precious than all the shooting practice you might invest in.

In the long run setting up and tuning your own equipment saves time and money. Depending on your level of commitment, for all of the tools you'd need for a full-service bow shop of you're own, you're facing an investment of from $500 for basic, portable tools, to $1,200 for professional-grade tools. This means the difference between slower, portable options that can be taken into the field during remote bowhunts or more efficient, bench-mounted options.

This may represent an intimidating start-up cost, but by having a handful of friends chip in, or maybe even starting a local bowhunter's co-op, you can share the burden of initial setup. A small toolshed shop, or some basement or garage space and the right tools will set you up for complete archery independence.

TOOLS OF THE TRADE

The right tools are absolutely imperative. Just like any vocation requiring specialized tools there are universal must-haves that will see you through almost any job. I've long operated with fairly basic tools, including a handful of fletching jigs and high-speed cut-off saw, economy bench-mounted bow vice and bow press, and a small soft-sided satchel of hand tools doubling as a field emergency kit with the addition of a basic portable bow press.

Bow Square

A basic bow square—sometimes referred to as a T-square—includes a cross section holding bowstring clips and a longer extension 90 degrees to this. The shorter, bowstring-attached section holds a finely

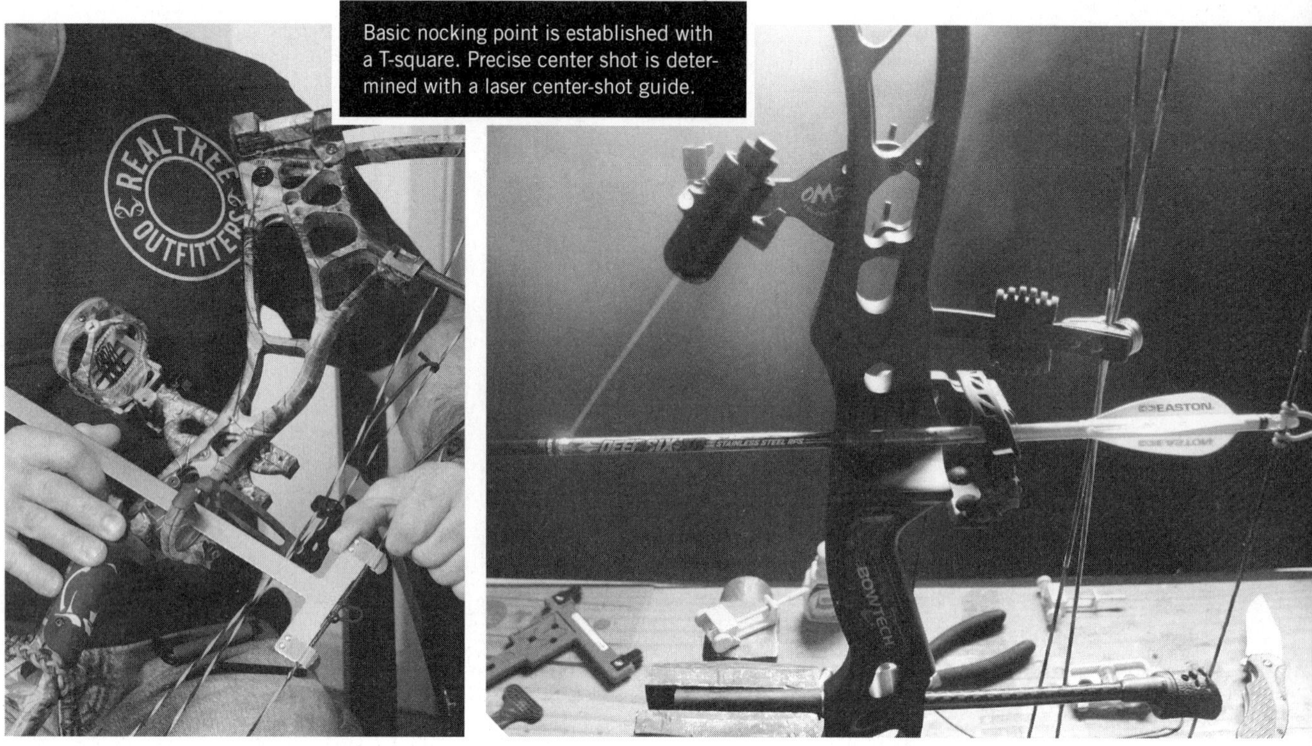

Basic nocking point is established with a T-square. Precise center shot is determined with a laser center-shot guide.

graduated ruler showing nocking-point center, the longer extension a standard 1-inch-increment ruler showing brace height. The bow square is clipped to the bowstring and moved up and down until the extension sits atop an installed arrow rest, indicating where the nocking point should be located, including zero-square and nock high or low in 1/32- to 1/8-inch increments. There are more precise ways to establish a nocking point, but for day-to-day nocking-point indexing and confirmation this is a fast, simple and affordable tool.

Laser Center-Shot Guide

Installing a new arrow rest should be taken a little more seriously than bolting it on the riser, eye-balling the center shot and calling it good. The arrow rest must work in harmony with the bow's cams and bowstring, and the arrow riding across it, to provide consistent accuracy. A laser center-shot tool takes all guesswork out of the equation. A laser center-shot tool, like October Mountain Products' OMP Tru-Center 2.0 Laser Alignment Tool, allows checking the center shot precisely from bowstring and nock to the arrow tip to get it perfect the first time. Now, some bow and arrow combinations will require slight tweaks inside or outside this center line to accommodate minor spine and draw weight incompatibilities, but it provides as accurate a starting point as humanly possible. The center-shot tool is attached to the riser or atop the installed bow sight with thumb screws, then a windage-adjustable, swiveling head that carries a bright red laser is tilted up and down a nocked arrow to reveal its relation to the bowstring and arrow rest. The laser can also be used to detect cam lean by shooting the laser beam across cam flats, split yolks then used to pull a tilted cam straight and improve accuracy.

Bowstring/Bow Level Set

One of my secrets to super-fine bow tuning is R.S. Archery's Bow Tuning Level Set and bow vise. This is used in addition to the bow square, which I consider a confirmation tool, for more precise nocking-point or string-loop placement. The set consists of a bowstring-attached level that clips to the serving and a spring-loaded level that attaches to an arrow laid over an installed arrow rest. The bowstring level is first clipped onto the bowstring serving and used to level the bow vertically and horizontally while it's held in a bench-mounted bow vise. The arrow level is then clipped to an arrow shaft set across an engaged (drop-away) launcher or rest arms and used to establish precise nocking point at the nock end, its graduated hash

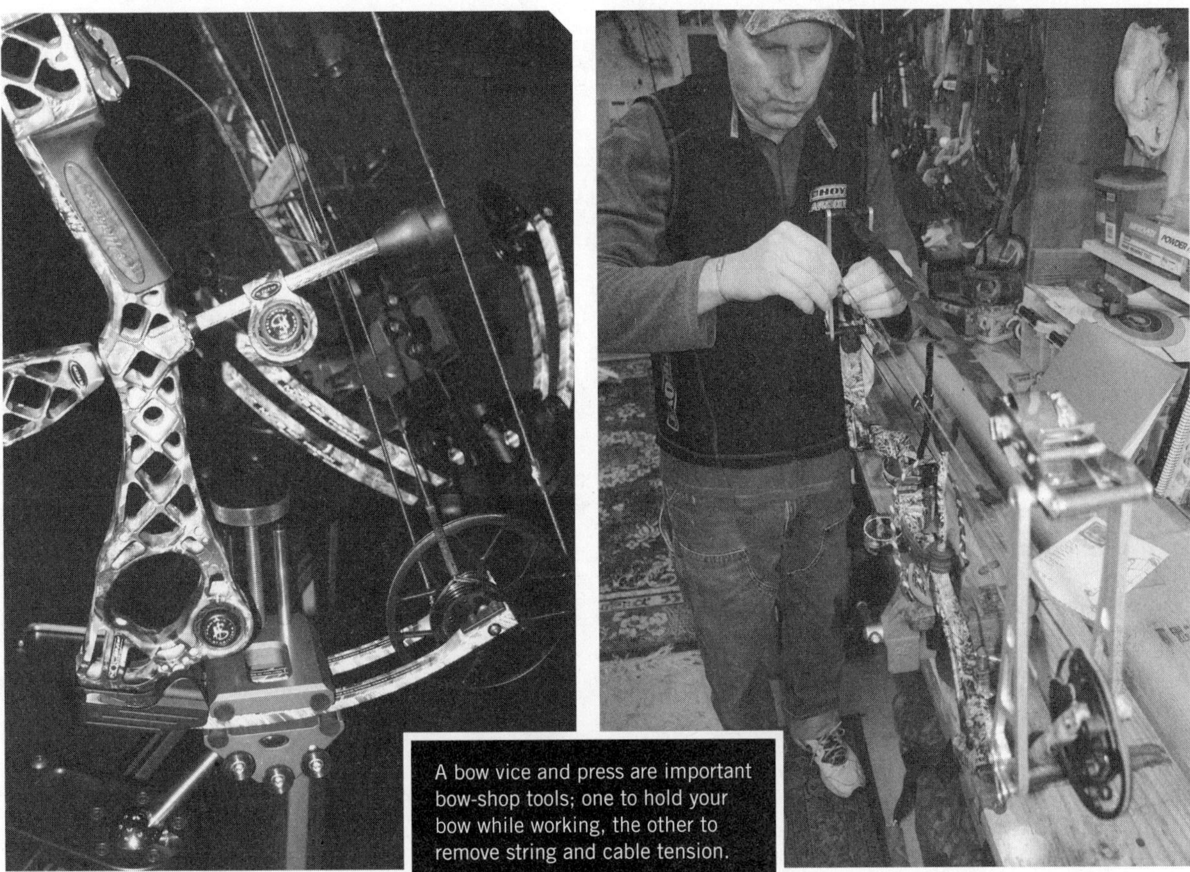

A bow vice and press are important bow-shop tools; one to hold your bow while working, the other to remove string and cable tension.

marks allowing zero level or nock high in 1/16-inch increments. I then mark the exact point with a silver felt-tip marker and proceed from there. The Bow Tuning Level Set also allows you to precisely establish second or third axis on the aperture-attached bubble levels of bow sights.

Bow Vice

A bow vice is part of using the Bow Level Set effectively. I once used an old solid-steel stabilizer attached to the bow and clamped in a standard bench vice for this work, but found that an actual bow vice is faster and less problematic. Bow vices come in a wide range of price points, but affordable models accomplish the same tasks as pricier units. Since I do a lot of home bow work I splurged on an R.S. Archery's Parallel Limb Bow-Vise H-D, its 55-degree leveling block and quick, secure and easily manipulated locking system makes it well worth the extra money. Back when I worked in retail, a cheaper Apple Archery Economy Bow Vise served me well.

Bow Press

A bow press is a necessary evil for all home bow mechanics and will also represent your largest investment. Whether installing new bowstrings and buss cables or replacing major parts such as a cracked limb or bent axle following an accidental dry fire, or everyday chores like installing peep sights, string silencers, eliminator and speed buttons, adjusting buss-cable timing or tweaking a leaning cam via a split-yoke system, releasing tension from the string and cables is necessary. Bow presses are certainly offered in affordable portable models that are useful for field work or at home if the price of a full-size model is out of the question, or there's not room for a bench-mounted unit. Full-size, bench-mounted bow presses are where real money comes in, but they make jobs faster, easier and much safer.

Two of the best deals in full-size bow presses include Apple Archery's Edge Economy Bow Press and Last Chance Archery's EZ-Green. Apple's Edge Economy Bow Press allows limb-tip (parallel) or conventional compression without introducing harmful limb torque, and is compatible with long

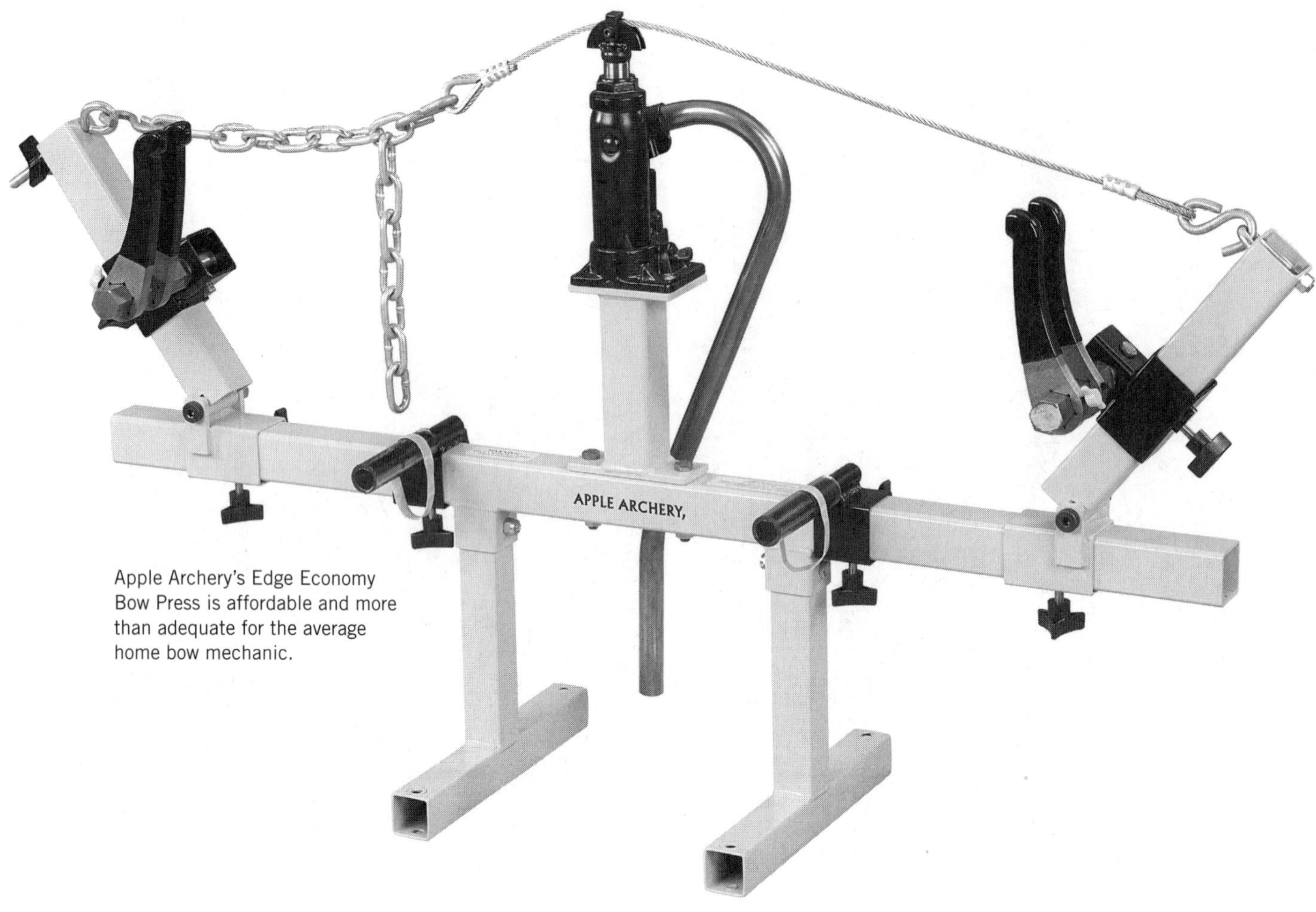

Apple Archery's Edge Economy Bow Press is affordable and more than adequate for the average home bow mechanic.

or short risers. Last Chance's EZ-Green is the press I use in my own shop—highly affordable, bench mounted, bare-bones but highly functional. The EZ-Green was designed especially for home bow mechanics and is compatible with any bow design.

For years I got along well with an affordable portable press from Bowmaster, which I still own and take along on remote or long hunting trips for emergency repairs. It slows the tuning or repair process, but are absolutely functional.

That Bowmaster I mentioned is now in its second generation, which includes special L-brackets to help accommodate modern parallel-limb bows. The G2 Portable Bow Press is smaller than the original and its L-brackets hook on the limb tips and a center-screw mechanism pulls limbs together to release string tension. It can be tightened with the included cross-piece, or with an appropriate size socket and ratchet wrench for faster take-up. RAM Products' Ratchet-Loc Portable Bow Press includes limb brackets, rubber-coated connection pins and a heavy-duty ratchet strap to remove tension from bowstrings and buss cables for maintenance or repair, even on bows with parallel limbs. Both models are compact enough to travel with or tote into wilderness backcountry.

Other Tools

I don't think there's a week that goes by that I don't use Allen wrenches to tinker with something bow related—from installing and adjusting sights and rests to changing draw-length modules or going over bows inch by inch and tightening screws or bolts to avoid potential disasters. I own two folding sets, big and small, that allow me to drop one into a pocket while sighting and tuning, or for packing when traveling – air travel has a funny way of loosening bow and accessory screws during transport. I own another, full T-handle set for regular home shop use.

Other tools that I find necessary include a string splitter, nocking pliers and string-loop tool, cigarette lighter, and basic tap-and-die set. String splitters help while changing peeps without the need to

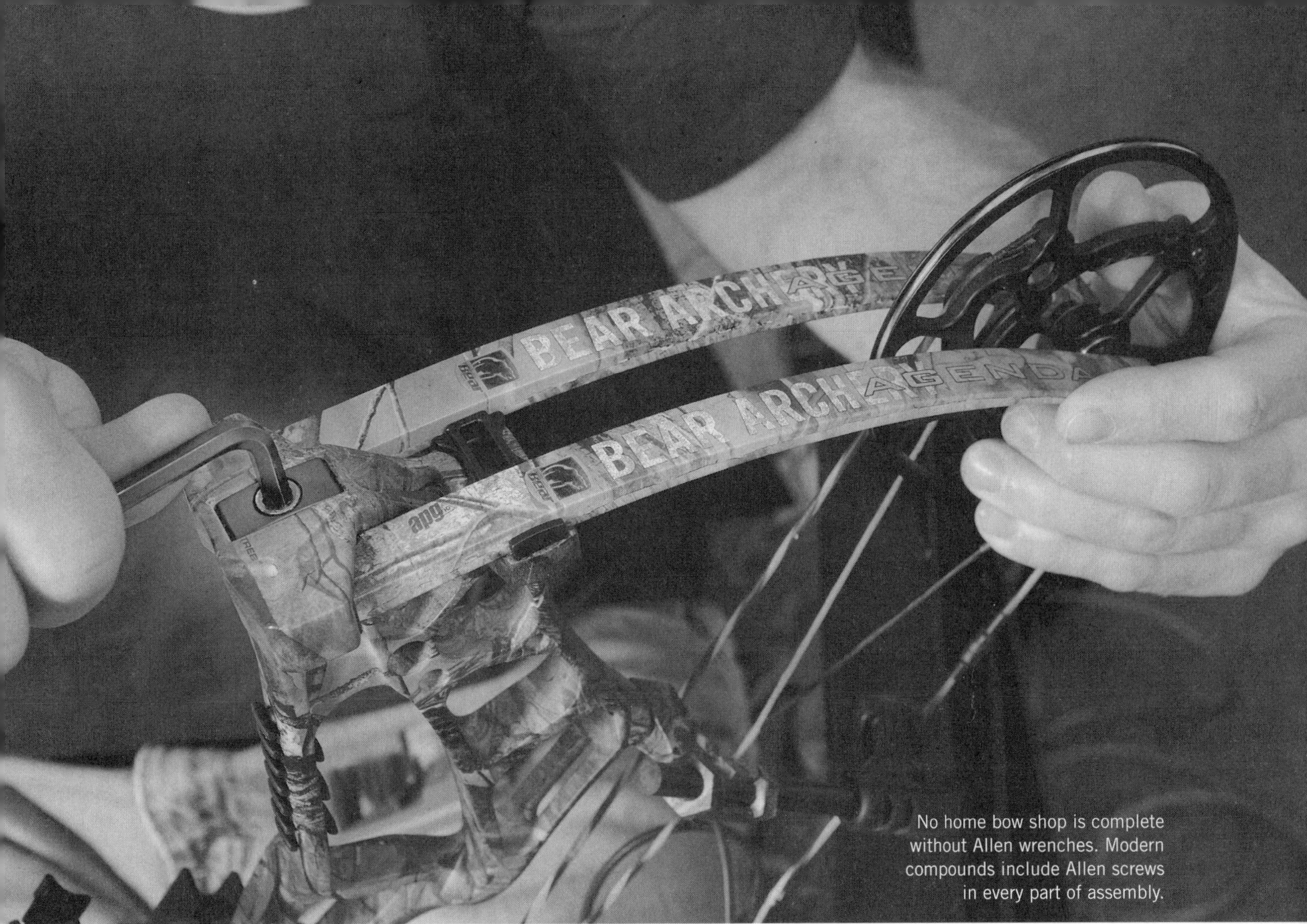

No home bow shop is complete without Allen wrenches. Modern compounds include Allen screws in every part of assembly.

press the bow, or to replace worn split-string silencers and similar jobs. They should have polished edges to avoid damage to string fibers during insertion. All-in-one nocking/archery pliers can be used to install and remove brass nocking points, pull serving tags tight and cinch string loops after installation. Easton Technical Products makes a useful one. Convenience-store butane lighters are used to burn tag ends after serving peeps, lashing drop-away rest activation cords or re-serving bowstrings. A basic tap-and-die set isn't an absolute necessity, but can save the day should you accidently strip or bugger an important accessory tap by over-tightening or cross-threading an attachment bolt.

INSTALLING THE REST

We touched on rest installation tools earlier, namely R.S. Archery's Bow Level Set. Of all the accessories you'll attach to your bow, none are as vital to accuracy as a properly installed arrow rest. To begin, bolt the rest to the riser, assuring it sits level to the arrow shelf, while pushed as far forward as possible without hindering the operation of the drop-away mechanism. Bolt it tight. With bows holding dual rest taps, and when there is enough room, I double bolt rests for added insurance. Rest elevation is adjusted to correlate to the mounting taps when viewed from the arrow-shelf side. This is the pivot point of most compound bow risers and provides correct height adjustment. Nocking-point position must revolve around this rest position, though slight adjustments to rest elevation can be made while fine-tuning nocking-point height – sometimes an easier option than moving an entire string loop or nocking points.

More care is required while setting rest windage, or center shot. Clamp the bow in a vice and level it. Step back three to four feet and sight along the cam flats and note the attitude of a nocked arrow in relation to the bowstring. An arrow tip pointing inside or outside the bowstring line should be adjusted until it sits directly behind the bowstring and is in line with the cam flats.

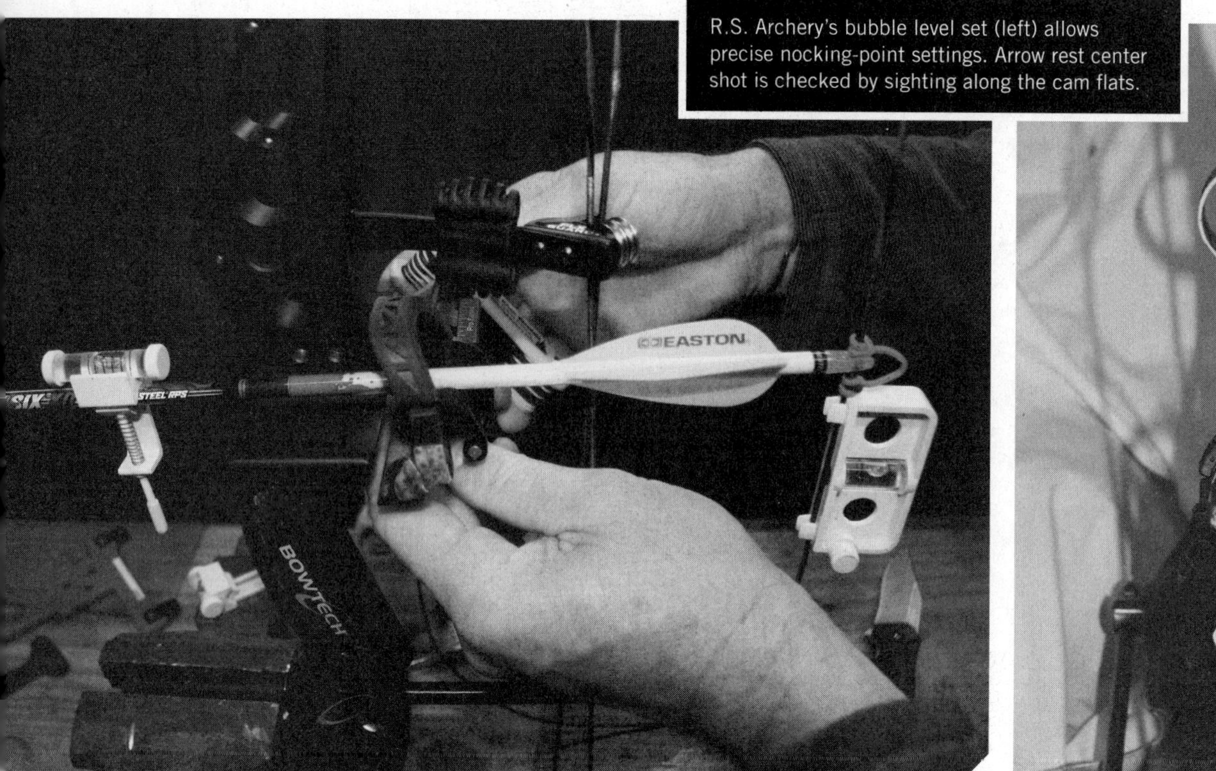

R.S. Archery's bubble level set (left) allows precise nocking-point settings. Arrow rest center shot is checked by sighting along the cam flats.

Now attach a laser center-shot guide directly to the riser with the laser head pointing forward on a new bow without accessories, or atop the sight bracket quiver mounts and pointing backward. Some low brace height bows, or those equipped with "bridged" risers, may require removing the sight completely, as buss cables or the riser bridge will interfere with the laser head when pointed back. Adjust the laser windage until it centers on the bowstring serving. Be precise, and assure the laser is aligned with the exact bowstring center.

Now pivot the swiveling head to run along the length of a nocked arrow holding a field point. If the laser begins to run off the left side of the shaft, adjust the rest arm away from the riser. If the laser runs off the right side of the arrow shaft, move the rest arms inward on right-hand bows, reverse this for left-hand bows. The goal is for the laser to run along the middle of the nocked arrow, all the way to the very tip of a sharp field tip. During fine-tuning some slight adjustments may prove necessary to accommodate slight eccentricities in the cam or riser attitude, or precise arrow spine with particular points or broadheads, but this is as precise a beginning as possible. The rest is now ready for fine-tuning.

SETTING THE PEEP

Setting the peep is another intricate step to bow set up. Start by tying a small piece of bright thread or rubber band to the bowstring in the general area you think the peep will be installed. Roughly sight in your bow sight for elevation and windage by standing 10 yards away from the target and shoot without a peep until the arrows impact slightly high of an established dot. Then draw your bow several times with the front sight installed and move that thread or rubber band up and down the string until you must sight through it at full draw while tightly anchored and set into a comfortable head position. Sometimes it helps to close your eyes, draw your bow and anchor solidly and settle into a relaxed feel before opening your eyes to note the position of the bowstring marker. When that marker hits the correct spot after several relaxed draw cycles, mark it with a silver, felt-tipped pen.

The bow must now be pressed and the bowstring pressure relaxed to allow inserting the peep on your mark. Avoid the temptation to shortcut the process by shoving a string separator through the bowstring, as today's bows are strung tighter than ever and modern string materials, while much stronger, are also

For absolute reliability through an entire season your peep should be served thoroughly and tightly into the string.

quite fibrous and easily damaged by abrasion. I use string separators only to replace peeps or string silencers already in place and providing an established gap to work into. Ideally the peep is placed between two separate but equal fiber bundles, marked by different material colors, to assure even pressure to each side of the peep and square rotation to the eye for each shot. This is less critical with peeps that include alignment tubing (a system I avoid whenever possible due to speed erosion and the added confusion or a potential breakdown), but it's still best if such systems sit square to the eye at full draw.

Square and consistent peep rotation is absolutely imperative with Tru-Peep-style peeps without alignment tubing. Today's creep-free string materials and pre-stretched finished product make this approach more practical. Once the peep is installed the bow press is backed off, string tension returned and peep attitude noted. Draw the bow multiple times to assure proper vertical positioning, while also checking rotation. The rare cam system introduces additional rotation to the peep after drawing, but most peeps, if sitting square at rest, will come back square after pulling to full draw. If the peep remains flush after initial installation, tie it in temporarily and shoot it 10 or 20 times to see how it settles in after break-in.

If peep rotation must be tweaked after shooting, return the bow to the press to relieve tension and transfer single strands of string material from one side of the peep to the other in even increments. Remove from the press and test again. This can prove to be a tedious trial-and-error process, but is vitally important, as a peep that turns anything other than square to the eye while drawing on game is unacceptable. Work with it until it is perfect, and then serve it into place securely.

To serve a peep into place start with a basic overhand knot above or below the peep (serve with existing string twist, not against it), make five to six tight turns of serving by hand over the tag end and bowstring, then pull the tag away and create five or six additional tight turns over the bowstring only. At this point you should have begun tightening the string split. While holding the existing work tightly to the bowstring, thread the loose end of the serving material through the open split (either side is fine at this point), then make four turns around one side of the split and to the peep, with two tight turns around the peep aperture proper (it should include a groove to accommodate serving material). Next thread the serving material through the opposite side of the string split and thread/wrap four turns to reach the beginning of the split opposite of the one already served. Make five to six tight turns around the bowstring only, and pull the split tighter. Lay a loop of extra serving material against the string, open the loop pointing away from the peep, make five or six more tight turns over this material and the bowstring. Now thread the serving tag through the open loop, pull tight to the bowstring, and then use the served-over loop to pull the serving beneath the wrapped serving and completely through. Use pliers if necessary. It helps to wax the loop to help it slide beneath the other serving wraps more easily. You'll now have a served-in peep with loose tags of serving material at each end. Pull these tags tightly toward the peep from each end with pliers. Trim to about 1/8 inch long and very carefully melt the tags to create a ball of material serving as a stop. Avoid heating the bowstring material – which is extremely vulnerable to heat. Dab a drop of super glue into each serving end and rub it in—likely an unnecessary step, but it provides bulletproof insurance.

The author adds a served nocking point below the nock inside his string loops to impart upward pressure and improve accuracy.

CREATING STRING LOOPS

More and more bowhunters every year adopt a string loop. String loops offer an accuracy advantage by leaving nock throats perpendicular to the arrow and static on the bowstring throughout the draw cycle, reduce center-serving wear and allow letting down without dislodging the arrow. No matter your nock-point option, string loop or direct hook-up below clamp-on brass nocking points, establishing precise placement is important. As already discussed, the most accurate way to establish nock-point location is with R.S. Archery's Bow Level Set. Be sure to first set your arrow rest to the proper height, and use the same arrow during measurements that you'll be hunting or shooting with. I once used white correction fluid to mark nocking–point position, but found it sometimes lacks durability, so have since adopted a silver felt-tip pen, a color that shows up well on any string material.

Installing a string loop involves taking a pre-measured piece of string-loop material and tying two opposing cow-hitch knots around the bowstring serving in the correct spots. That pre-measured length is from 4 (smallest loop possible) to 4-1/8 inches (standard loop), with the ends melted to create small balls of stop material to prevent knots from slipping under pressure. The knots themselves come easier with practice.

To start, with bow sitting in your lap or on a bench, riser pointing away from you, place the loop material under the bowstring, longer end pointing toward the riser. Wrap it around the bowstring and around the backside of the loop material and over the top of the bowstring again. Wrap it around the bowstring and insert the loop material through this newly created loop. Pull it tight to the melted ball end. Bend the material to the right to create a closed loop, the material tag placed over the top of the bowstring. Wrap it around the bowstring and thread the loop material through this created loop, pull it over the top of material and back beneath the bowstring, around the bowstring and through the smaller loop to complete the second cow hitch.

The actual string loop will now be flat to the serving, then open it by inserting a smooth needle-nose pliers and opening handles to pull the loop tighter. Move the loop ends up and down the serving to the appropriate marks you determined earlier, before cinching them tight with a string-loop tool or needle-nose pliers jaws. Micro adjustments can be made by twisting the string loop up and down the bowstring serving like a nut on a bolt. If this proves difficult due to the string loop being cinched too tightly, use the rest's elevation adjustments for finite tuning. Always double-check the positioning with a bow level before adding a small drop of glue to the inside of each string-loop knot.

OTHER NOCKING OPTIONS

Those who wish to hook up dual-caliper releases directly to the bowstring and serving, or those shooting compound or traditional gear with fingers, will normally employ a clamp-on brass nock. Painstaking positioning with the Bow Level Set is still important, especially while shooting a release attached directly to the serving. Standard procedure for decades has been to add dual brass nocking points above the nock with the bottom nocking point establishing the actual arrow nock positioning, and the upper as security against slippage due to upward pressure applied by release jaws. The only problem I have with this approach is that brass nocking points are heavy and any weight added to the middle of the bowstring erodes arrow speeds. I prefer to add a single brass nocking point and add serving as a safety stop above it. The serving material is lighter and just as secure. I've also eliminated brass nocking points altogether by creating a ¼-inch long nocking point above the nock, double-layered to provide the thickness required to prevent upward nock slippage, then super glue is applied and rubbed in after to increase the durability.

A rubber eliminator button is added below the nock while using the serving-direct hookup approach, eliminating wear caused by hard release jaws after repeated shooting. The eliminator button also prevents string pinch that can cause arrows to dislodge and fall off the bowstring after letting down without shooting. Most bowhunters who use this approach also added an extra layer of serving material below the eliminator button to absorb the brunt of abuse caused by release jaws. This ½-inch section of extra serving is replaced regularly to avoid damage to the main serving beneath.

Finger shooters need but a single nocking point located on the bowstring serving just above the arrow nock. This is nothing more than a locator point really, a point to align the nock to each shot for consistency. For this reason alone I long ago abandoned brass nocking points for finger shooting. They're heavy and groove my finger tabs. Instead I create serving-material nocking points. I start with slightly heavier serving material than the main bowstring serving, lay down an open loop with one tag end and wrap over that with the opposite end. I create a single layer of serving material, maybe three or four turns, before carefully turning back over those turns already laid down. When I reach the beginning I thread the loose end through the created loop, pull it tight to the bowstring and pull

Brass nocking points are easy to use but also heavy. Served nocking points are lighter and allow faster tuning for clean arrow flight.

Pins should center in the sight aperture, not crowd into the top or bottom. This provides faster target acquisition and aiming.

on the loop tag until it pulls the tag end beneath the created ball. I snip the tags short, burn them carefully and mash the melted material flush with my thumbnail to eliminate protrusions. I then apply super glue, working it into the ball of material and allow it to dry. This nocking point can now be worked up and down the bowstring serving like a nut on a bolt, allowing precise placement and fine-tuning. When I find a location resulting in perfect arrow flight, a drop of super glue is added to the upper edge of the nocking point to hold it in place.

SIGHT CONSIDERATIONS

Technically, anywhere your sight aperture happens to land after installation should allow unobstructed shooting, as long as the pins within are sighted properly. But this can result in pins bunched to one end of available aperture space, which isn't acceptable to me. Since my sighting system includes centering the round pin guards inside round peeps, I want my pins centered within the aperture to help my eye naturally center the sight during fleeting shot opportunities. Besides this, noncentered pins can mean running out of latitude at the bottom of the aperture needed for longer shots. Once I sight a bow in, if I find the pins aren't centered, I'll mark the pin gaps on the bow riser with a pencil, move the aperture for center, and then move the interior pins back to those established marks, shortening the sighting-in process.

While sighting in, thoroughly consider your most common aiming needs. Let's say you're a whitetail hunter who hunts thick cover where shots seldom exceed 25 yards. Do you really need 20, 30 and 40 yards from a three-pin sight? Maybe 15, 20 and 30 yards would make more sense. Conversely, let's say you're bowhunting pronghorns during rainy weather and know that snake-belly stalking will be the likely mode of operation. Shots are sure to run to the long end, so you've installed a five-pin sight. Now ask yourself, how likely is it you'll actually receive a 20-yard shot on open-country pronghorn? Might you be better served with pins set from 30 to 70 yards?

After sighting in I use Loctite Threadlocker on all sight bolts and screws to assure they won't work loose, and install aftermarket silencing accessories, like Mini LimbSavers, to eliminate small tuning fork hums upon release. A large rubber band—or those rubber bracelets so popular today—wrapped around a sight aperture really goes a long way toward making sights quieter.

PAPER AND BARE-SHAFT TUNING

If you've followed the previous setup advice closely your bow is likely fairly well tuned without further manipulation—at least for field-tipped arrows, and likely even while shooting mechanical broadheads. Fixed-blade broadheads, the fastest bows, long-range shooting and the tiny 12 rings of 3-D archery might also ask for further fine-tuning. To determine if bow tuning or human error is to blame for imperfect arrow flight, or less-than-stellar arrow groups from compounds shot with release – paper tuning is in order.

Paper tuning is nothing more than shooting arrows through taut paper at very close range to determine how arrows are behaving as they exit the bow. Obviously you'll need some way to hold a large sheet of paper taut while shooting, preferably at shoulder level. Commercial paper tuners—like Specialty Archery's professional-grade, stand-up Paper Tuner or more affordable, and highly portable, Paper Tune-It from 30-06 Outdoors are certainly available, and well worth the investment.

Staunch do-it-yourselfers can also construct their own paper tuner quickly and cheaply. Start by creating a simple, 2- to 3-foot square frame from inexpensive ½- by 1-inch wood, with longer extensions or legs left on the bottom to stand the frame in front of a target. Next, stretch plain white paper across your frame and anchor into place with a staple gun. Place the papered frame in front of a safe backstop to capture arrows when shot through the paper.

Now, using the arrows you'll be hunting with, and field tips matching broadhead weight, step three to five feet in front of the paper face. Draw and shoot through the paper, executing your best shooting form. As arrows pass through the paper they create tears, revealing how the arrows are behaving off the arrow rest. The goal is a clean arrow punch with three clean fletching slits.

An imperfectly tuned bow will create ragged tears

to the right or left, high or low of center. This indicates an arrow coming off the rest slightly askew. Flight is corrected by adjusting the rest, choosing a different arrow spine or tip weight.

Here is what those tears reveal for right-hand shooters – the reverse for left-hand shooting:

Paper tear to the right: Arrow is exiting the bow nock right. This indicates an arrow rest adjusted too far inward (toward the riser), an arrow with a spine that is too stiff or a tip weight that is too light. To correct such flight, move the rest away from the riser, working in small increments; choose a "softer" spined arrow of 250/.400 inch instead of 350/.340 inch deflection, for instance; or choose a heavier tip like 125 grains instead of 100 grains, for example.

Paper tear to the left: Arrow is exiting the bow nock left. This indicates an arrow rest that is adjusted too far outward (away from the riser), arrow spine that isn't stiff enough, or tip weight that is too heavy. To correct such flight, move the arrow rest toward the riser; choose a stiffer arrow spine of 350/.340 inch instead of 250/.400 inch; or a lighter tip of 100 grains instead of 125 grains.

Tear high: Arrow is exiting the bow nock high. Your nocking point or string loop is situated too high. Adjust it downward or move the rest/launcher up slightly.

Tear low: Arrow is exiting the bow nock low. Your nocking point or string loop is situated too low. Adjust it upward or move the rest/launcher down slightly.

Combination Tears: You may also find a tear, say, left and high, or pointing to the 10 o'clock position, just as an example. In these situations it's always best to work on one plane at a time, left and right first, and then up and down.

While shooting a release and modern launcher or drop-away-style arrow rest you should be able to produce a clean, "bullet-hole" punch and vane slices by working in small increments until perfection is achieved. Remember though, if you're shooting fingers some amount of horizontal tear is possible – and slightly high and left tears are common for right-hand shooters using a split-finger approach, because the bowstring rolls around the finger tips and away from the riser. Paper tuning allows you to minimize these effects, but some sideways push-away from the riser is acceptable.

If you're unable to create clean arrow punches after extensive corrections, or if tears prove somewhat random, you may be dealing with fletching contact. It's not unheard of for even a drop-away rest to result in fletching contact with launcher arms. The quickest way to know for sure is to spray-coat the entire fletching end of the arrow with foot powder and shoot it into a target. Any contact with rest arms will be revealed by scuffed-off areas of removed foot powder. Repositioning an indexable nock will generally solve the problem, though

Paper tuning reveals how arrows are exiting the bow and what adjustments must be made to promote laser-straight arrow flight.

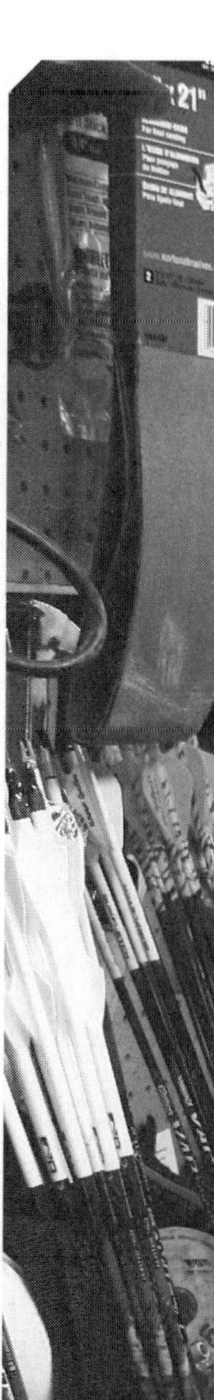

you may need to adjust a drop-away to fall faster – normally by tightening or shortening the activation cord, or by increasing the drop-spring tension when possible.

Bare-shaft tuning is generally most useful for tuning finger bows, particularly traditional bows. It is much the same as paper tuning, but instead of paper you are shooting an arrow stripped of fletchings (I add a length of duct tape to the arrow's rear to compensate for the weight of fletchings and mimic F.O.C. balance). Stand three to five feet from the target and shoot this bare shaft. Shaft attitude in the target face, just like paper tears, reveals how the arrow is exiting the bow. The same adjustments made in paper tuning apply here as well, though with traditional bows nocking point positioning and brace height (adjusted by adding or subtracting twists to the bowstring) can influence left-and-right arrow attitude due to the dynamic influence of fingers, as well as side-plate thickness. This is determined through trial-and-error experimentation. Overall though, with single-string bows, arrow spine and point weight are how recurves and longbows are tuned.

SERVING BASICS AND RELIABILITY MAINTENANCE

Bows are subjected to plenty of repetitive use and field battering. One of the most common wear points is the center serving found on all bowstrings; installed to eliminate nock and bow-arm slap wear to the actual bowstring material. Bowstring center serving requires periodic replacement, a job that is easy to accomplish if you own a string server. I own a couple serving tools, one each from Bohning Archery and Cavalier Archery/Arizona Archery

Learning to serve your own bowstrings allows you to replace worn or failing center serving, even in the middle of a hunt.

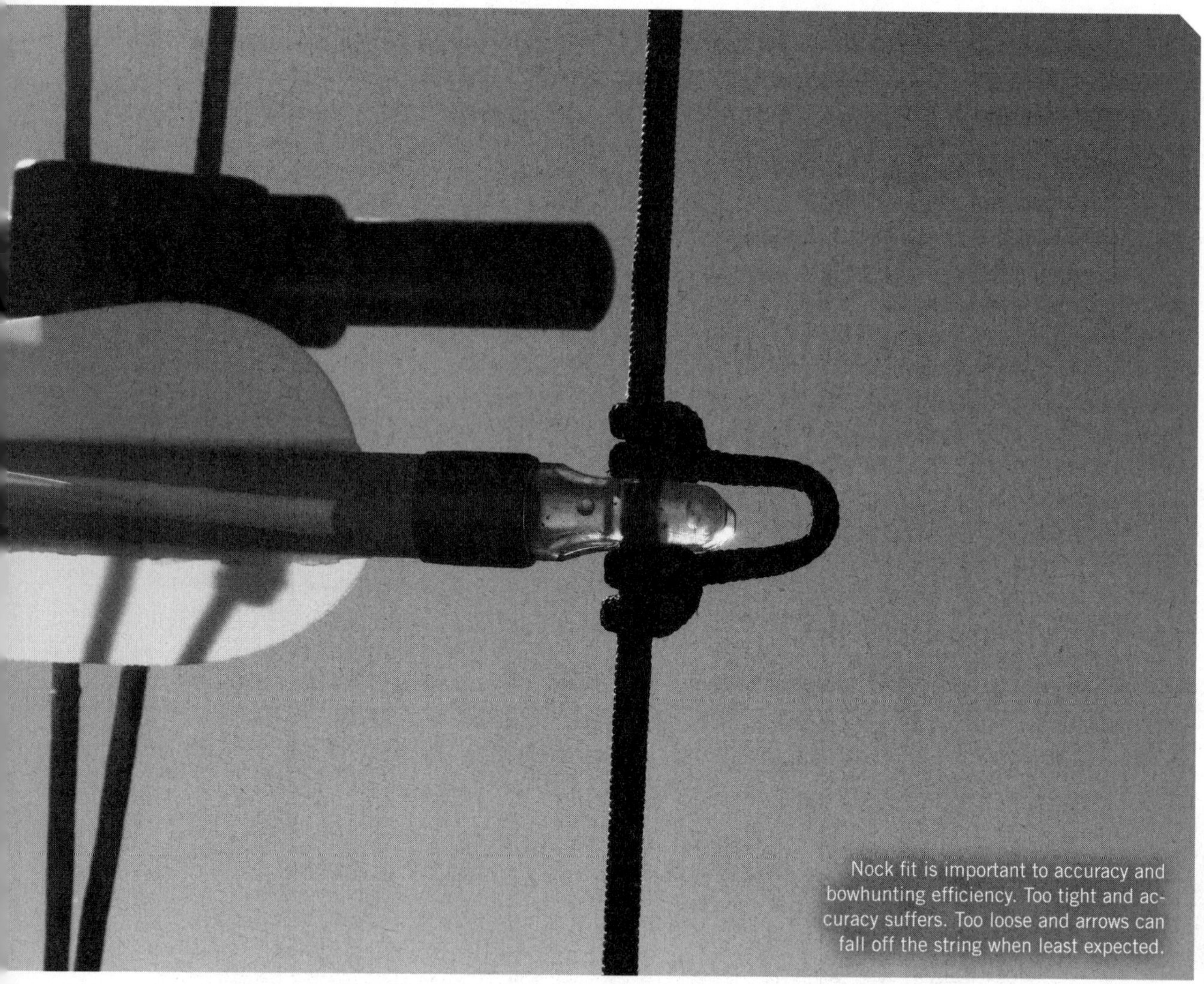

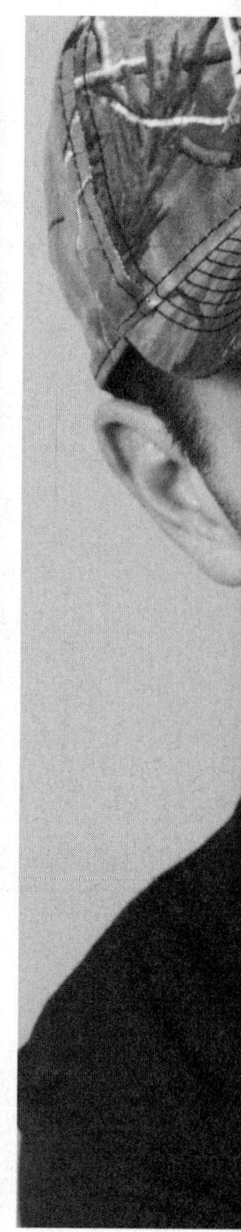

Nock fit is important to accuracy and bowhunting efficiency. Too tight and accuracy suffers. Too loose and arrows can fall off the string when least expected.

Enterprises (AAE), each retailing for around $20. Serving tools make quick work of replacing fraying or failed serving, their special serving-routing systems and tension bolts assure smooth, neat jobs often more reliable than original factory serving.

This also allows you to choose a serving diameter most compatible with the nocks you use most often. I find Bohning's .021-inch Braided #62 best for my needs, for instance, though I've used thicker serving on compounds with especially thin string materials.

A Quick Note On Nock Fit

Top-notch accuracy is only enjoyed when nocks fit the bowstring perfectly. You want a nock that isn't too tight – which would delay nock separation and cause premature serving wear, nor too loose – which would allow the arrow to fall off the bowstring at the worst possible moment or "rattle" off the serving during separation. Nocks should clip onto the string securely, but not so tightly they cannot be easily slid up and down the string serving with light pressure. If you nock an arrow and point the tip at the ground, allowing it to dangle, it should swing without falling off the bowstring, but a sharp rap of the fingers should cause it to pop loose.

Different nock brands and models own various throat diameters. When possible, visit archery pro shops that will allow you to audition a wide variety of styles until a perfect fit is discovered. Once you've discovered that perfect fit, stick with that nock religiously.

Serving diameter becomes trickier, as consistency in this area is also vitally important. If you've found a perfect fit, but are forced to replace serving due to normal wear, take a piece of that serving and carefully compare it to new material to find a perfect

Thoroughly waxing bowstrings and cables periodically helps to prolong their life and assure consistent performance in wet weather.

match – using a micrometer isn't out of the question. If your current serving doesn't offer a good fit with the nocks your arrows wear, don't hesitate to remove it and replace it with material that does. Once you've discovered an ideal serving diameter, pen it on the back of the bow's limb face so it's always handy.

Serving Application

Having your bow's center serving unravel in the middle of a big hunt can be just as disastrous as a cracked limb, except that re-serving a bowstring is so much easier to remedy. Serving a bowstring is much the same as serving a peep, but easier due to the addition of a serving jig. Start by tying an overhand knot, serving over the tag end of the beginning serving and bowstring five to seven turns, before pulling the tag aside and serving over only the bowstring. After reaching a point where you wish to tie the serving off, place a loop of spare serving over the string, serving over this and the bowstring five to seven turns. Cut the serving material, tuck the tag through the created loop while maintaining tension before pulling it beneath the overlaid serving with the loop. Use pliers to pull each end tight toward the center. Remember to serve with the existing twist of the bowstring material, as serving against the established twist can cause the serving to loosen. Cut the tags to about 1/8 inch and carefully melt them a with butane lighter. Add a drop of super glue to each end knot and rub it in with your fingers for increased reliability.

Wax For Longevity

It's also important to keep bowstrings and buss cables thoroughly waxed between hunts. This minimizes abrasion from dirt and debris, and protects

A comprehensive, compact field repair kit should be included any time you leave home, allowing you to take care of problems in the field.

from UV damage. This is especially true if your bow is subjected to persistent rain, muddy or dusty ATV rides, or bouncing rides in the bed of a pick-up. Bowstring wax is quite inexpensive and offered in easy-application tubes that are easy to drop into a hunting pack, bow case or field kit. Periodic use of string cleaners and conditioners, like Scorpion Venom Anti-Venom String Cleaner, prolongs the life of expensive bowstring and buss-cable sets—which can run in the excess of $100 today.

String wax and slippery silicone-based rail lube also help crossbow strings and cables last longer. Crossbow strings and cables, even more so than compound strings, are subject to intense wear, especially the bowstring riding atop the rail. Waxing your x-bow's bowstring regularly, and keeping the rail treated with a slippery lubricant will mean fewer maintenance problems and more reliable performance over the long haul.

Field Repair Kit

When I'm attending a big bowhunt far from home, especially forays to places like Canada, Alaska or Africa where bow shops can prove rare to nonexistent, I assemble and pack a basic field kit to address unforeseen breakdowns or problems. An example of the tools in my own field emergency kits include Goat Tuff's compact, lightweight GT Arrow Fletcher and a package of BloodVane fletching cartridges, which can be slipped over shaft ends and adhered into place in seconds without the need for the fletching jig. I also include the aforementioned Bowmaster's Portable Bow Press and new rubber-

Learning to repair your own equipment can save important hunts. There are no bow shops in the wilderness.

coated Limb Brackets to make it compatible with split and parallel-limb compounds. Easton Technical Products' Archery Essentials 12-Piece Pro Shop Tool Kit provides all the important tools needed to work out equipment glitches, Real Avid's Bowsmith multi-tool filling in the blanks that the Easton kit does not. Finally, I include Bohning's Mini Server, which includes 27 feet of .021-inch 62XS serving material. This leaves me ready for all but catastrophic bow failure and has saved several hunts.

BOW & CROSSBOW STORAGE

Compound bows and crossbows will do just fine between hunts and during the long off-season if left strung, but should both be protected from intense heat – especially avoid leaving your weapon inside a hot vehicle or in a sweltering summertime attic. Prior to each off-season I thoroughly wax the bowstrings and cables, wipe steel parts with a light lubricant, clean away any accumulated dirt, dust, grime or blood, and place my bow or crossbow in a soft or hard case. This case is stored in a relatively dark, cool place, like a spare-room closet, basement or store room.

Hopefully you have come away from this chapter confident that you can set up and service your own gear. The right tools and a little knowledge go a long way toward saving you money, assuring your gear is tuned to perfection, and that a minor breakdown won't ruin your bowhunting season or that one big hunt.

How well do you function under pressure? Mental prep and deeply ingrained shooting skills help you convert on tough shots.

CHAPTER 17

TAKING ARCHERY TO THE NEXT LEVEL

EVENTUALLY, DURING YOUR bow-and-arrow journey, you'll begin to want more from archery and bowhunting. For many this includes holding out for better trophy quality, maybe transitioning into more challenging traditional gear. For others this means breaking out of the whitetail shell and addressing black bears or wild boars close to home, or making annual trips out West to fulfill dreams of mule deer, pronghorn or elk. For me this eventually led to forays that greatly expanded my horizons and challenged everything previous bowhunting experiences had delivered. In part this included DIY adventures in the Alaska wilderness for caribou and moose, later the extreme conditions faced stalking mountain goats and brown bears, and ultimately multiple African safaris, including, with time, Big-5 dangerous game. These are bowhunting adventures offering new and exciting challenges, but also extreme mental hurdles representing real fear, extreme environmental elements, and foreign surroundings and or game animals. This is a perfectly understandable evolution, from casual backyard bowhunter to adventure seeker, as variety truly is the spice of life.

But that is not what I have in mind here, in and of itself at least. What I have in mind is asking more of yourself and your shooting capabilities, and especially dealing with debilitating mental stumbling blocks. I call this getting over the hump. It includes exponentially increasing hit-to-miss ratios, elevating your ability to successfully address dynamic hunting situations and convert on fleeting shot opportunities, extending maximum effective range—most of all, keeping yourself tightly wound when faced with season-making shots. Ironically, the kind of extreme adventures I've alluded to often require bowhunters to step up their game.

There is always room for improvement, even for the intermediate to "expert" bowhunter (a term that has always made me a bit uncomfortable) with many tagged animals to their credit. This usually involves breaking through a current plateau you've been stalled on for years. It means stepping outside of your current comfort zone and striving to improve performance in any situation. In the big picture, this involves whetting shooting form to a finer edge, expanding or honing skills already acquired.

In Africa, you make it bleed, you pay – adding pressure to every shot. Proper preparation leaves you confident in every shot.

On a micro level, this means sharpening the cerebral portion of your shooting program and taking a stronger, more confident mental game into the field that will allow you to achieve what you currently think is out of reach, while also remaining calm in the face of pressure. Or, if not calm in the real sense, at least maintain the ability to operate at a level required to pull success from difficult situations.

Everyone derives different pleasures from archery and bowhunting. Some only wish to use backyard archery or casual bowhunting as a way to blow off steam or relieve the stress of everyday work and family life. If that is all you require of archery and bowhunting, good for you. You need no instruction from me. If on the other hand you want more from archery and bowhunting—to win more 3-D trophies or fill more hunting tags—you'll need to work harder to take shooting your bow to the next level. Here is some advice for moving in that direction.

GETTING THE RANGE

Even in the age of laser rangefinders, more animals are missed due to misjudged range than any other factor. Arrows, even those from the fastest high-tech compounds, travel an arching path on the way to a target. Misjudge the range—or receive a bum reading from a modern rangefinder—by just 5 yards and you'll miss completely. Misjudge the range by fewer yards and you'll wound the animal, a worse outcome to my mind.

Of course nearly every modern bowhunter today owns and employs a high-tech laser rangefinder—or at least I hope so. The bowhunter who forgoes this modern machinery is either a hard-core traditionalist who shoots recurves or longbows and shuns technology completely, one who sits in trees in thronged vegetation and never, ever shoots past 30 yards, or is a cheapskate or a fool—or both. Few bowhunters have any business taking any shot past 40 yards without first confirming the range with a rangefinder. That being said, bowhunters who work to maintain eye-ball range-judging skills have a decided edge during fluid bowhunting encounters. I didn't say "No bowhunter," I said "Few." I can name any number of scenarios when quick decisions and old-fashioned range judging resulted in putting tags on exceptional animals—including both of my Boone and Crocket Coues whitetails and a B&C Newfoundland woodland caribou as highlights.

Shooting tight groups on the range and shooting well in the field are two different things, but the former can lend confidence to the latter.

"Hunts of a lifetime" can really put the pressure on, but proper preparation can make you mentally ready for the most stressful shots.

Admittedly, I had a jump in this business, having guided big-game hunters for years before laser rangefinders. In the days before Bushnell brought the industry its first affordable, civilian laser rangefinders it was a guide's job to feed his client an accurate range estimate before each shot. A guide's reputation and post-hunt tips were on the line. I had to be on the money, too, as the slower bows and heavier aluminum arrows of the day made today's arrow flight appear laser-like by comparison. Mostly the Eastern whitetail hunters were at a loss in the wide-open and unfamiliar West.

I spent a lot of time honing range-judging skills. I did a lot of stump shooting and small-game hunting, roving across deserts or through woodlands with a couple of Judo Point or blunt-tipped arrows. I'd pick a cow patty, cactus pad, stick, dirt clod or pinecone, or spy a jackrabbit or prairie dog, at an unknown distance, guess its range and take a shot. If I missed slightly high or low I'd shoot my second arrow to confirm I'd misjudged the range and didn't muff shooting form somehow. After shooting I'd step off the range to the target to reconfirm my estimates. That also instilled the idea of compensated range on steeply tilted ground and better imprinted arrow trajectory in relation to shooting obstacles. There is no better practice for bowhunting than stump shooting in the same terrain types you'll be facing come opening day. Treestand hunters, for instance, should seek steep banks or hillsides and practice shooting downhill extensively. Long-range shooters should seek open ground and stretch themselves to their limit—if for no other reason than introducing a dose of reality.

Weekend 3-D tournaments—the kind with unmarked targets, not target-head marked-range shoots, which defeats the whole purpose of 3-D competition—are also a great way to hone range-judging skills. Life-size targets set in realistic surroundings give you an ideal opportunity to test not only range-judging skills, but also to make that one shot count – as there are no mulligans in 3-D if you are playing by the rules. I also find myself guessing ranges during everyday life—walking across a hardware-store parking lot or inside a grocery store—and stepping them off to confirm. With enough practice eye-ball range judging becomes second nature.

Certain tricks help you become more proficient, especially in unfamiliar terrain where topography

The author engages in endless off-season roving or stump shooting, practice that he considers in many ways is superior to punching paper and foam.

Summer unknown-distance 3-D shooting is excellent practice for bowhunting, including the competitive pressure often felt.

and vegetation vary from that at home. One of the most important aspects of eye-ball range judging, as it pertains to 3-D targets or live animals in particular, is avoiding the inclination to guess the range based on the target or animal itself. Targets vary greatly in size and form. Instead pick a rock, patch of ground or grass clump immediately beside the target and address it as if you were stump shooting. This typically results in more accurate range estimates.

More importantly, learn to break the ground between you and the target into tangible increments. For example, you can give me a pretty accurate estimate of what 10 yards looks like, right? If not, step off 10 long steps, mark it and study it up close and from a distance. When addressing a target envision that same 10-yard "ruler" and count how many are required to reach it. With enough practice judging range in this manner can become nearly automatic. When shooting across open space—a deep gully or point-to-point in mountains—you can also learn to use pin gaps as a basic range gauge by determining the average back-to-belly measurement for area deer, for instance, and what gap it fits into at various ranges. A 30-yard deer might fit nicely between 50- and 60-yard pins; the 20- to 30-yard pin gap correlating to 50 yards, just as round-number examples.

Getting More From Laser Rangefinders

It's common to think of modern technology as infallible, but like any tool laser rangefinders are prone to limitations. To operate as designed, laser rangefinders send a laser to the target, the laser bounces off that target and returns to re-enter a microprocessor, which measures the interval between initial laser pop and return. The microprocessor translates that time into yards or meters. Two problems can arise: that laser encounters an obstacle on the way to the target, and the receiving processor does not "catch" the returning laser bounce. The first is self explanatory. If your rangefinder's laser encounters the smallest grass stem or leaf on the way to the target it will provide "short" readings. Conceivably, in windy conditions, a laser could be intercepted on the return trip by a waving grass

A large part of 3-D shooting is learning to judge range with your eye; a skill that can come in handy during fleeting bowhunting encounters.

There isn't always time to employ a laser rangefinder on game. Honing eye-ball range-judging skills can result in more punched tags.

stem. Failure to capture returning lasers bounces is generally more prominent at longer ranges, and can be caused by unsteady hands, the rangefinder housing moving slightly during activation so the returning laser misses the processing window. Receiving a misreading, or a no-go pop, is normally remedied by steadying the unit—using both hands or pushing the unit against your bow or other object. The more compact the rangefinder, the more likely this problem is to surface.

The issue of laser obstructions is likely the most common frustration with modern rangefinders. It's fairly common to encounter an animal well within bow range, a shot wholly possible, but after repeated attempts a clean laser reading isn't forthcoming. For instance, I remember a gorgeous pronghorn buck bedded on the back side of a grassy ridge. By slipping over the top of the ridge the buck was plainly visible, a shot entirely feasible but longish, but I just couldn't get a laser pop through the sparse grass that shielded me. My broadhead-tipped arrow would arch right over that grass and drop into the buck's vitals beautifully. Out of the purest frustration I eventually raised higher on my knees to get a clean laser path, but the sharp-eyed buck instantly sensed me and bolted.

In hindsight—and playing armchair quarterback from the comfort of my desk swivel chair—I might have ranged the grass beyond the buck, made an educated guess on how much ground needed to be subtracted to move back to the buck, and aimed accordingly. But, that was years ago.

Aggressive Ranging

Keeping a clear head is what getting the range off of something other than animal hide is always about. If it proves impossible to get a direct pop, leave it alone and move on. Sometimes you can "paint" the animal while using SCAN mode and watch the provided readings carefully until a yardage pops up that you intuitively believe is right, but again, this requires some degree of eye-ball range-judging skills. Here is yet another reason to keep eye-ball range-judging skills sharp—the ability to

Laser rangefinders are indispensible to modern bowhunters, but by no means infallible without proper precautions.

recognize red-flag pops while attempting to secure a precise laser range through scattered debris. When in doubt, range obvious obstructions to imprint that range, and accept no range to the animal itself that closely mirrors this.

But again, don't remain fixated on animal hide. If you can range something in the animal's general vicinity situated on the same plain, don't hesitate. Pop a range—from an overhead tree trunk or branch, a rock or patch of open ground to one side—get the range and make the shot happen. Be aggressive, but also strive for accuracy with these off-target laser pops.

Just as often, laser ranges are obtained before an animal moves onto a particular patch of ground. When a shot appears imminent, like when stalking or calling for instance, I'm constantly taking laser pops on the ground before me. An elk may be 80 yards away but moving in my direction after responding to a call, but I'm taking inventory of every shooting lane he could conceivably enter. As he moves into range, even if he's still screened by brush, I'm anticipating his next move and attempting to remain three steps ahead of him, ready for instant action when he steps into a clean shooting lane. Opportunities can last but a finger's snap. Don't waste that opportunity working to get a laser pop off the animal itself. You should already know the range, based on a particular rock or grass clump, before that animal steps clear, already drawing your bow for a quick shot. Stay on top of developments—don't wait for opportunities to drop in your lap.

Missing Obstacles

Laser rangefinders also prove useful to help avoid arrow collisions with overhead obstacles. Let's say you've slipped over the lip of a sudden canyon edge after dogging a bugling bull elk for several miles, finding him standing broadside at a laser-marked 42 yards. You start to draw but notice overhead fir branches that long hours of stump shooting and intuition tell you will just barely interfere with the apex trajectory of your shaft or just barely clear. Do you hope for the best and shoot anyway? The bull is horning a sapling and not going anywhere for the moment. He's a monster bull and you want to make it good. So you pop the branches in question, seeing they are 23 yards, ditching the rangefinder in a silent hip pouch. You hit full draw and place your 40-yard pin in the middle of the bull's ribs, but take just a moment to consult your 20-yard pin. As suspected it is just at the bottom edge of those branches. You take a long step backwards to lower your stature, creating more space between those branches and your 20-yard pin and trip the shot. The arrow flies clean and the bull is all yours!

This procedure can also be used on smaller holes through brush, "threading the needle" to reach vitals beyond as it's sometimes called. Let's say a rutting whitetail has paused near your stand, trying to figure out where that grunt you produced came from. You have a solid idea of how far that buck is after previously ranging objects around your stand, but a single forked oak branch hangs between you and that buck. There is an opening through that fork, but is it wide enough? Use your rangefinder to find out. Range the top edge of the fork, come to full draw, place the proper pin on the buck, consult your pins again to see if a pin correlating to the range of the fork is buried in wood or leaves. If it isn't, let 'er rip!

Ranging Off Level

One factor of laser rangefinders that every archer must be conscious of is ranging steeply uphill or down. The problem with laser rangefinders is that they range, well, straight as a laser. When shooting steeply downhill or from an elevated stand—or uphill, more likely on Western game—a straight-line range will cause you to shoot high. This is a geometrical factor called Pythagorean Theorem, but basically all you need to know is that angular distance is always shorter than line-of-sight distance.

Adjusted range is most easily determined from a treestand. While earmarking ranges around your stand, instead of taking laser pops directly off rocks, sticks, stumps or patches of dirt at ground level, take readings off of tree trunks on the same level you sit. By taking ranges in this manner you've received the compensated range for anything standing at the bases of those trees. This can prove more problematic when operating from the ground, say when dogging bugling elk in mountain terrain or coming at a bedded muley from above, but it's still possible under the right conditions. Whenever possible, attempt to range treetops on the same level as you stand to receive the correct range for any animal situated at the base of that tree—or at least a usable approximation.

Shooting steeply downhill can confuse the range-judging routine. Tilt-compensated laser rangefinders offer a solution.

Steep uphill shots are another matter. Unless a bighorn ram or mountain goat billy stands on top of sheer cliff, allowing you to pop a straight-line range into a vertical-cliff base, you're going to be left guessing. But you can make that a best-guess estimate. Say you're looking up a steep hillside at a bugling elk. Take a straight-line pop to that animal. Now turn around, and with the laser rangefinder attempt to find a tree at that very range (granted the downhill slope mirrors that of the uphill slope). Range that tree's top to get a compensated range. In areas without trees, obviously, you're outta luck...

Technology to the Rescue

Of course, technology commonly solves our most common reoccurring vexations. In regards to overhanging branches, Nikon offers the The Truth Laser Rangefinder with ClearShot Technology. The unit includes an interior mechanism that allows inputting your bow's actual speed; afterward a second red dot situated above the sighting dot shows the level to which arrows will clear at a given range. Range an animal, and as long as the upper dot is clear of brush, you'll receive a clean shot to that animal.

More common is angle compensation. Halo Rangefinders calls theirs AI Technology, Bushnell ARC (Angle Range Compensation), Nikon ID (Incline/Decline) Technology. What they all have in common is providing compensated ranging on steep uphill and downhill shots. This technology does require a careful approach, starting the rangefinder on the level before carefully tilting it to address the target to assure dead-on readings. They are especially useful for treestand and mountain use, and this feature adds only about $100 to the cost of the unit, on average.

SUPER TUNING YOUR BOW

For the average bowhunter paper tuning is as far as you need to take the process. A clean arrow punch is normally all you need to shoot even fixed-blade broadheads at moderate ranges. But if you want more from your equipment, one-hole accuracy with fixed-blade broadheads and more consistent accuracy at longer ranges, you'll need to push tuning to the next level. This is accomplished through in-line tuning.

In-line tuning was conceived specifically for fine-tuning compound bows shot with releases. It provides feedback regarding precise rest alignment. To begin, stand 20 yards from a large target face and fire a three- to five-arrow group at a small aiming point located on the upper edge of your target. Strive for a technically perfect shot each time and heed the bubble level on your sight to assure you're holding your bow perfectly plumb. Now hang a chalk line from or hold a carpenter's bubble level to the arrow located as close to the center line (elevation is of no concern) of the group as possible. Create a plumb/vertical line below that arrow. Walk back to 30 yards and shoot another group while holding your 20-yard pin on the same aiming point used for the first group. Continue moving back in 10-yard increments and assembling groups, always holding the 20-yard pin on the original aiming point at every range – enlarge the aiming point if necessary to see it as the range increases, until groups become inconclusive or you run out of target. All groups, regardless of range, should group on the vertical line.

Persistent grouping to the right indicates a rest that needs to be moved left (work in very small increments), left groups meaning the rest should be moved right for right-hand shooters, the reverse for left-handed. A perfectly tuned bow should consistently assemble arrows on the vertical line, no matter the range.

The next step is to assure broadheads and same-weight field tips impact exactly alike. Assemble six arrows, three with field tips and three with broadheads. Create a clean face with butcher paper and create a new spot and vertical line. Start at 20 yards again. Shoot the broadhead arrows and mark the group before pulling, followed by field points – shooting all into a single group will likely result in broadheads damaging the fletchings, or field tips damaging broadhead blades. Note any discrepancies. Broadheads that shoot higher than field tips signal a need to lower your arrow rest or raise your nocking point—again only slightly. The opposite is true if broadheads group below field points. If your broadheads impact left of the field points, move your rest right; vice versa for right impacts. Recall

In-line tuning reveals tiny tuning flaws in your equipment and helps you super-tune gear for increased long-range accuracy.

that you're making adjustments by tiny degrees, like hair-widths. Broadheads and field tips weighing exactly the same should group as one from a well-tuned bow—end of discussion.

EXTENDING MAXIMUM EFFECTIVE RANGE

Your maximum effective range, or MER, is the point at which you can assemble five out of five arrows into the circumference correlating to the vital area of the animal you're pursuing. Eight inches for pronghorns or small deer, 10 inches on average for large deer or black bear, 14 inches for elk, just as examples. Taking the life of another living creature is damn serious business and two out of three isn't good enough. Range is most emphatic to bowhunting because bows and arrows are inherently short-range weapons, even as technology advances, and getting close is still the name of the game. Extending your maximum effective range by only a small margin brings more animals into your bowhunting sphere over the course of a season, increasing your odds of success with each yard added.

That's straightforward and grounded in common sense, but to put this into sharper perspective let's do some math. Let's say, just for the sake of argu-

Increasing your maximum effective range—meaning five out of five shots in the vitals—only 10 yards will put more game within reach.

ment, your current MER—five out of five arrows into the kill zone—is 20 yards. Let's also pretend you occupy a treestand allowing unrestricted shooting in all directions. Since scent is always a factor in bowhunting, let's also remove a 20-degree wedge downwind of that position, the "stink zone" any big-game animal will vacate immediately. With a 20-yard MER you're master of 1,187 square yards (don't ask me for the formula, I'm a writer. An engineer buddy ran the numbers for me). That's a decent chunk of ground when put into those terms. But...let's say you double your MER. What is gained? A MER of 40 yards means you're now in command of a whopping 4,748 square yards, three times more ground or slightly more than an entire acre (39.25 yards). If you wish to command 2 acres, your MER need only be 55.5 yards. As you can see, a minor gain in MER makes a huge difference in potential shot opportunities.

If you've run out of ideas to improve your shooting, don't be too proud to hire a professional shooting coach.

Now with this gain in range capabilities comes much responsibility. Target groups should never be confused with field capabilities while under the pressure of shooting game. In most cases, I'd say it's safe to assume the average bowhunter looses 15 to 20 percent of their MER while shooting at game, particularly trophy-size game (whatever that might mean to a specific shooter). Food for thought...

And I always come back to that five-of-five qualifier. Two out of three doesn't cut it in the field.

Shooting-Form Tune-Up

The first step in extending your maximum effective range is determining what part of your shooting form or routine is currently holding you back. I've guided enough sports to witness the camp hotshot, the guy shooting lights out at 90 yards on the camp targets, but can't hit a 1,000-pound bull elk at 20 yards broadside in the field. This is strictly mental and something I'll delve into more deeply later in this chapter. What I'm talking about here are strictly physical aspects of shooting form that are preventing you from shooting your best – though at some point in your shooting journey all shooting form is technically mental, but let's not split hairs.

We've already discussed all of these points in great detail in Chapter 5, "Shooting Your Bow." But if you're to break through your current glass ceiling those "rules" must be revisited and examined in greater detail. Obvious accuracy robbers are improper grip, incomplete follow-through and anchor, and a less-than-ideal release. Remember that small influences are exponentially compounded as the range increases. Fine-tune these four aspects of shooting alone and you're well on your way.

I generally accomplish such fine-tuning by blind or blank-face shooting. By blind I mean literally blind. This is best performed with a hunting partner, taking turns watching one another to assure safety. Start by pulling a blindfold over your eyes and shooting into a large backstop, which allows you to feel every small aspect of the shot. It doesn't matter whatsoever (save safety) where your arrows go, it's all about the feeling and mental visualization of the perfect shot, working through each step of the shot process while seeing it in your head in great detail. Removing visual feedback also generally removes anxiety, allowing you to reprogram your mind for a relaxed shot sequence.

When alone and unable to safely shoot blind, blank-face shooting is the next best approach. This means wallpapering your target in clean paper and leave your eyes open, but perform the same feel-based, aim-free shot process. Pick a clean patch of target to shoot into for each shot, and don't give a thought to where arrows hit, aside from obvious safety. When I feel myself growing glitchy I return to these shooting exercises to calm my nerves and reinforce a flawless shot sequence.

The self-aware archer may be very well aware of chinks in their shooting regimen. I know, for instance, that I have a tendency to rush every shot, especially under pressure, failing to really settle in and allow the release and the shot to happen on its own. When this bad habit grips me I somehow need to get every shot off under some unspecified time frame. It's a symptom of target panic that I must work on diligently to keep in check. My shooting training, therefore, is largely based on calming these symptoms. You, on the other hand, may have no idea what is holding you back. That is why I always encourage bowhunters to swallow their pride and seek the assistance of a professional archery coach, or at least a highly seasoned archer who can watch you shoot and point out deficiencies. This provides a starting point to help you make your practice sessions more productive, moving forward instead of reinforcing bad habitats that erode shooting accuracy.

I mentioned it before, but it bears repeating: I really believe in the power of video. Have someone video you shooting five or more shots, or simply set the video camera on a tripod and film yourself, without the distraction or pressure of outside influences (which a good shooter should be able to withstand, by the way). Study these videos carefully, taking notes on what improvements can obviously be made and others that might need a little work. Prioritizing your shooting flaws is also important. You can't work on all your problems at once; it's simply too overwhelming. Pick the most debilitating and work to rid yourself of just that one bad habit before moving on to the next. Remember, psychologists remind us that no fewer than 21 days are required to rid yourself of any bad habitat in any lasting manner. Be persistent, remain disciplined, and bad shooting habits can eventually be erased.

Stepping Back

Interestingly enough, if you wish to extend your maximum effective range, you'll have to step well out of your comfort zone—meaning literally stepping away from your target. There is more to long-range shooting proficiency than nailing a single-pin mover sight to your bow with pre-set yardage tape set to 100 yards. You'll need to earn this. Long-range shooting is partly diligent, savvy practice, but to an equal extent overcoming mental hurdles. Shooting well at long ranges is about first building confidence and dispelling inherent disbelief. In theory, if you must shoot a multi-spot target at ranges less than 25 yards because a single-spot target would almost certainly result in blasting nocks off, your 60- to 70-yard groups shouldn't expand beyond the dimensions of the vital areas of average big-game animals. I've even seen formulas offered,

Super-tuning your gear and shooting skills will tighten up groups at long ranges, equaling more in-field success on game.

translating close-range groups into measured arrow clusters likely to result at longer ranges. Groups, say, increasing 20 percent for every 10 yards added, just as an example. This is pure-and-simple hogwash. Such formulas fail to take into account the mental factor, which largely stem from a fear of missing, and the knowledge that added range increases the likelihood of that outcome.

Modern archers, with all their bowhunting education brainwashing, have assumed an ethics of mediocrity that did not burden archers of old and their hugely inferior equipment. It's as if bowhunting education has no room for qualifications, so all archers must live by the lackluster standards set by those with lackluster passions for bettering their shooting skills.

Still, the fear of missing is stronger in some than others. This can be alleviated to some small degree by investing in a larger target. I own a 28" x 47" BLOCK Range Target for this reason alone. Most of my anxiety, though, is grounded in the fear of losing expensive arrows, as my backyard includes swallowing brush and grass. To alleviate this anxiety I used our tractor bucket to push up a decent-size earthen backstop behind our targets. Should I miss the entire target—which will happen when you begin stretching your limits—I'll invariably find my arrow stuck into the side of that backing dirt pile. This allows me to concentrate on shooting, and forget about recovering arrows afterwards. A levee or pond dam, large pile of sand or haystack can serve the same purpose.

By stepping away from the target, I mean stepping well back. During hunting season I generally warm up with a handful of 20-yard shots, then move back for a few 30- and 40-yard shots before preparing to climb into a stand. During the off-season, when I'm striving to extend my maximum effective range, I warm up at 60 yards and move back to shoot at 80, 90 and 100 yards. Beginning this shooting program after a winter without any significant amount of shooting and a spring of short-range turkeys, is always humbling. Eighty-yard arrow groups I can't take in with both arms are commonplace, but with enough persistence I begin bearing down, concentrating that much more intensely, and groups begin to slowly shrink. By the end of summer, with early archery seasons looming, 80-yard groups have dwindled to the circumference of any big-game animal's vital area and 100-yards groups are less than a foot in diameter.

Now, understand, I generally have absolutely no intent of shooting at unwounded game at such ranges. But after a summer of practicing at such extreme ranges, shots taken at 40 to 60 yards seem like child's play. And I did qualify that statement with "unwounded." If I get involved in some goat rope where a friend or I have gut-shot an animal and that animal pauses on open ground at 110 yards, I'll without a doubt poke another hole in him someplace. When attempting to recover any wounded animal, any additional holes you can introduce to the equation bring you that much closer to recovery.

Long-Range Gear

Early in my bowhunting career long-range shooting—at, say, nongame prairie dogs or jackrabbits—meant pin stacking, or holding existing pins (20, 30 and 40 yards normally) well over the target while counting gaps established by those pins. It wasn't very precise, as can be imagined, entering the realm of *Beverly Hillbillies'* Kentucky Windage. That situation is no longer necessary. Run-of-the-mill bow sights can now hold five pins, serving bowhunters well from 20 to 60 yards; or 30 to 70 if you're anticipating longer shots and start the sight-in process at 30 yards. More common today is the seven-pin sight, theoretically leaving the bowhunter ready for any shot from 20 to 80 yards. Such a sight is like a four-wheel-drive truck. You likely won't use it to its full potential 95 percent of

Don't rely on "Kentucky windage" for long-range shooting. Instead, invest in a sight with enough pins to allow point-on aiming.

Mover sights are excellent long-range tools, but a clear head is required when presented with a shot to assure the range is dialed in correctly.

the time, but when you need it, you need it desperately. Such a sight saved my butt on one of my most recent bull elk. I'd taken a quartering-away shot at 43 yards, daylight draining away fast and threading the needle through a basketball-size hole in second-growth firs. When the 6x6 cleared the brush I could see that I had bitten off a bit more than my arrow and broadhead combination could chew. I sprinted a wide loop to cut him off, finding him standing at a guesstimated 85 yards, and gave him another one, which slammed into his lower shoulder with very little penetration. The first shot nipped the liver and a single lung, and killed him. But I trailed him from the blood left behind by that low shoulder hit.

A lot of pins can prove obviously confusing. That's where all of that long-range summertime practice pays off huge, making you more familiar with your pin layout and corresponding yardages. If you're in the habit of switching equipment setups or just sights between seasons—early-season pronghorn and elk versus November rutting whitetails for instance—it's wise to assure the pin layout on your three-pin sight closely mirrors that of your five- or seven-pin sight. Adopt a color-code order and stick with it, in other words. For me that's green (the brightest fiber-optic hue to my eyes), yellow, red; repeated to the bottom of the stack. This can prove a bit tedious, purchasing extra pins and doing some musical chairs to get them arranged correctly, but will help avoid unwanted confusion when shooting under pressure. In general, I prefer fixed pins, as bowhunting is seldom static and unexpected shot opportunities are common, and I don't like to be left scrambling when presented a sudden shot opportunity. I also prefer multi-pin sights with graduated-diameter pins, like

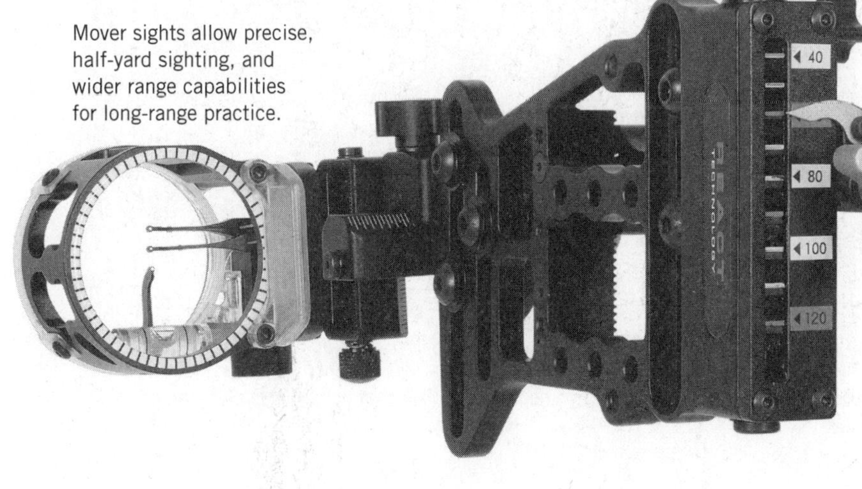

Mover sights allow precise, half-yard sighting, and wider range capabilities for long-range practice.

those from TRUGLO, including larger .029-inch pins up top, medium .019-inch pins in the middle and finer .010-inch pins on the bottom. This allows brighter aiming points for closer shots and finer pins for longer shots.

That being said, there is a lot to be recommended in a quality mover sight in long-range situations. They allow dialing range more precisely—no best-guess gapping for odd ranges, like 33 or 47 yards, just for example—not only adjustable for any even yardage, but half yardages as well. True long-range shooting seldom entails the urgent time frames presented at closer ranges. At the least, long-range shots should include a bit more contemplation, including reading the game animal's body language to determine if a shot should be taken at all. Swiveling heads, darting ears, stomping feet or a generally nervous nature should signal a pass on any shot beyond 35 yards, as the potential for string jumping is too great.

The problem I've experienced with mover sights is that I'm too absentminded to be trusted with them. I recall a certain Texas wild boar hunt where a movable sight caused some small amount of embarrassment. Earlier in the morning I'd stalked a behemoth boar, crawling to within 35 yards as he entered an isolated copse of tangled mesquite. I anticipated him weaving back out of that thronged cover and onto open ground so I waited with the sight locked at 35 yards. He never reappeared. I suppose he slipped out the opposite side of that tangle undetected.

Hours later, trudging up a nasty, thick arroyo choked with wild plums, I jumped a triple sounder of hogs of all shapes, sizes and color schemes. The first volunteer stopped at 18 yards. I was thinking how courteous it was of him to offer himself broadside like that, already counting him bagged and listening to the progress of at least 30 other hogs at seemingly every point of the compass. I dumped the string and watched in dismay as my arrow flew a foot high. I wasn't given much time to ponder that easy miss as I stepped around a bush to the grunting of another heavy hog, who was also courteous enough to pause broadside inside 20 yards. I snugged the brightly glowing pin into his armpit and let loose. That arrow, too, flew high. What the…?

I had the presence of mind to hold even lower on the next hog, this one walking up a side draw at 25 yards. The arrow buried in its spine and dropped it on the spot. While I didn't feel inclined to argue with success, I still wondered how this could be? That's when I happened to glance down at the mover sight's yardage tape. Thirty-five yards – of course!

Several sight companies have solved the issue of abrupt short-range shot opportunities, combined with the adaptability of a mover for longer shots. Two or three pins are added to the top of the stack to address typical 20-, 30- or 40-yard shots, the bottom pin also serving as the mover aiming point when the head is pivoted or geared downward for longer shots. The top pins serve only when the sight mechanism is bottomed out, the bottom of the actual mover. G5 Outdoor's Optic sights include one or three fixed pins and a gear-driven pin that moves within the aperture while allowing the fixed pins to remain in place and available.

One piece of advice that I would offer if you choose a standard mover sight is to bottom the aperture/sight head out and work from there to sight it in for your closest expected range, be that 10, 20 or 30 yards. This accomplishes two important things: First it provides wider travel options allowing more yardage latitude—many models out

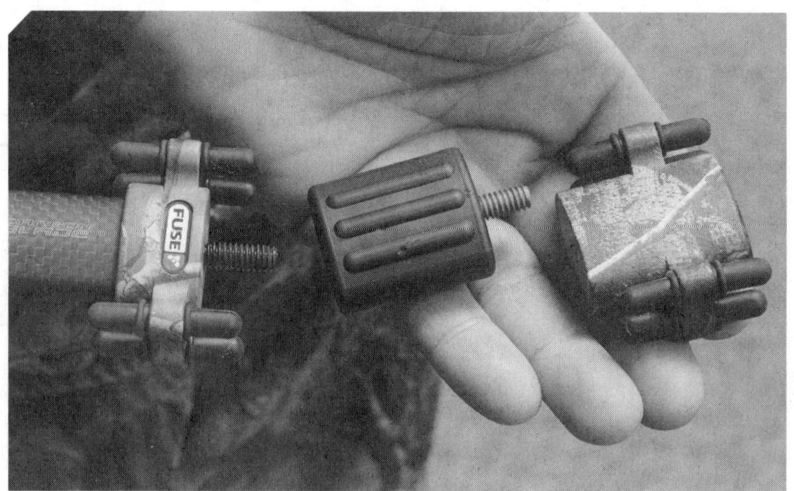

When ranges stretch, bowhunters need a stabilizer that actually steadies the shot, such as something in the 10- to 12-inch class.

to 100-plus yards. Second, this also allows you to bottom the sight to your shortest range by feel, without taking your eyes off of the target. If you'll get into the habit of bottoming the sight between shots, or when an encounter goes south, you'll always be starting from a known point, and avoid the mistake that I made on those Texas hogs. On a couple mover sights I've used this required drilling a tiny hole in the yardage-indicator face and creating a solid stop by inserting or cementing a small finishing nail.

Stabilized Shooting

Long-range shooting and the fine degree of aiming required on distant targets requires added stability. While less convenient and even somewhat unwieldy for the kind of crawling, stalking bowhunts normally resulting in longer-than-average shot opportunities, when ranges stretch beyond 45 yards, I choose a stabilizer in the 10- to 12-inch class. The job of a stabilizer is ultimately to stabilize—especially in settings where shot noise and vibration control is less critical as animals react to shot noise most violently when the ranges are shortest, as intimacy breeds immediacy. This stabilizer should include weight set out on its end, slowing torsional influences by dampening nervous twitches and muscle spasms, and should be adjustable to best accommodate your individual bow setup or shooting preferences. I prefer long stabilizer models including bladed (FUSE Carbon Blade) or skeletonized (Trophy Ridge Static, TRUGLO Carbon XS, as examples) extension bodies, as they allow breezes to pass through, minimizing wind buffeting while aiming.

Stabilizers should also be about balance. A well-behaved bow is always a plus, but especially imperative for long-range accuracy. Your bow should sit level in the hand while at rest and especially at full draw while the shooter supports the bow using an open, cradling grip. You should never be required to split your focus to coax your bow to sit up straight, all concentration should be invested in the shot and aiming small at a target way over yonder. A longer stabilizer will generally accomplish this, but it can sometimes become necessary to add stabilizers to the rear of the riser (when a rear tap is available), or install a solid or attitude-adjustable V-bar or offset stabilizer to compensate for the side torque introduced by heavy, tool-less sights, chunky drop-away rests and especially fully loaded, bow-mounted quivers. This can come at the cost of carrying ease, but a bow is of no use for long-range shooting at any weight if it doesn't promote dead-steady aiming.

Well-balanced bows are vital to long-range shooting. This allows your concentration to be focused on aiming and not manipulating bow attitude.

A wrist sling should also be part of the stabilization program, and a drop-away rest added for ultimate forgiveness.

A STRONG MENTAL GAME

If you have made it this far you are obviously heavily invested in thoroughly understanding and implementing solid shooting fundamentals and quality shooting practice. If you have been shooting a bow for a good number of years, I'd also wager the only major difference between you and shooting machines like Howard Hill or Levi Morgan is the ability to apply all-consuming concentration on demand. This might be said of any sport for which you have a modicum of talent, including sinking golf putts, hitting fastballs or sinking basketball free throws. The mind is a powerful computer, but tapping that power requires practice and programming.

Taking a moment to visualize the perfect shot before drawing your bow can boost performance under stressful conditions.

I'm sure you've noticed how much better you shoot while alone and untroubled on an abandoned public range or your own backyard. Conversely, it's also common to hear archers complain that they never live up to their full potential while shooting with a group of friends during 3-D tournaments. While shooting alone, after a good day at work or during a carefree weekend, your mind focuses easily. You're relaxed, untroubled and free of distractions, easily falling into The Zone, arrow's covering your SPOTs nearly effortlessly. But, while making the rounds during a 3-D tournament you're swapping hunting tales and retelling jokes; essentially catching up with friends and not completely focused on shooting.

Now, translate this into an encounter with game while stalking or sitting in a treestand—working to set the shot up initially with those last quiet steps, positioning for the impending shot and drawing your bow without being detected, the burning desire to collect a set of trophy antlers or needed meat for the freezer, what your buddies will say if you miss, maybe even ending the discomfort of a long, cold sit. Whatever the case, the shot itself can easily get lost in the mental static.

Bowhunting icon Fred Bear once said, "The whole body from the toes to the top of the head must be involved in every shot." The bigger problem is that to enjoy a 3-D tournament with friends, to assure shot timing is perfect and you get to shoot at an animal at all, this concentration cannot remain constant, or perpetual.

I recall, for instance, when I first began to become highly competitive in local and regional traditional-class 3-D tournaments. I had become the guy to beat, but early on I could only manage to maintain that level of performance by shutting myself off completely from everything and everyone around me. I was committed wholly to the shooting, completely disengaged from the social aspect of an archery gathering. I became greatly annoyed when those around me didn't take the shooting as seriously as I did. So it should come as no surprise that I was openly regarded as an arrogant scat dispenser by many who I shot with. Maintaining this level of concentration over a two-day shoot was also mentally exhausting.

As my confidence annealed, especially after marrying my wife, who held archery passions of her own and didn't exactly appreciate being ignored on the 3-D course, I learned to lighten up. I did this by learning to turn concentration on and off at will. This ability became particularly useful while directing arrows at real animals.

When bowhunting dangerous game, a strong mental game is imperative. Breathing exercises will help calm frazzled nerves.

To arrive in this place requires practice. In the beginning you must seek conditions completely free of distractions. You will need that solitude and disruption-free atmosphere to help enlarge your visualization skills—seeing yourself performing flawlessly in your mind's eye to ultimately help boost mental acuity during the shot.

This is first about relaxation. One of the easiest ways to instill mental calm is by practicing physical breathing exercises before each shot. To begin, inhale slowly and deeply through your nose only. Hold that breath momentarily, and then release it slowly; enough to bend a candle flame but without extinguishing it. As you exhale repeat the word "calm" or "relax" silently. After three or four deep breaths you should feel yourself beginning to relax. This is also something you can do on stand, or just before drawing your bow, in preparation for a shot at game.

You should also be working to instill healthy mental visualization skills, especially during solo backyard shooting practice. Work to use the creative side of your brain, actively visualizing yourself performing positively. While first developing these skills keep things simple. Envision your arrow going into the bull's-eye while shooting, for instance. Work outward from there.

As your visualization skills become more refined, work to make them more realistic, engaging all of the senses. This means you're not only seeing the perfect shot, but feeling it, hearing it, even smelling it. During the downtime on stand strengthen your visualization skills by imagining various scenarios around you, how you will respond, casting yourself as a successful performer. Go through an entire shot sequence mentally; from first sighting a buck you want to shoot, hearing his hooves crunch leaves, smelling the crisp autumn air, to getting the range, positioning yourself to address the target, anchoring, the feeling of settling into perfect shooting form, executing a smooth release and following through, finally seeing your arrow sink into the SPOT. Strive to feel the excitement, your pulse surging, and falling into the calm necessary to make a technically perfect shot. Such detail requires practice, but the awesome thing is once your visualizations become vividly real, your mind has a difficult time distinguishing between reality and what is visualized. Through visualizations you execute dozens of successful shots, experiences that provide confidence, and that confidence translates into calm under pressure.

Beware though, if at any time during your visualization exercises should your thoughts veer into negative territory, quickly and aggressively redirect those thoughts by literally visualizing a STOP sign, and switch channels to visualize past triumphs and positive scenarios.

Mental visualization exercises are used by the world's elite athletes to boost performance and give them a competitive edge. You can also use that power to make yourself a more effective predator. Once you learn to use mental visualization to turn that switch on and off on demand, combining that skill with the physical aspects of honed shooting form, you'll enter the field a more confident and deadly bowhunter; meaning fewer misses on trophy game and more filled tags.

CHAPTER 18

EQUIPMENT DIRECTORY

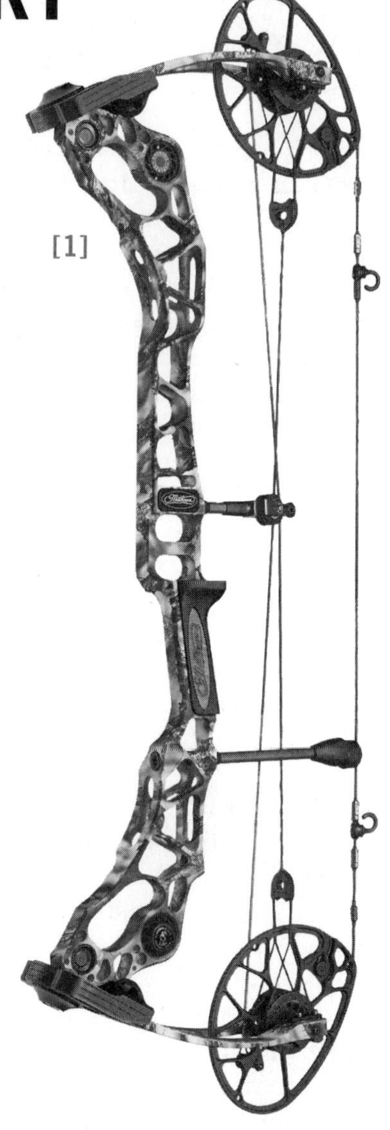
[1]

BOWS

Mathews

www.mathewsinc.com

[1] The CrossCentric Cam system powering Mathews' Halon is based on proven No-Cam Technology, including Advanced Vectoring System (AVS). The result: silky-smooth draws and impressive speed. Halons come in 5, 6 and 7 models; correlating to brace height. All are 30 inches long and weigh 4.5 pounds. Each hold stable, wide bridged risers, FlatBack Grips, Harmonic Damper top and Harmonic Stabilizer Lite below, and short, wider, torsion-free split limbs. The system is efficient, vibration free and quiet. Further silencing comes through Reverse Assist Roller Guard (also eliminating lateral torque), Dead End String Stop and MonkeyTail string silencers.

[2] Based on the Halon, the Halon X is designed to give shooters added forgiveness. The Halon X measures 35 inches between the axles, weighs 4.95 pounds and includes a forgiving 7-inch brace height. It's powered by a perimeter-weighted, 75/85-percent let-off Mini CrossCentric Cam incorporating accurate No Cam ST Technology, pushing arrows to 330 fps. The long riser—equipped with Mathews' Harmonic Dampers, Roller Guard and string stop—holds split, parallel limbs. The double-bridged riser is extremely rigid to provide a stable, vibration-free shooting platform. Draw lengths are offered from 26 to 30.5 inches.

Mission Archery

www.missionarchery.com

[3] Mission Archery's 4.27-pound Ballistic 2.0 offers bowhunters a lot of bang for their buck. This 28.5-inch dynamo produces arrow speeds matching bows costing much more. A wide range of draw lengths (26-30.5 inches) and weight adjustments (50-70 pounds) are included. Its 80-percent let-off AVS Cam System is designed to eliminate torque and assure smooth draw cycles. The precision-milled aluminum riser is well balanced, pivoting limb pockets creating a wide lateral base to reduce limb torque and increase stability. Parallel quad limbs are silent, the 7-5/8-inch brace height is highly forgiving. Mathews' Harmonic Stabilizer Lite, Dead End String Stop and MonkeyTail string silencers ensure silence.

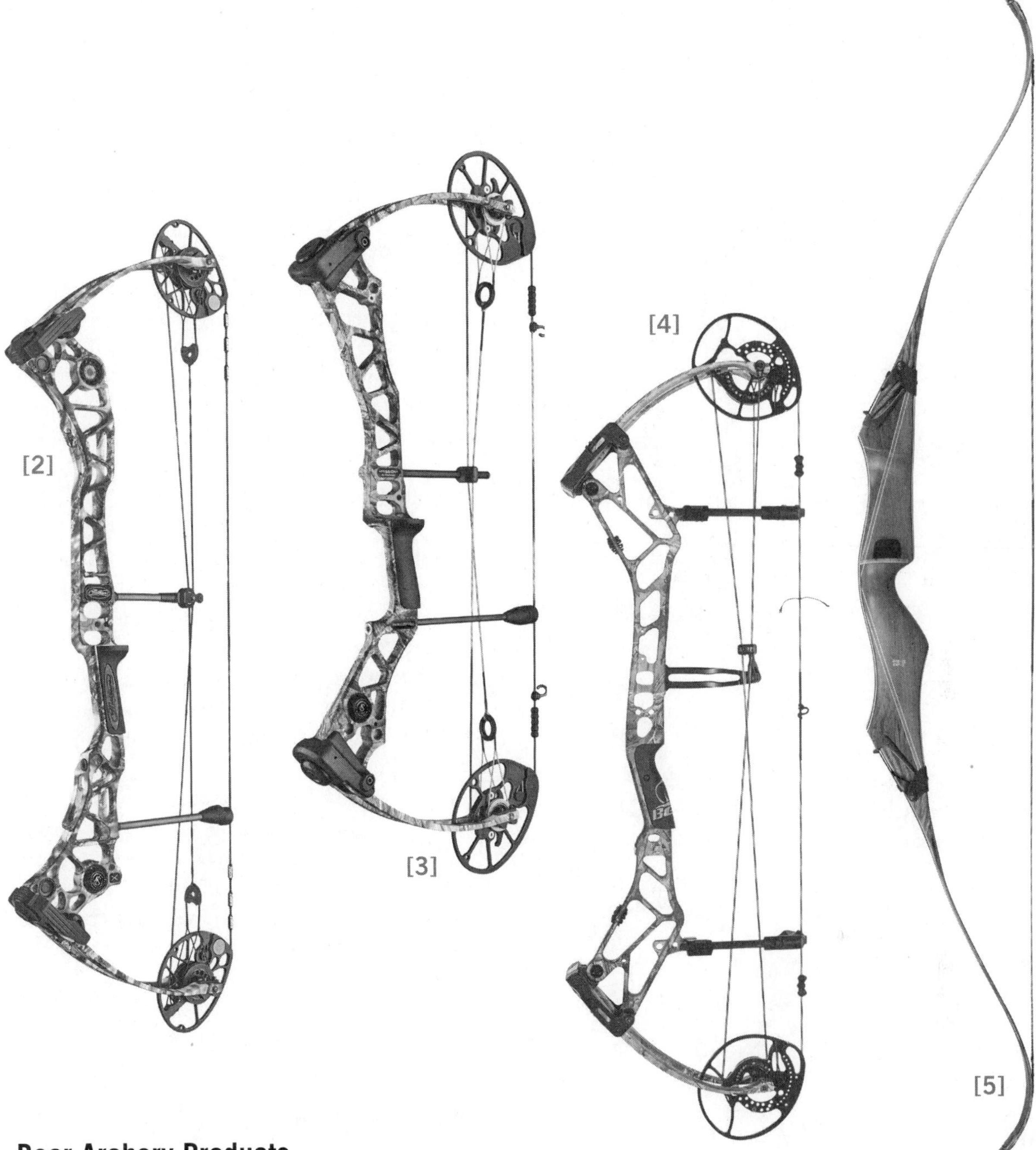

Bear Archery Products

www.beararchery.com

[4] Bear's 4.2-pound BR 33 is forgiveness incarnate. Its 80-percent let-off EAZ Hybrid cam is smoooooth, while providing 330 fps arrow speeds. String- or limb-stop options are included. The BR 33 includes a perfectly balanced riser milled from 7075 aluminum, torque-killing Hinge Guard, 7-inch brace height and highly efficient Max-Preload Quad limbs. Limbs are held in streamlined, pivoting pockets, holding rubber silencing inserts like those on the riser. Zero-stretch strings hold combination rubber speed buttons/silencers, captured after release by bi-dimensionally adjustable dual, offset string suppressors.

[5] Bear Archery's Takedown Recurve was Fred Bear's favorite, a design he perfected in 1969 and carried until his last hunt. Today's fine-shooting Takedown still allows instant assembly without tools or bolts. Mixing A or B risers and #1 or #3 limbs creates 56-, 60- and 64-inch bows. The crowned shelf holds a Bear Hair Rest and leather side plate, a Dynaflight 97 Flemish-twist string included. Choose from black maple or black maple/African Bubinga in draw weights from 20 to 65 pounds, left- or right-hand.

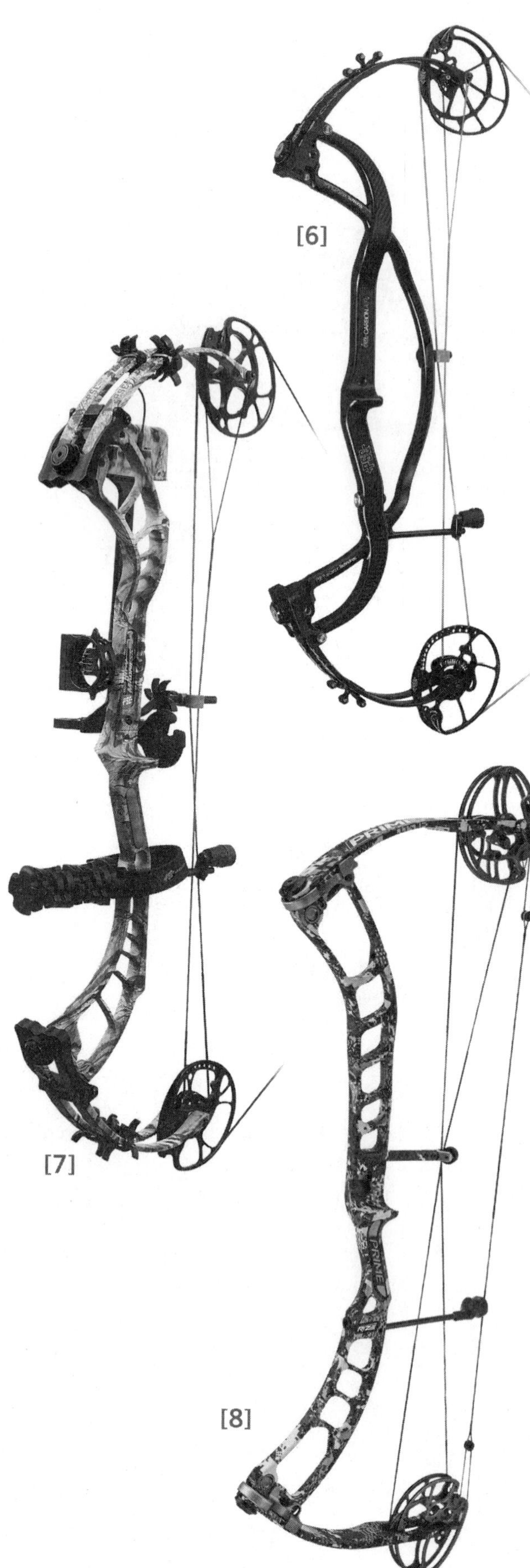

PSE Archery

www.pse-archery.com

[6] PSE's Carbon Air is a showcase of space-age technology. The 32-inch, 3.2-pound bow includes PSE True Carbon Technology built around Proprietary Structural, Rigid Acoustic Core (S-RAC)—carbon laid over acoustic foam—suppressing noise, vibration, and insulating against cold. Titanium makes up limb and pocket hardware, the 80-percent let-off HD hybrid cam remarkably smooth for a bow producing 340 fps arrow speeds. CenterLock Speed Pocket and preloaded, beyond-parallel X-Force limbs lend speed through a 6-1/8-inch brace height. The carbon riser holds machined-aluminum inserts, stainless steel stabilizer bushing, adjustable Backstop 4 and Arch Bridge handle. Shock Modz Limb Dampeners complete its silent nature.

[7] PSE's Bow Madness 34 RTS (Ready To Shoot) includes all accessories needed to start shooting, including Strider sight, Whisker Biscuit rest, Spire stabilizer, Raven quiver, neoprene wrist sling, red aluminum peep and string loop. Just add arrows and some practice. The bow is fueled by a high-performance hybrid cam delivering speed, precision and a wide adjustment range from 24.5 to 30.5 inches. The forged-aluminum riser proves rigid and vibration free shots, combined with past-parallel X-Force limbs to launch arrows to 342 fps, while also providing a comfortably smooth draw with 80 percent let-off. The 34¼-inch axle-to-axle length and 6-inch brace height provide a balanced mix of forgiveness and speed.

G5 Outdoors/Prime

www.g5prime.com

[8] G5 Outdoors engineered the riser on their 33-inch, 4.3-pound Prime Rize to provide a more pleasant and forgiving shooting experience. The riser is milled from unsurpassed 82X aluminum, making it stronger and more vibration free. The Rize's Sherpa Attachment Mounting System allows attaching nearly anything, its Flexis FlexShock damper assuring shot silence, articulated Ghost Grip Side Plates provide consistent and comfortable hand placement. The unique Prime Parallel Cam System pushes arrows to 335 fps via a 6.75-inch brace height, while also eliminating cam lean. The patented, adjustable Flexis-AR roller cable guard eliminates riser torque for easy accuracy.

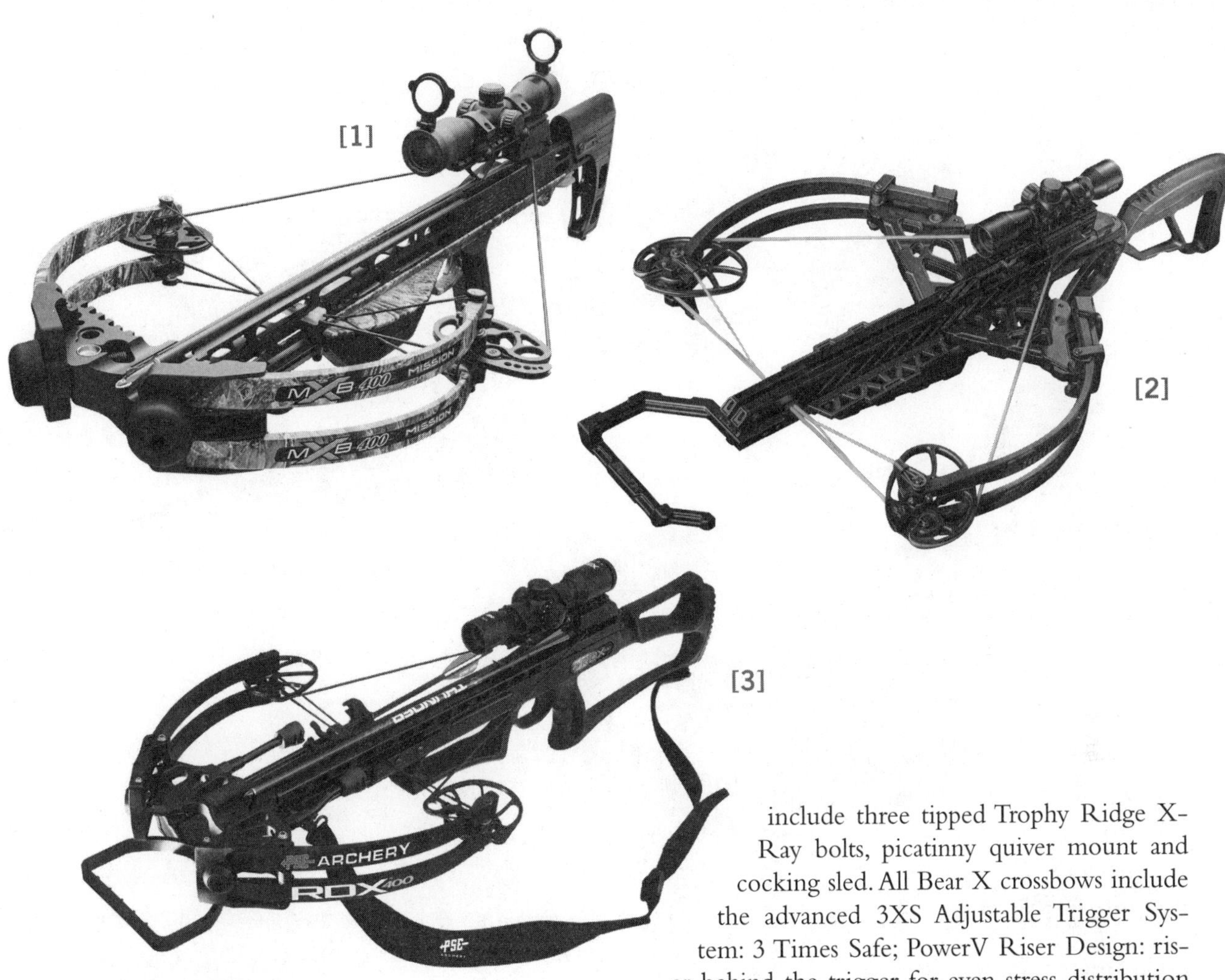

CROSSBOWS

Mission Archery

www.missionarchery.com

[1] Mission's MXB-400 offers 400 fps top speed via a 14-inch power stroke and a lightweight chassis. The MXB-400 uses proven technologies such as RSS Tread, making conventional foot stirrups obsolete, PCC Anchor eliminating the possibility of string-hook jumps and BIAS Rail to minimize weight and enhance downrange accuracy. Dual X-Cams reduce recoil while generating screaming speed. The MXB-400 accepts Mission's new RSD (Removable Silent Draw) cocking system and includes a scope.

Bear X

www.beararchery.com

[2] Bear X's affordable Bruzer FFL produces 335 fps with only a 125-pound draw weight and 14-inch power stroke. The 9-pound crossbow is compact and holds a Trophy Ridge XF425 scope. Packages include three tipped Trophy Ridge X-Ray bolts, picatinny quiver mount and cocking sled. All Bear X crossbows include the advanced 3XS Adjustable Trigger System: 3 Times Safe; PowerV Riser Design: riser behind the trigger for even stress distribution and increased efficiency; PowerLink Cable Routing Hangers: extending limbs slightly and allowing yoked cables to clear cams for better tuning; Forward Facing Limbs: FFL – moving riser weight between hands for optimal balance; and GaffStep Stirrup: combination stirrup/hanger.

PSE Archery

www.pse-archery.com

[3] PSE's supercharged reverse-draw RDX 400 is engineered to push bolts to blazing 400 fps speeds. The RDX 400 includes an independent machined-aluminum barrel and composite stock, patented PSE X-Tech limbs, crisp 3-pound trigger and field-serviceable capabilities. The overall package includes silencing string stops, XO 3x32mm illuminated scope, anti-dry-fire and auto-safety trigger, five-bolt quiver, three 20-inch Thunder Boltz Carbon Bolts with 100-grain tips, 22-inch discharge bolt, deluxe neoprene no-slip sling, deluxe crossbow case, speed loader cocking device, cocking rope, rail lube and foot stirrup.

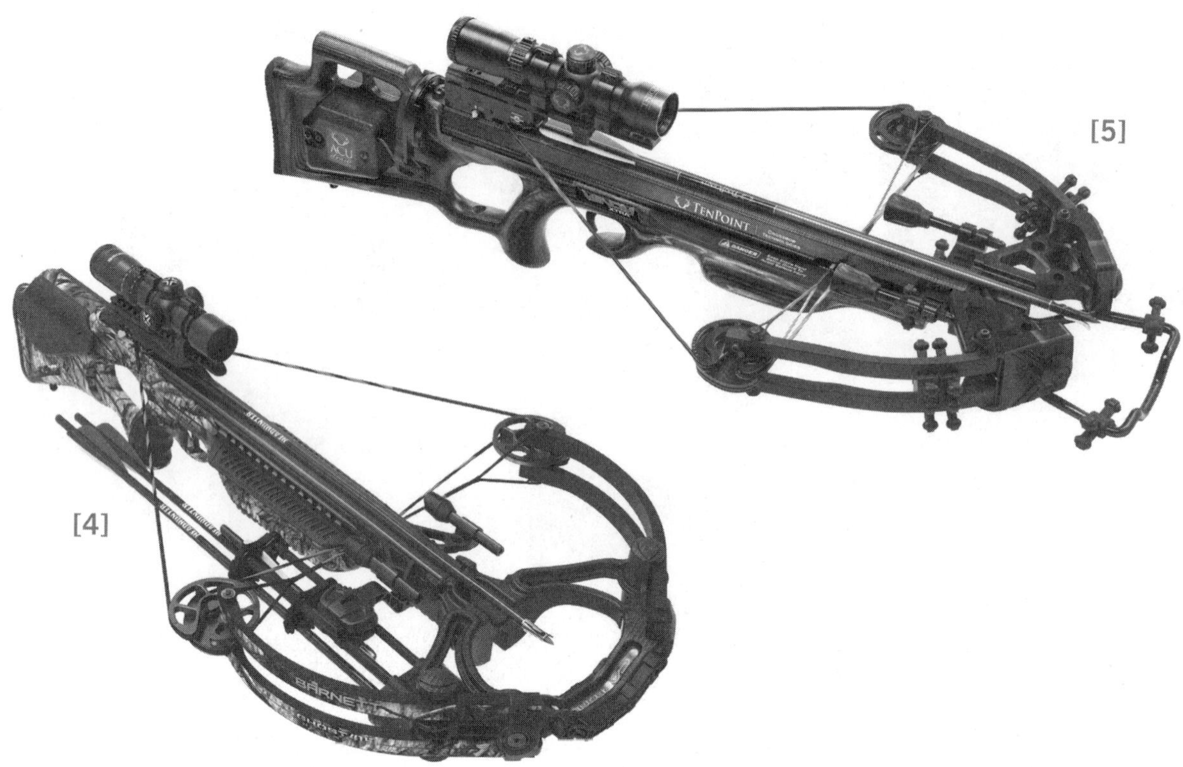

Barnett Crossbows

www.barnettcrossbows.com

[4] The Ghost 415 Revenant from Barnett launches bolts to 415 fps; high speeds generated by a compact crossbow weighing only 7 pounds. Proprietary Carbonlite Riser Technology (CRT) with adjustable buttpad shifts balance toward the shooter's shoulder, improving feel and accuracy. TriggerTech Technology provides "benchrest" level trigger pulls for added accuracy. Shooting rail and 7/8-inch picatinny rail are precision CNC machined, a bristle retainer keeping bolts in place between shots, and Crosswire string and cable system assure long life and reliability. Ghost 415 Revenant packages include rope-cocking device, three-slot quiver, three 22-inch Headhunter bolts and illuminated 1.5-5x32mm scope.

TenPoint Crossbow Technologies

www.tenpointcrossbows.com

[5] TenPoint's 6.7-pound Venom Xtra features a precision-crafted, laminated wood stock with non-slip rubber buttplate and semi-gloss finish. Its carbon-fiber barrel is set on rubber inserts to reduce noise and vibration, a redesigned handguard keeping shooters safer. XLT riser, IsoTaper Limbs and HE2 (Hybrid Eccentric 2) cams fuel 372 fps speeds from 185 pounds of draw weight. TenPoint's Dry-Fire-Inhibitor and 3.5-pound T3 auto-engaging safety trigger are included. Packages include choice of two cocking mechanisms, RangeMaster pro scope, bolts, quiver, Side-Mount Quiver bracket, soft case, String Dampening System (SDS) and Bowjax limb, stirrup, barrel and retention-spring dampeners.

Wicked Ridge Crossbows

www.wickedridgecrossbows.com

[6] Wicked Ridge's redesigned Warrior G3 is lighter, narrower, safer and faster. This crossbow includes a stout machined-aluminum riser and PolyOne OnForce semi-skeletal stock providing a 6.6-pound carry weight. WL12 limbs and Energy Wheel cams with DynaFlight 97 string and yolked cables produce 320 fps from 155 pounds. The pass-through fore-grip design is safer and more stable. The stock is fitted with TenPoint's DFI (Dry-Fire-Inhibitor) and 3.5-pound T3 auto-engaging safety trigger. Affordable packages include TenPoint 3x Multi-Line Scope, three Wicked Ridge aluminum bolts and quiver.

Carbon Express Crossbows

www.carbonexpressbow.com

[7] Carbon Express' X-Force Advantex gets you into crossbow hunting quickly with a lighter, better-balanced feel and narrower front profile for increased maneuverability. Split limbs improve performance, a new stock design improves fit and comfort. The precision trigger mechanism provides an incredibly crisp pull, including anti-dry-fire technology for safety. Single-point and traditional sling mounts are included. The crossbow comes ready to hunt with lever-action three-bolt quiver, three heavy PileDriver 20-inch crossbolts with practice points, 4x32mm scope and rail lubricant. This highly affordable crossbow weighs only 6.9 pounds and includes a 165-pound draw weight pushing bolts to 320 fps.

Horton Crossbow Technologies

www.hortoncrossbows.com

[8] Horton's reverse-draw Storm RDX—voted a best buy by two prominent hunting publications—are now available with an upgraded Premium Package featuring a lighted TenPoint 3x Pro-View 2 Scope. Further options include a budget-price Dedd Sled 50 manual cocking mechanism, or a top-end ACUdraw automated cocking mechanism. It also comes with a detachable quiver and three carbon crossbolts. The lightweight Dedd Sled 50 is made from PolyOne OnForce Long Glass Fiber Nylon and reduces crossbow drawing weight by 50 percent. The 8.2-pound Storm RDX propels bolts to 370 fps with 165 pounds of draw weight. The RDX cam system includes dual string stops, and the bull-pup stock design is comfort and fit adjustable.

ARROWS

Easton Hunting

www.eastonhunting.com

[1] Easton's D6 4mm Full Metal Jacket is one of a kind. These arrows combine an alloy outer jacket over an ultra-slim carbon core holding Injexion Steel G HIT inserts and direct-fit G Nocks. The focused mass and thin profile penetrates like no other arrow and results in decreased wind drift. In 330 spine they weigh 11 gpi for reliability on the largest game, and include .002-inch straightness tolerances and 2-grain matched weight.

[2] Easton's Da'Torch provides long-range shooters near perfection. These lightweight, .205-inch-diameter shafts hold X Nocks with UNI Bushing and longer HP Inserts (brass inserts available to boost F.O.C.). With .001-inch straightness tolerances and 1-grain matched weight they offer top-notch accuracy potential; in 6.3 gpi 480, 7.2 gpi 400 and 7.9 gpi 330 spines. They include a handsome white Easton logo crest.

Beman

www.beman.com

[3] Beman's ICS Precision Hunter gives bowhunters looking for a midweight arrow the accuracy potential needed to instill confidence. Precision Hunters include unsurpassed .001-inch straightness tolerances and 1-grain matched weight per dozen. They accept standard Super Nocks and CB Inserts, offered in 500 (7.3 gpi), 400 (8.4 gpi) and 340 (9.3 gpi) deflections.

Carbon Express

www.carbonexpressarrows.com

[4] Carbon Express' CX Maxima BLU RZ features game-changing Maxima RED Technology, but in a lighter 8.45 gpi payload. They include .0025-inch straightness and 1-grain matched weight. The "RED-Zone" center and stiffer ends lends the BLU RZ unsurpassed broadhead flight from the fastest bows. They come in 150 (.502-inch deflection), 250 (.413-inch) and 350 (.346-inch).

PSE Archery

www.pse-archery.com

[5] PSE Archery's cross-wrapped Radial X-Weave Pro shafts include near perfect .001-inch straightness tolerances and 1-grain per dozen matched weight. QuietCoat treatment, which penetrates beyond the surface to last longer, makes them silent across arrow rests, helps them penetrate deeper and assures easier extraction from high-density foam targets. They weigh 8.6 gpi in 300 (.359-inch) spine.

BloodSport Archery

www.bloodsportarchery.com

[6] BloodSport's .165-inch inside-diameter Evidence arrows include 1-grain matched weight and .001-inch straightness tolerances. Rugged Wrap Construction makes for uncompromising reliability along with a 60-grain R.O.C. (Reliable Outsert Component) System – a two-part 7075 aluminum component protecting the shaft front from splitting after hard impacts. Evidence arrows also include a wide Blood Ring to capture blood and bodily fluids during pass through, helping bowhunters make informed trailing decisions after hits. Look for them in 300/11.7, 350/10.2, 400/9.1 and 500/8.2 spine/gpi combinations.

Gold Tip

www.goldtip.com

[7] Gold Tip's .166-inch internal diameter Kinetic Pierce holds direct-fit, "G-Nock"-diameter GTO nock and 9.8/250, 9.1/300, 8.3/340, 7.6/400 and 6.6/500 gpi/spine specs promising a good combination of flat trajectory and deep penetration, plus complete reliability following punishing impacts. Platinum-grade includes .0025-inch straightness specs and .5-grain matched weight, and also include GTO nocks and protective collars. A .006-inch straightness version is also offered.

CROSSBOW BOLTS

BloodSport Archery

www.bloodsport.com

[8] The Witness crossbolt from BloodSport is designed specifically for today's high-performance crossbows, using Rugged Wrap construction to make them stronger and maintain .003-inch straightness tolerances. They include BloodSport's Blood Ring – plainly showing shooters what kind of hit was made after a shot based on blood or fluid hue. They're offered in 300-grain 20-inch models and 325-grain 22-inch models.

Carbon Express

www.carbonexpressarrows.com

[9] Carbon Express offers seven different crossbow bolts, but the Whitetail Crossbolt has emerged as the company's top seller. These 20-inch bolts use the latest technology to help them fly faster, straighter and hit harder. Choose from 20- or 22-inch models, complete with half-moon nocks or universal flat nocks, and weighing 430 grains finished with a 100-grain point.

Gold Tip

www.goldtip.com

[10] Gold Tip's Nitro X-Bolt is designed to wring top performance from the most powerful crossbows. They include added mass and a stiffer spine, increasing kinetic energy and withstanding the massive energies produced by today's fastest crossbows. Look for them in .005-inch straightness or newer .001-inch Nitro Pro, in 20-inch or 22-inch lengths. Both weigh 13.9 gpi.

Beman

www.beman.com

[11] Beman's White Box Crossbow carbon bolts are affordable and hunt ready. They come in boxes of six, are made of a super-strong, multi-laminate carbon with all components already installed and ready to shoot. They weigh 400 grains, including 4-inch vanes, inserts, half-moon nocks and even field points. This weight-matched bolt is 20 inches long and designed to compliment today's faster, more powerful crossbow models.

Easton

www.eastonarchery.com

[12] Crossbow hunters can now enjoy the added penetration potential and unsurpassed accuracy of Easton's Full Metal Jacket in an x-bow bolt. Easton fuses a carbon core to an alloy jacket to produce bolts with .003-inch straightness and precisely matched spine/weight for accuracy, plus the added mass needed to assure deep penetration on the largest game.

BROADHEADS

Bloodsport

www.bloodsportarchery.com

[1] Bloodsport's Wraith Broadhead System includes a "Scooptail" ferrule compatible with several blade designs. Scooptail/cutting-tip ferrules snowplow a passageway for greater accuracy and penetration. Choose from Deepcut (1.125-inch cutting diameter), Widecut (1.5 inch) and Treestand (1.125 inch with step blade rear to exaggerate entry holes from powerful bows), all weighing 100 grains. Each .030-inch-thick blade reverses to double its usable life.

[2] Bloodsport's Grave Diggers are hybrid fixed/mechanical designs delivering maximum devastation. Cut-on-contact models include a 1-inch cut-on-contact fixed blade, and the Chisel Point features a trocar tip and replaceable blades, both with additional 1.75-inch deployable blades. A patented retention system keeps blades tight in flight, but always opens on impact. The 100-grain models include 7075 aluminum, 125-grain models have steel ferrules.

Quality Archery Designs

www.qadinc.com

[3] QAD's dependable, accurate Exodus is 100-percent stainless steel, with short-profile over-the-blade technology. The Rock-Buster Hardened SST cutting tip leads a 1.25-inch cutting diameter made of .040-inch-thick blades. Choose solid-blade

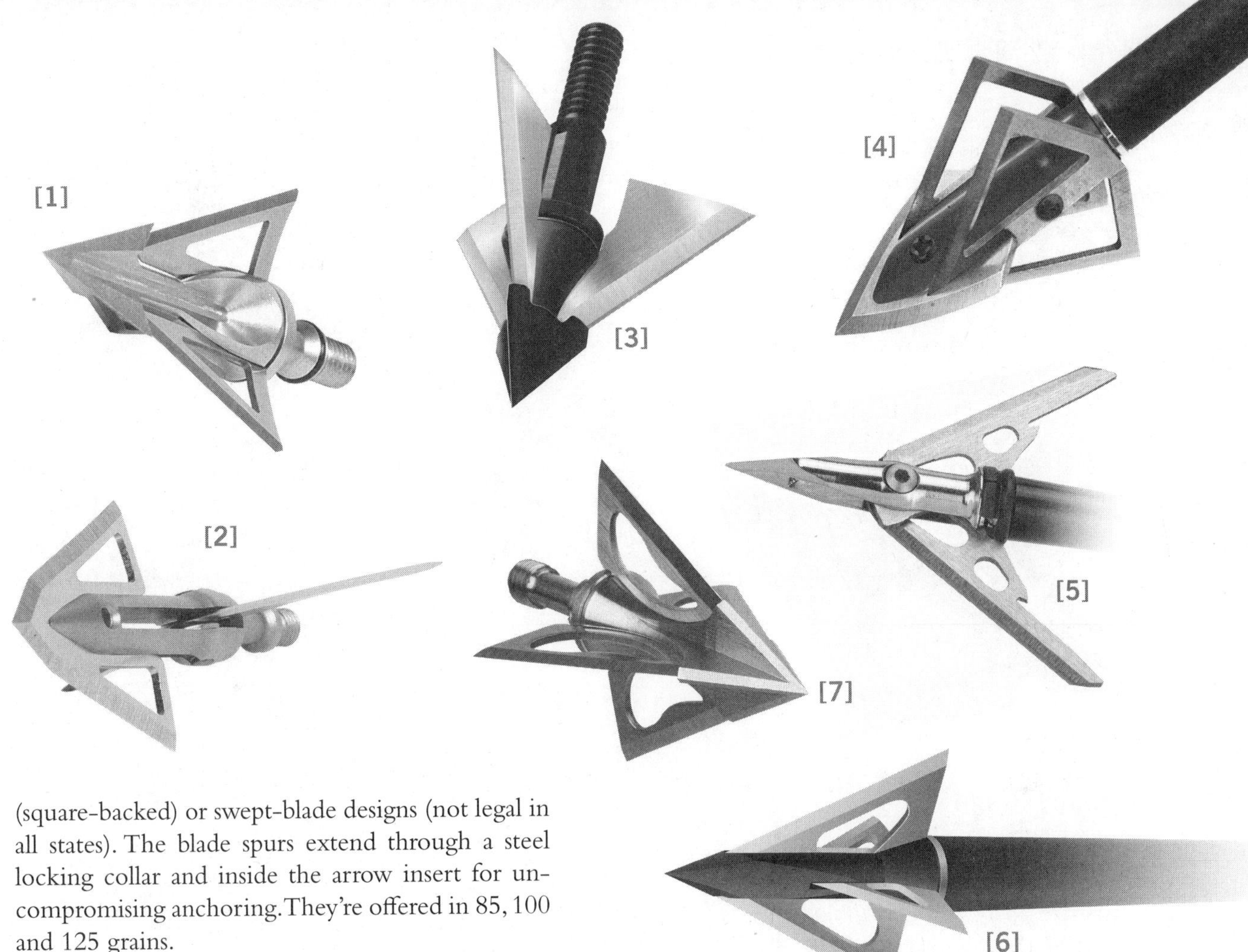

(square-backed) or swept-blade designs (not legal in all states). The blade spurs extend through a steel locking collar and inside the arrow insert for uncompromising anchoring. They're offered in 85, 100 and 125 grains.

Carbon Express

www.carbonexpressarrows.com

[4] Carbon Express' 100-grain, cut-on-contact Shuriken includes wide, twin "bleeders" that bore devastating H-like wound channels. Hard-anodized aluminum ferrules hold 5/8-inch-wide, .058-inch-thick nose blade, and two vented, .058-inch-thick, 1.5-inch-wide "bleeders" slotted into the leading edge and anchored to opposing ferrule sides with steel screws. They're extremely accurate and create wide blood trails.

Rage Broadheads

www.ragebroadheads.com

[5] Rage's Hypodermic +P is a streamlined mechanical designed for low-energy bows, or for the largest big game. The one-piece stainless-steel ferrule includes a cut-on-contact tip and the .035-inch-thick blades sweep back to create a 1.5-inch cutting diameter. Shock Collars make them extremely reliable, and each three-broadhead package includes an aerodynamically and weight-matched practice tip.

Slick Trick

www.slicktrick.net

[6] Slick Trick's ViperTrick includes an indestructible Super Steel ferrule with a cutting tip. The ferrule holds cross-locking (Alcatraz BladeLock System) .035-inch-thick, German-honed Lutz blades. They're spooky sharp and withstand the most punishing bone hits. The four-blade design includes 1-1/16" x 7/8" cut in 100- and 125-grain models. These mini heads provide field-point accuracy even at high speeds.

Wac'em Broadheads

www.wacemarchery.com

[7] Wac'em Broadheads have stainless-steel ferrules with milled-in cutting tips. These mini fixed blades wear .027-inch-thick replaceable stainless blades held in place by a brass retention ring. The four-blade is offered in 85-, 100- and 125-grain models, each with 1-1/16-inch cutting diameter. They offer pinpoint accuracy combined with the deepest possible penetration. Tips can be re-sharpened on any flat stone.

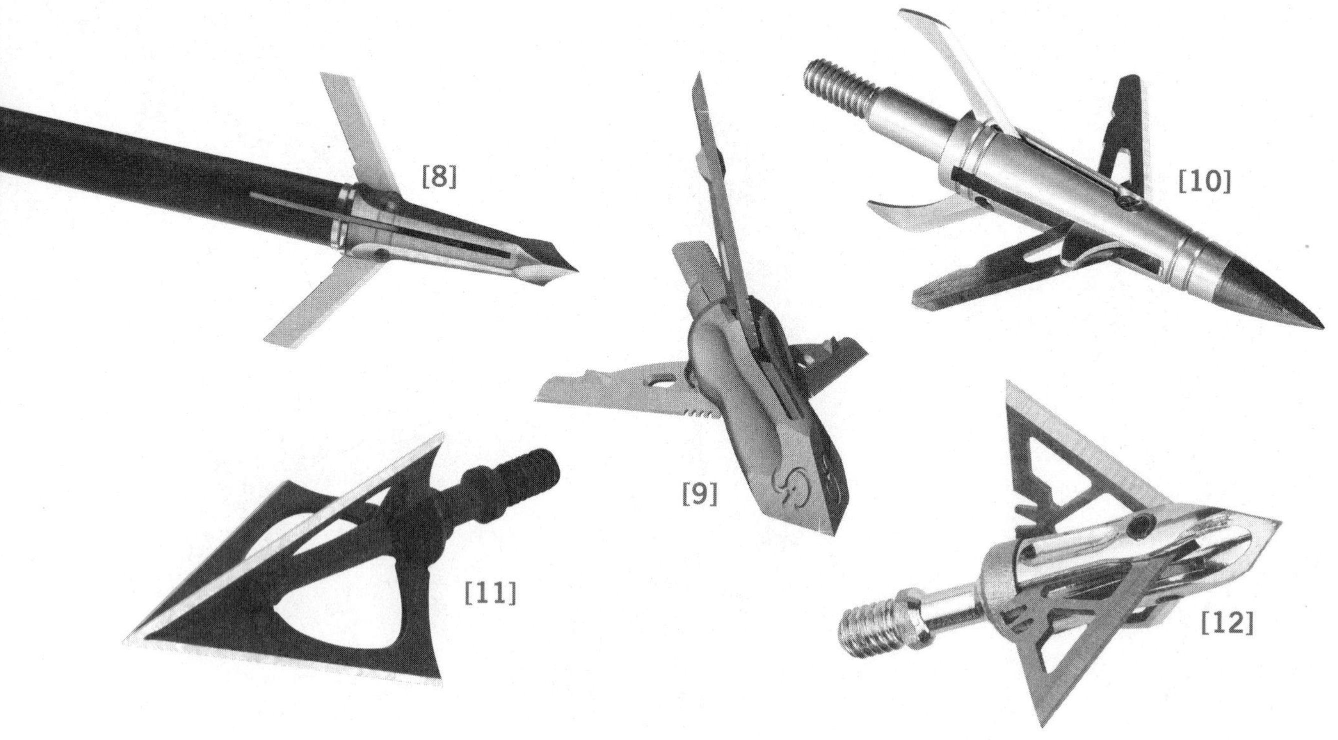

Trophy Ridge

www.trophyridge.com

[8] Trophy Ridge's 100-grain Rocket Steelhead is in a class of its own. The three-blade mechanical maintains true field-point dimensions in flight, the all-steel, one-piece ferrule with cutting tip and titanium-nitride coating is tough as nails. Its three thick blades open to 1-1/8 inches on impact. This combination assures deep penetration on the biggest game, combined with field-point accuracy.

G5 Outdoors

www.g5outdoors.com

[9] G5 Outdoors' Metal Injection Molding Technology creates the 100-percent stainless-steel, rear-deploying T3 mechanical. Its three expandable blades open to 1.5 inches, secured in flight by a Spider Clip system offering two deployment tensions. Lighter clips accommodate most situations, stronger clips provided for high-speed bows or crossbows, or shooting through pop-up blind screens. The tip cuts on contact, MIM blades riding in deployment slots on smooth, molded protrusions.

New Archery Products

www.newarchery.com

[10] NAP's Spitfire DoubleCross broadhead is made for high-energy rigs to produce maximum cutting action. The four-blade design delivers 3 inches of cutting trauma in a head weighing 100 grains. Two-stage deployment starts with 1-7/8-inch-wide, .030-inch-thick main blades and finishes with 1-1/8-inch-wide, .027-inch-thick secondary deployable bleeders. The design includes the bone-splitting NAP Trophy Tip and clip retention for reliability from even the fastest crossbows.

[11] New Archery Products' three-blade HellRazor is a cut-on-contact broadhead assembled via photon welding to create a one-piece broadhead that is awesomely strong. The 1-1/8-inch cutting diameter offers an ideal balance of in-flight stability and penetration potential, the spooky-sharp, cross-cutting blades assuring generous blood trails. The blades can also be re-sharpened after use. They're offered in 100- and 125-grain options.

Muzzy Broadheads

www.muzzy.com

[12] Muzzy's Trocar Switch is an adjustable-cutting-diameter broadhead that provides bowhunters with one head for all needs. The Switch includes an all-steel ferrule with a milled cutting tip for deeper penetration. The .035-inch-thick blades can be moved to 1-, 1-1/8- or 1¼-inch cutting diameters and locked securely. Two-degree offset blades work with fletchings for ultimate accuracy, all-steel construction assuring nail-tough reliability.

BOW ACCESSORIES

Tru-Fire Releases

www.trufire.com

[1] Tru-Fire's C4 introduces affordability to a thumb-activated, T-handle release. The hammer-throw, four-finger C4 is injection molded from stout carbon-composite material and covered in soft rubber for noise reduction and comfort. The sear closes over the string loop to be left hanging before the shot. Its hexagonal thumb barrel is adjustable to six positions, and its internal parts precision milled and heat treated for long life.

[2] The Spark from Tru-Fire is a dual-jaw caliper release with wrist strap engineered to be more compact and fits 4.5- to 8-inch wrists. Spring-loaded jaws, linear bearing system and Tru-Forward adjustable trigger combine to assure smooth shots. Tru-Fire's Foldback ring allows flipping the release back 180 degrees when not in use, and wrist adjustments are made via a 10-point buckle strap. The head includes 3/8-inch travel adjustment.

TRUGLO

www.truglo.com

[3] TRUGLO's Carbon XS Xtreme five-pin sight includes ultra-lightweight (4.2 ounces) carbon composite construction; featuring a longer mounting bracket to improve the sight radius, extended windage and elevation adjustments, larger aperture and extended Pro-Bright Pin Technology aiming points that are stronger and brighter than ever. The peep-alignment ring glows in the dark, and the sight is covered in Tru-Touch Black, Realtree Xtra, APC Pink, Lost and Lost AP rubber coating.

[4] TRUGLO's Carbon XS Stabilizer is weight adjustable with two stainless-steel weights and comes with a sling, providing perfect bow balance that promotes proper shooting form. It also includes a vibration-dampening suspension system that's adjustable for custom balance, and designed to reduce vibrations and noise. Nonreflective Tru-Touch soft coating provides further shot dampening. They're offered in 7- and 9-inch camo models.

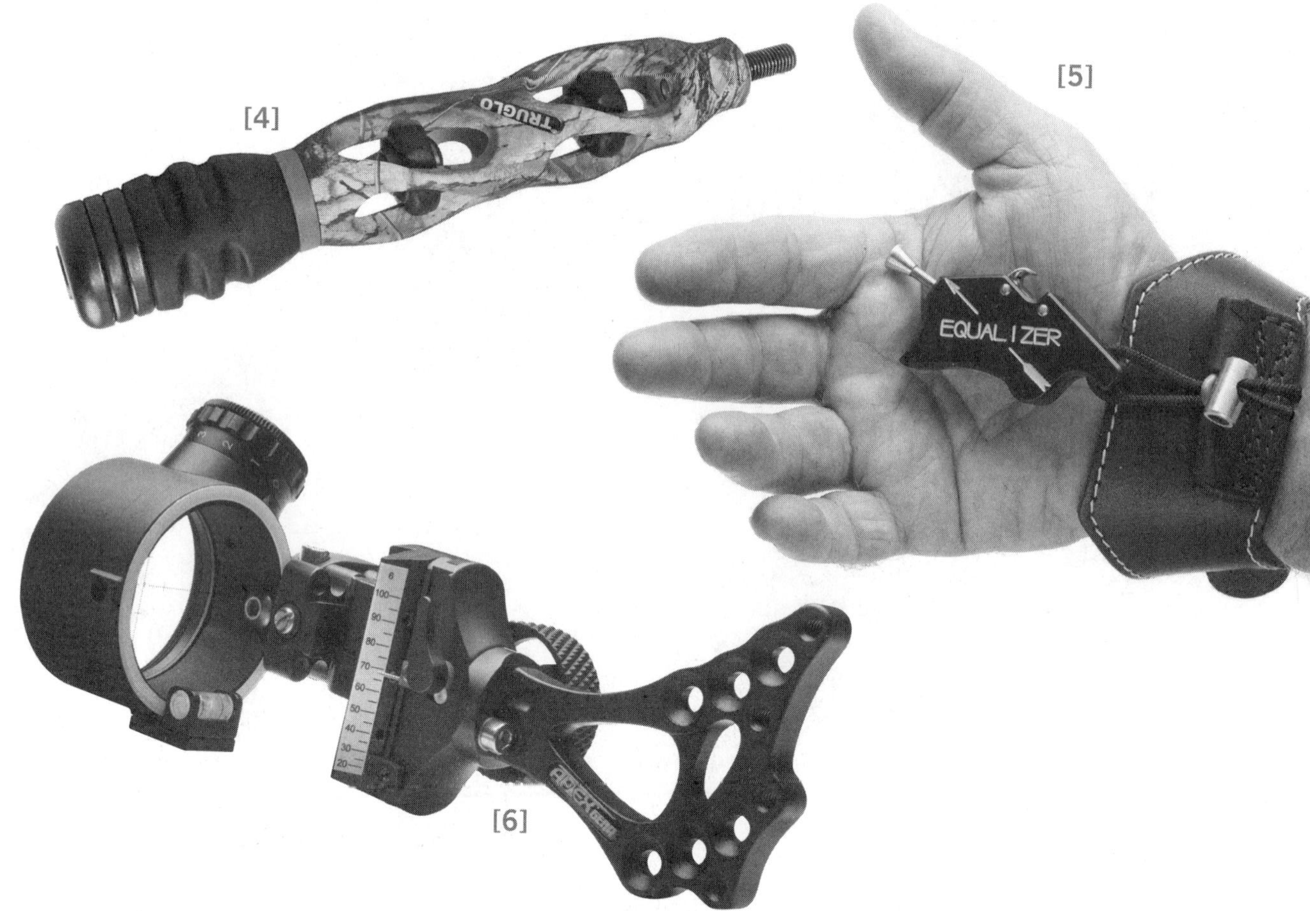

Goat Tuff Products

www.goattuffproducts.com

[5] The Equalizer release from Goat Tuff allows short-draw and low-poundage shooters to increase draw length up to 3 inches by setting the trigger in front of the string-loop sear, boosting arrow speeds 10 to 15 fps without increasing draw weight. It features a unique plunger trigger and draw-finger shelf promoting solid shooting form. The body is milled from aluminum, all internal parts polished stainless steel. Wrist-strap options include double-tongue metal buckle or Velcro closure.

Apex Gear

www.apex-gear.com

[6] Apex Gear's Covert Pro Sight features the PWR-Dot Illuminated Center-Dot Technology scope with adjustable, green LED center dot and 11 brightness settings controlled through a click-stop rheostat (not legal in all states). The mover sight is perfect for failing eyesight or those seeking a finer long-range aiming point. The 1.8-inch diameter aperture includes micro windage and elevation adjustments. Gravity-Line rotation adjustment aligns aiming-point movements through gravity, assuring that treestand or difficult angled shots don't cause trouble, in addition to holding an illuminated second- and third-axis adjustable bubble level. It comes with more than 60 pre-marked yardage tapes and adjustable yardage pointer for precise range dialing according to bow speed.

New Archery Products

www.newarchery.com

[7] New Archery Products' Apache Carbon drop-away rest weighs only 4 ounces, including the carbon full-containment arrow cage. A side slot allows faster loading and the containment cage is padded with sound-dampening foam for silence. Laser-etched graduations allow precise tuning, Quik-Tune design fast and easy set-up and tuning. Every aspect of the rest, from the bearing-equipped launcher, carbon containment cage to aluminum mounting and adjustment bracket is designed for silence and reliability.

Quality Archery Designs

www.qadinc.com

[8] QAD's UltraRest HDX delivers 100 percent arrow containment and drop-away fletching clearance with bow speeds to 400 fps. The rest is precision tuned, requiring no adjustments. Lock-Down Technology eliminates launcher bounce-back, held at 90 degrees before the shot for unsurpassed accuracy, dropping only when the bow is fired, not during slow let-downs. The launcher is covered in laser-cut felt and the body features rubber dampeners for quieter shots. The USA-made rest includes a limited lifetime warranty.

Trophy Ridge

www.trophyridge.com

[9] Trophy Ridge's vertical, in-line pin sights block less target area and allow lining up on an animal's front leg during high-pressure shots. Trophy Ridge's React technology requires sighting only 20- and 30-yard pins for dead-on sighting out to 60 yards. Trophy Ridge's React V5 sight provides both of these features in one sight; five pins set vertically and linked through React technology for quick sighting. The V5 includes lightweight but tough Ballistix CoPolymer construction (the strength of aluminum but 25 percent lighter), second axis leveling, tool-less adjustment and a rheostat light.

[1]

[2]

[3]

OPTICS & SCOUTING TOOLS

GSM/Stealth Cam

www.gsmoutdoors.com

[1] Stealth Cam's G45NG Pro is compact and includes a matte-finish camouflage case. Adjustable PIR, plus 100-foot day and night maximum range are some of its features. DVR mode allows writing over existing images if your SD card fills up. PIR-triggered stills can be taken in 2, 6, 8, or 14MP, and theReflex Trigger provides sub-½-second triggering. The unit allows includes HD video with sound and Time Lapse with PIR override. NO GLO or Black Out IR flash is invisible to animals and humans. The unit also includes Burst Mode, Matrix Blur Reduction technology and operates on six AA batteries.

Browning Trail Cameras

www.browningtrailcameras.com

[2]The Strike Force HD Elite from Browning Trail Cameras includes a proprietary camouflage case, .4-second trigger speed and sub-1½-second recovery. It overwrites the oldest images or videos on a full SD card, allows continuous 720p HD sound video as long as motion is detected (up to 5 minutes in daylight) and has self-adjusting IR illumination—among other highlights. BuckWatch time lapse mode, 10MP resolution, "Zero Blur" technology, plus Rapid Fire image capturing are also part of the package. The camera also features a 55-foot detection range and operates on eight AA batteries.

Muddy Outdoors

www.gomuddy.com

[3] Muddy's Pro-Cam 12 is a 12MP trail camera capable of capturing two- to eight-photo bursts, includes time lapse and 1280x720 HD video with sound. It includes a .6-second trigger speed with invisible flash via 36 HE LEDs. The unit is very easy to program and includes a backlit LCD screen for easy viewing any time of the day. It includes a 70-foot range and operates on six AA batteries allowing up to 10,000 images. The case features a nonreflective bark pattern.

Bushnell

www.bushnell.com

[4] Bushnell's Trophy Cam Aggressor HD provides one-year battery life on eight AA batteries. PIR sensitivity is adjustable, plus it has a .2-second trigger speed and sub-1 second recovery. The unit captures up to 14MP stills or 1080p HD sound video. The case includes a removable ARD (Anti-Reflection Device) LED cover and stronger cable-lock channel and latch system. Two Low-Glow IR models and two No-Glow Black LED units are offered—48 Black LEDs providing 80-foot range, or a 100-foot range is possible with 36 Low-Glow LED units.

[5] Bushnell's Trophy Xtreme series offers exceptional, yet affordable performance. All include rugged, green rubber coating, fully multi-coated lenses and BaK-4 prisms in rugged, fog proof and waterproof chassis. Binoculars include ergonomic design for easy handling, built-in and secure lens covers, three-step twist-up eyecups and large focus knob. Spotting scopes include compact porro-prism design, adjustable sunshade, compact tripod/window mount, waterproof hard and compact soft cases. All include the No Questions Asked Lifetime Warranty. Look for binos in 10x50, 12x50 and 8x56 configurations, spotters in 16-48x50 or 20-60x65.

Day 6 Outdoors

www.day6outdoors.com

[6] The PlotWatcher Pro from Day 6 perfected time-lapse technology to allow keeping tabs on larger patches of ground without impacting hunting sites, by capturing an image every few seconds without PIR triggering. Images are then automatically spliced together, allowing you to view a 12-hour day in three minutes. Many conventional trail cameras have time-lapse capabilities, but batteries are quickly exhausted in that mode. This unit takes millions of images and saves them in TRU-Video format for up to four months on one set of eight AA batteries.

[8]

Cuddeback

www.cuddeback.com

[7] Cuddeback's IR Plus is an affordable scouting camera with exceptional performance, including ½-second trigger speed and 1-second recovery in 8MP resolution. Cuddeback's super-simple setup makes deployment easy, its Genius Mount allowing mounting a bracket and sliding the camera into place, and optional mounts allow panning, tilting and locking. Its 24 IR LEDs reach to 50 feet; the camera operates on eight AA batteries for six months. Detection zone is adjustable and images are taken in 4:3 format.

Halo Rangefinders

www.halooptics.com

[8] Halo's XRay 800 laser rangefinder includes a color LCD readout display and 800-yard capabilities from reflective targets. AI Technology compensates for sloping terrain and allows continuous ranging in Scan Mode, with readings accurate to within one yard. The eyepiece provides 6X magnification and the housing is water resistant. The rangefinder operates on one CR2 lithium ion camera battery (not included) and comes with a one-year warranty and nylon carry case.

[9]

Nikon Sport Optics

www.NikonSportOptics.com

[9] Nikon's Prostaff 3S binoculars, in 8x42 and 10x42, are lightweight and compact for easy portability. Prisms include high-reflective silver-alloy coatings and multilayer lenses for bright, sharp viewing. Turn-and-slide rubber eyecups with click adjustments are comfortable and compatible with eyeglasses. A large field of view and ergonomic design ensure hours of comfortable glassing. They're rubber coated for durability and are fog proof and waterproof.

[10]

[10] Nikon's Arrow ID 3000 laser rangefinder meets the bowhunter's needs. Tru-Target and ID (Incline/Decline) technologies remove the guesswork from important shots at game. The 4X monocular includes multilayer coatings for brightness, the housing is rainproof and includes a silencing neoprene case. Tru-Target Technology allows selecting between First Target Priority or Distant Target priority for accurate ranging in wooded environments. ID technology provides precise yardages in steep topography.

PACKS & CAMOUFLAGE CLOTHING

Rancho Safari

ranchosafari.com

[1] Rancho Safari's Catquivers offer a sturdy daypack and dependable arrow quiver in one. The Catquiver VI.5 includes a main compartment with 1,340 cubic inches for spotting scopes and tripods, plus a plethora of external pockets and exterior compression straps to keep smaller gear organized and extra clothing instantly available. A water-bottle pouch assures you remain hydrated. The pack holds a Catquiver Mini arrow quiver across your back, remaining streamlined while protecting arrows, covering bright fletchings or delicate feathers and eliminating accidental deployment of mechanical broadheads – all while making arrows instantly available.

ALPS OutdoorZ

www.alpsoutdoorz.com

[2] The ALPS OutdoorZ Commander X is a highly versatile, full-size backpack made for the extreme backcountry bowhunter who wants to get off the beaten track. Its design includes a sturdy backpack and efficient packing frame with meat shelf all in one streamlined unit. This backpack is big enough to get you into remote backcountry with all of the gear and food needed for a week's stay, but when you tag that big one it quickly converts into a shelved pack board for comfortable transport of heavy meat, capes and bulky antlers. The overall construction includes bulletproof fabric and reinforced stress points to endure many years of rough treatment. Once in your hunting area the backpack lid doubles as a convenient fanny pack.

[1]

[2]

[3]

[4]

Sitka Gear

www.sitkagear.com

[3] Sitka's unique Tool Box treestand daypack is designed to organize, haul and hang everything needed for all-day stand sits. Breathable padded pack straps minimize perspiration and human odors, and the pack can be hung from a screw-in tree step by an incorporated hanging ring to provide access to the main compartment, seven slide-in pockets and four zippered pockets. It also includes side water bottle pouches. The 1,800 cubic-inch pack weighs 2.7 pounds unloaded and is covered in Gore Optifade Elevated II camouflage.

[4] For the true whitetail fanatic Sitka Gear offers Fanatic wear. This is one of the warmest outfits in existence, shelled in high-pile, super-quiet Berber Fleece, featuring a membrane of breeze-turning WindStopper and insulated with highly efficient Primaloft. Fanatic wear turns ultimate cold-weather comfort into ultimate stealth wear. The "fuzzy" Berber fleece is much quieter than typical polyester softshell fabrics and does an effective job of masking WindStopper rustle in the coldest weather. It you bowhunt from stands in cold weather, this is the outfit you have been waiting for. Fanatic is also offered in Lite series Bib, Vest and jacket for chilly early seasons, replacing Primaloft insulation with hexagonal grid fleece.

[5] The Timberline series from Sitka Gear includes a body mapped Micro Grid Fleece insulation to keep your core warm, and taped WindStopper fabric to turn biting wind. Reinforced jacket shoulders and sleeves, and pant knees, seat and hems stand up to rough treatment, making it the perfect outfit for cool early seasons in the high country or active hunting during cold late seasons. Technical four-way stretch material is water repellent and dries quickly. Both pieces are offered in Gore Optifade Concealment Open Country.

SCENTLOK TECHNOLOGIES

www.scentlok.com

[6] ScentLok's Nexus Series base layers include technical body mapping combined with the latest ScentLok odor management systems. Offered in Active, Summit and Arctic Weights, Nexus odor management is provided through Gold+ Alloy, technology that catalyzes and destroys bacteria at an atomic level, and Carbon Alloy two-pronged odor absorption. Nexus also includes cutting-edge moisture management, and lighter garments feature Coolcore Technology to keep wearers cool and dry in warm weather or during exertion. Nexus garments are paneled, articulated and flat-lock seamed to assure comfort.

Field & Stream

www.fieldandstreamshop.com

[7] C3 Everyhunt Lightweight Hunting Jacket and Pants from Field & Stream are perfect to take the chill off during early seasons. Two-way stretch fleece allows free movement combined with silence. NOSCENT C3 antimicrobial and Zeolite technology minimizes human odors, while hydro-Repel fabric sheds water during light drizzles. The collar includes a safety-harness slot, pockets include a zippered chest and dual hand-warmers. Pants feature a high waistband and side elastic, with articulated knees and five pockets. They are offered in Mossy Oak Break-Up Country and Realtree Xtra.

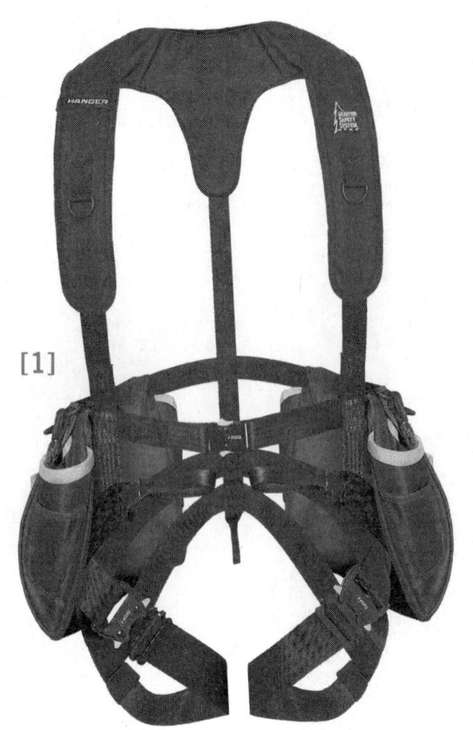
[1]

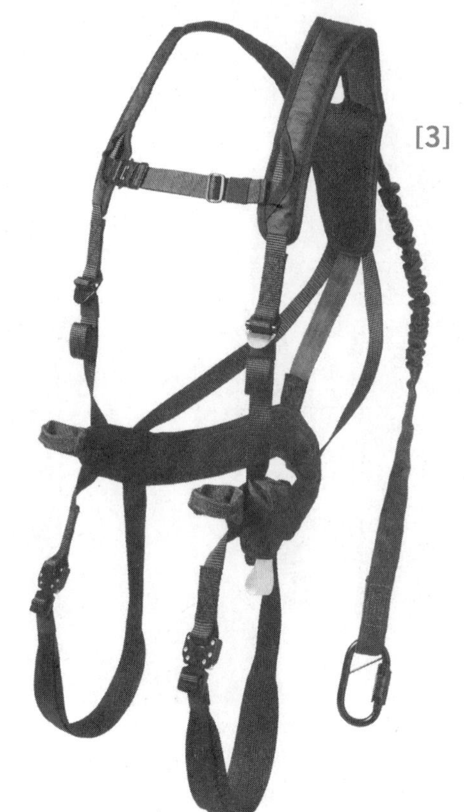
[3]

TREESTANDS & BLINDS

Hunter Safety Systems

www.hssvest.com

[1] Hunter Safety System has made hanging stands easier and safer. The HSS Hanger Harness is a utility safety harness featuring deep pockets to carry tools needed to hang stands—so you can keep your hunting vest free of human odors in hot weather. Tough nylon webbing and ballistic fabric ensure it lasts for years. It has ample storage space via deep, rigid, sliding pockets to eliminate multiple trips up and down the tree and are easily moved out of the way while working. The harness includes padded shoulders and comes with a lineman's climbing belt, and adjustable tree and suspension straps.

[2] A quality harness is worthless if you fall while entering or exiting a stand. Enter the LIFELINE, which includes a rubber Recon carabiner Cowbell sound dampener to eliminate stand clanks. The LIFELINE is made from heavy-duty mountain-climbing rope with incorporated reflective strip to help locate stands in the dark via flashlight. The LIFELINE is attached to the tree base and above your stand, then your harness is clipped in at the tree base. A simple prussik knot slides freely along the rope while climbing or descending, but cinches tight should you fall at any point. Thirty- and 42-foot versions are offered. The carabiner and rope are rated to 3,500 pounds.

[2]

Gorilla Gear

www.gogorillagear.com

[3] Gorilla Gear's G-TAC AIR Harnesses are some of the most comfortable around, their 30-inch proprietary tether allowing reacting to shots 360 degrees around your stand without tangling in your tether. This unique tether-webbing system also pro-

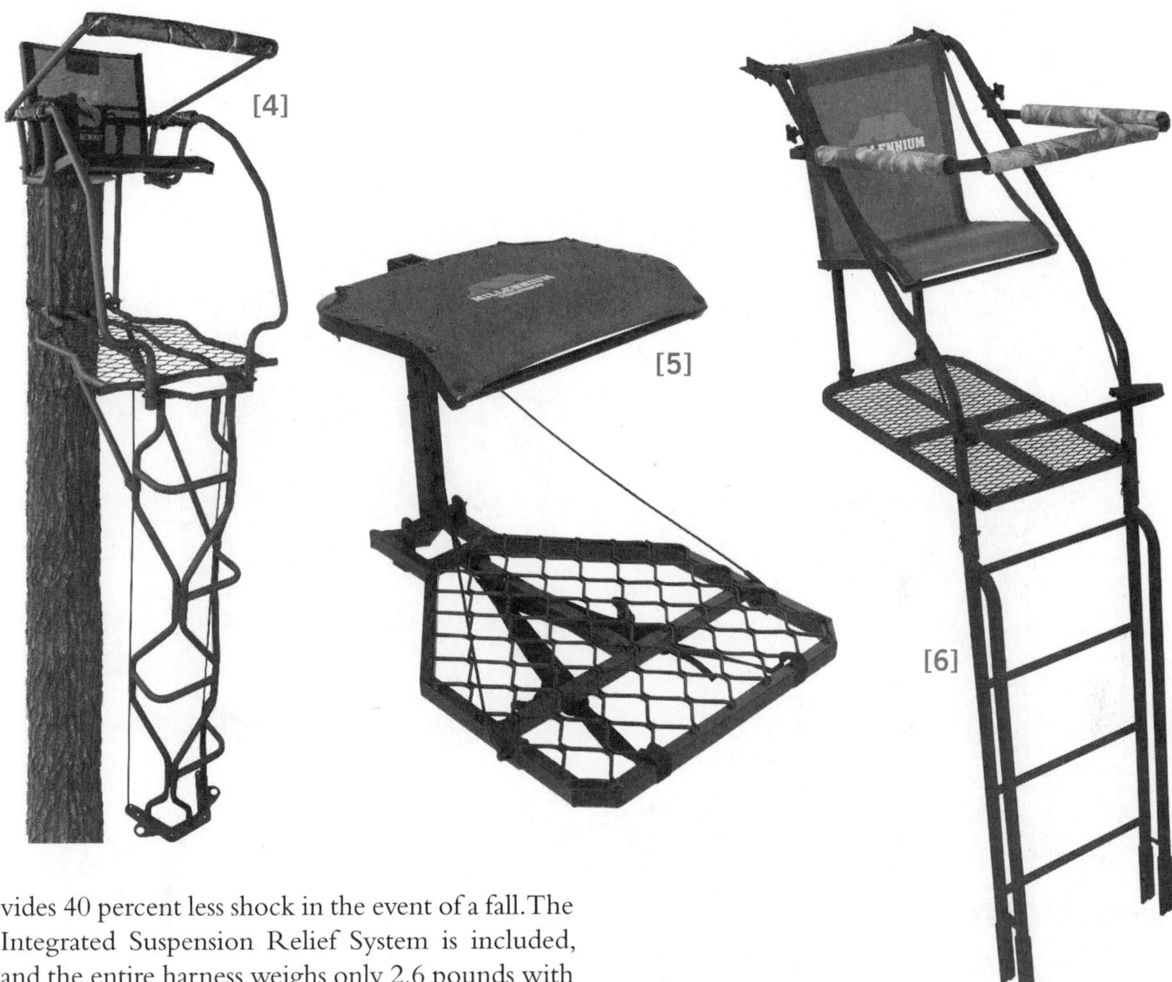

vides 40 percent less shock in the event of a fall. The Integrated Suspension Relief System is included, and the entire harness weighs only 2.6 pounds with hardware. Its tapered comfort-strap system and ergonomic design create maximum comfort while walking or sitting without sacrificing safety. There are also special cuts for women.

Summit Treestands

www.summitstands.com

[4] The Vine Series from Summit redefines hunting stands through "engineered concealment" and includes single and double ladders, the Back Country hang-on and Climbing Sticks. Each includes curved structural features to better mimic forest surroundings. All of The Vine stands include large, comfortable 16" x 18" mesh seats and built-in footrests – plus the ladder stands have mesh backrests and padded armrests. The 95-pound, 20-foot Single Ladder has a 24" x 25.5" platform, the 120-pound, 15-foot Double a 32" x 47" platform. The 22-pound Back Country hang-on has a 24" x 30" platform and 16" x 18" seat, and the 22-pound Climbing Sticks include four sections reaching 23 feet. All are constructed of sturdy steel.

Millennium Treestands

millenniumstands.com

[5] Millennium's M60U Ultralite Hang-On combines feathery 13.5-pound mass with huge comfort for all-day sits. It features the InterLockLEVELING System for crooked trees and a large, comfortable 16x20-inch ComfortMax Seat set 21 inches high. The SilentHunt Design uses nylon washers between all pivot points to eliminate squeaks, and quick and silent CamLock Receiver anchors the stand to the tree safely. The all-aluminum stand is weight rated to 300 pounds, and the 24" x 33" platform is surfaced with metal grating to create a non-slip surface in any weather. The stand comes with backpack straps to provide easy carrying.

[6] The L110 21-foot Single Ladder from Millennium is designed for all-day comfort and loaded with hunter-friendly features. The folding ComfortTech Seat, adjustable surround rail and folding footrest are all included, plus a large platform gives plenty of room to get off that important shot.

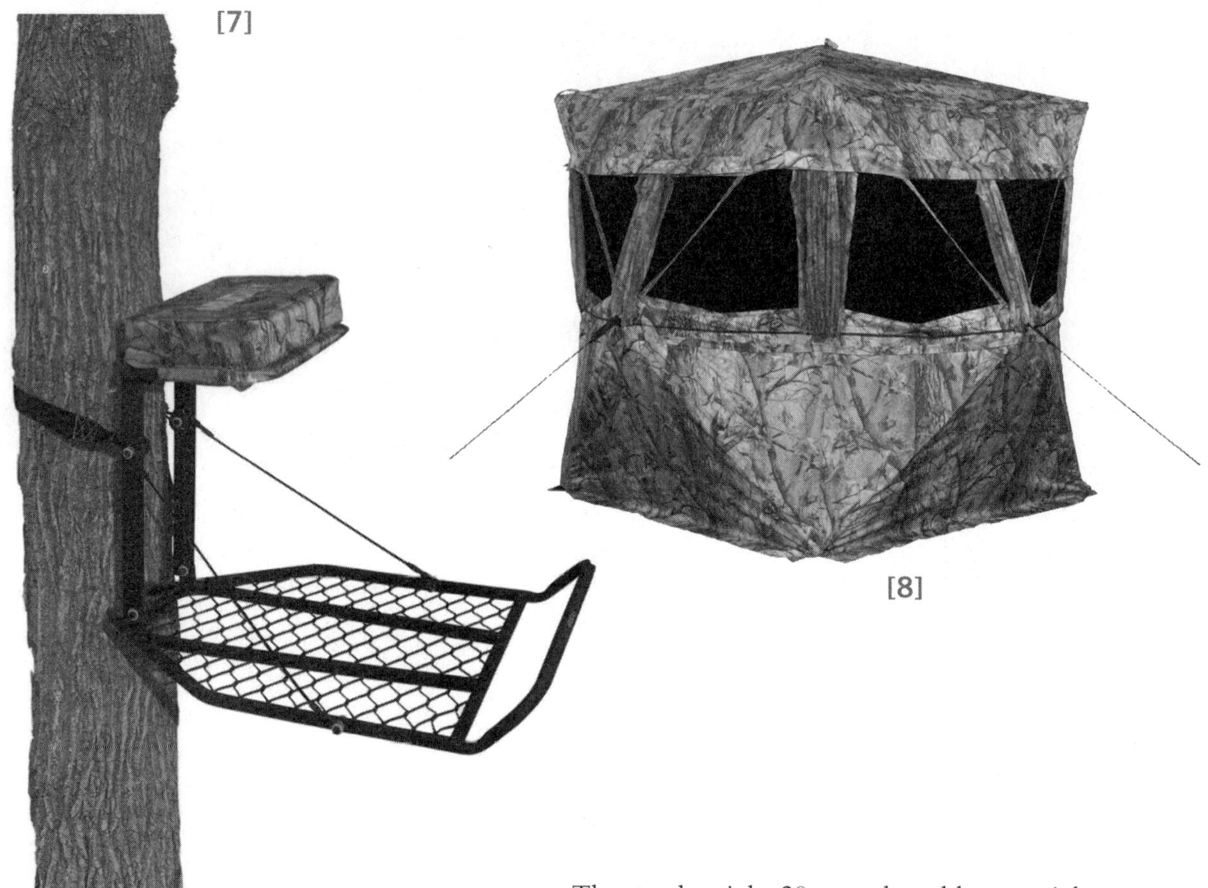
[7]

[8]

Height can be customized by adding or removing ladder sections, allowing you to create stands 8 to 21 feet high. The L110 Ladder features SteelTough Construction for strength and stability. The L110 makes the perfect stand for those who don't feel secure in an exposed hang-on stand.

Muddy Outdoors

www.gomuddy.com

[7] Muddy's The Boss XL treestand is a roomy 25" x 34" all-steel stand made for all-day comfort. It includes a fixed footrest, and a 22"-high, 12" x 18" seat with thick, water-resistant Triplex Foam cover. This seat also flips up when not needed. It quickly attaches to any tree measuring at least 9 inches in diameter with a 2-inch Silent Slide Buckle Strap. The stand weighs 20 pounds and has a weight rating of 300 pounds. It comes with a full-body fall-arrest harness. The wide expanded-metal platform assures sure traction in wet or icy weather.

[8] The VS360 portable blind from Muddy can be set up in seconds and features sliding, shoot-through mesh window covers for 360-degree viewing and shooting. The sliding, shoot-through mesh camouflage windows offer endless window configurations, allowing getting that important shot off no matter where game appears. The blind comes with nine steel stakes and an interior stake pocket, four tie-down ropes and oversize deluxe carry bag. The interior is black backed, the exterior water resistant, with a 77" x 77" footprint and 70" height. The blind weighs only 19.5 pounds and also features a zippered roof opening, two gear pockets and bottom scent-sealing skirt.

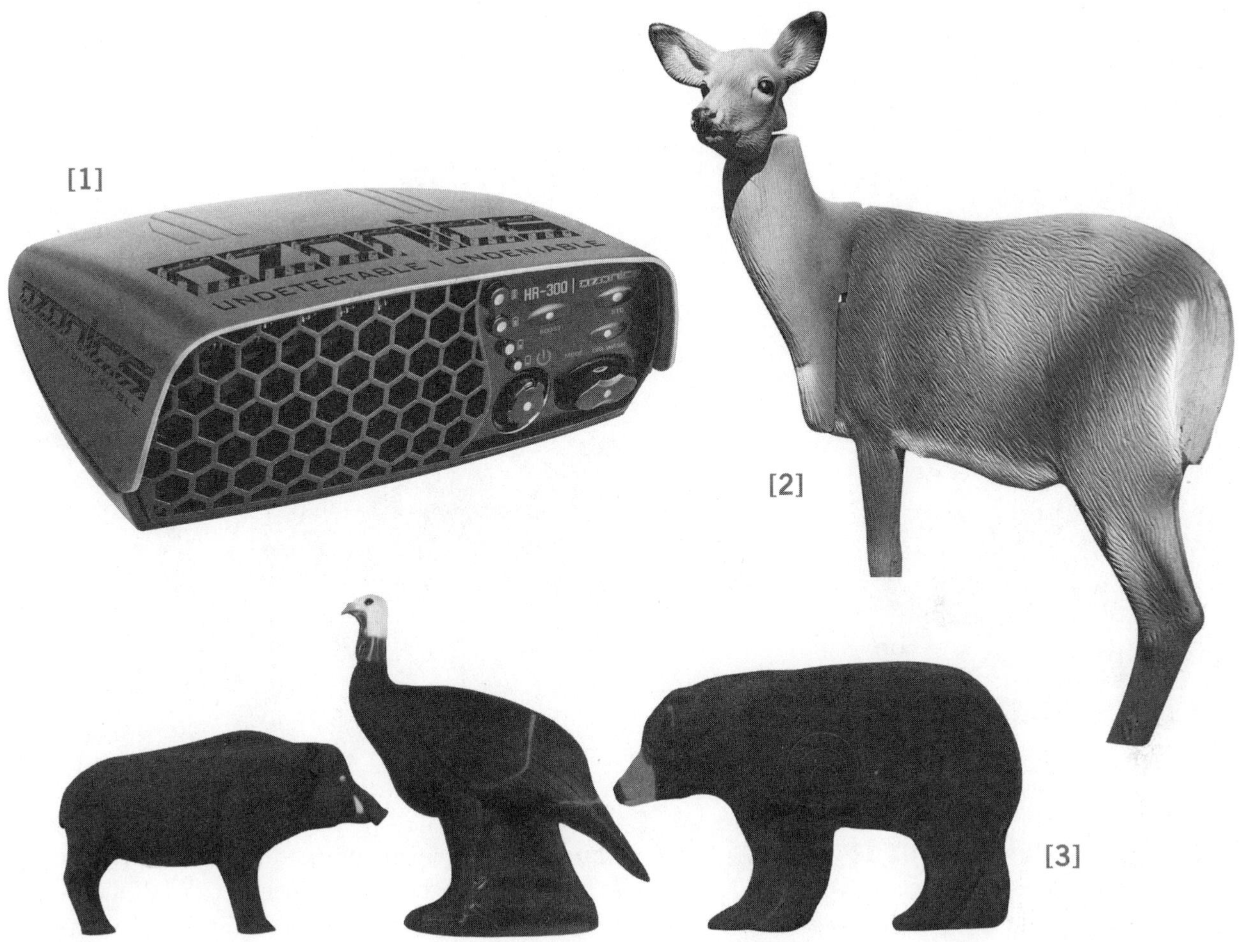

OTHER USEFUL BOWHUNTING GEAR

Ozonics

www.ozonicshunting.com

[1] Ozonics units neutralize odors with oxidizing ozone, and the HR-300 now produces 45 percent more ozone. The housing is ergonomic, with re-engineered internal components making it quieter and prolonging battery life. Its improved interface makes set up easy while wearing gloves or in the dark. Pulse Technology regulates output to match environmental needs. It's compatible with all existing Ozonics accessories, including the Kinetic Backpack for stalking bowhunters and Dri-wash Bag for de-scenting hunting togs in camp or at home.

Rinehart 3-D Targets

www.rinehart3d.com

[2] Rinehart's Deloma Series Doe Decoy provides realistic shape and ultra-quiet Rinehart foam construction. It features a patented design allowing natural head and neck movement on the slightest breeze. The anchor rod is situated behind the front legs so the body can pivot on the smallest puff of wind to create life-like movement to attract the wariest bucks. The decoy folds for easy storage and transport, held in a drawstring "Quiet-Tech" fabric, burr-resistant bag with a comfortable carry strap.

Shooter 3D Archery Targets

shooter3d.com

[3] Looking for affordable 3-D targets for quality off-season practice? Shooter 3D makes the most affordable in the industry. These durable, realistic targets are offered in Shooter 3D Bear (24 inches at the shoulder), Turkey (32 inches tall) and Hog (19 inches to shoulder). The weather-resistant, high-density-foam targets provide more realistic practice and are made to withstand thousands of shots. Bear and Hog targets include score rings on each side, the Turkey on sides, front and back. They all come with ground stakes.

[4]

[5]

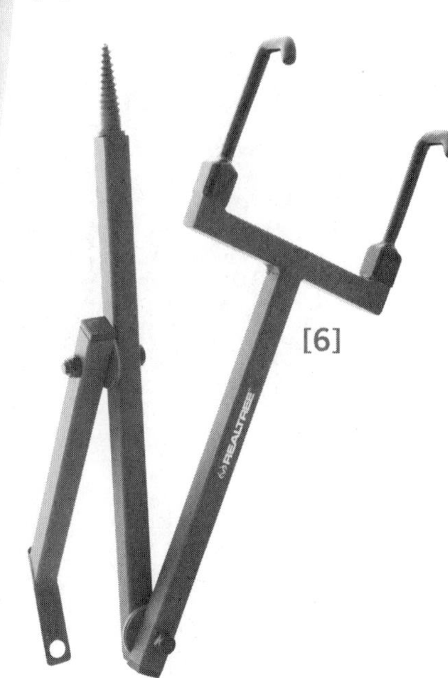
[6]

Heartland Wildlife Institute

www.heartlandwildlife.com

[4] Heartland Wildlife Institute Rack Maker Extreme food-plot seed is designed for planting during early fall, serving as a late-fall and early-winter hunting plot that will remain palatable long after hunting seasons finish due to its frost-tolerant ingredients with variable peak-attraction periods. It includes attractive winter oats, winter rye, forage soybeans and Rack Maker Brassicas mix.

Whitetail Institute

www.whitetailinstitute.com

[5] Whitetail Institute's Imperial Whitetail Fusion consists of selected seeds that perform as if "melted together." The blend contains an advanced, next-generation Imperial Whitetail Clover that proves more attractive and is nutritionally packed, along with augmented drought tolerance and lower fertilizer needs. Fusion is sold in 3.15- and 9.25-pound bags.

Realtree

www.realtree.com

[6] Realtree EZ Hangers are the most durable and reliable bow hangers around, available in 13-, 23- and 34-inch lengths. The hinged hangers allow treestand hunters to position their bows to minimize movement when that big buck arrives. The 34-inch EZ Hanger includes three pivoting sections for maximum adjustability. They silently swing out of the way when not needed, some models including a screw mount to hold POV cameras. Each includes a self-tapping lag-bolt base for quick installation. A Crossbow model is shown here.

Nutra Deer

nutradeer.com

[7] Nutra Deer's Antler Builder is ideal for establishing deer mineral licks to attract more deer to your hunting area, or act as a direct hunting site in states where that's legal. This mineral blend also helps does recover from the stress of winter and give birth to healthier fawns, and helps bucks to maximize antler growth. Antler Builder is nutritionally balanced and highly attractive, including the vitamins, essential minerals and micro minerals that bucks need to grow longer tines and heavier mass. Offer it year round to ensure a healthier deer herd.

Hi Mountain Seasonings

www.himtnjerky.com

[8] Hunting, game meat and jerky go hand in hand. Make delicious jerky from your own game meat

with Hi Mountain Seasonings Jerky Cure & Seasoning Variety Pack. It features five different flavors, including Original, Hunter's Blend, Bourbon BBQ, Jalapeno and new Spicy Lime Blend. Each individual packet includes enough spices and seasonings to prepare 4 pounds of meat, and detailed instructions allow preparing in 1- to 4-pound batches. The Wyoming-based company also offers kits for creating a wide variety of game-meat sausages, plus its own line of dehydrated meals for backcountry bowhunters.

Avian-X

www.avian-x.com

[9] Avian-X produces some of the most realistic rubberized and collapsible turkey decoys in the business, and the LCD Laydown Hen is one of the most effective, especially when used in conjunction with the LCD Jake or Strutter to illicit competition and jealousy. Dura-Rubber bodies are soft and quiet, but also ultra-realistic and tough. The LCD Laydown Hen simulates the true submissive breeding position of hen turkeys and gets gobblers really worked up. All Avian-X decoys come with drawstring carry bag.

Plano Molding

www.planomolding.com

[10] Plano's All Weather Bow Case is designed to provide uncompromising protection of your hard-earned compound-bow investment. It includes thick, rugged construction, plush crush-proof Pillar-Lock system interior and weather-resistant edge seal to keep your bow safe from harm and the elements. The ergonomic handle, high-density foam interior and integrated arrow storage are suitable for air travel. Interior dimensions are 6.75" x 16" x 46.5".